THE EARLY PLAYS

David Hare was born in Sussex in 1947. Upon leaving university he formed the Portable Theatre Company, which toured Britain for three years. He wrote his first play, *Slag*, in 1970, while Literary Manager at the Royal Court Theatre. Since then he has written thirteen plays, of which eight have been presented at the National Theatre, and seven original screenplays for cinema and television. His first feature film, *Wetherby*, won the Golden Bear at Berlin in 1985.

Contents

Introduction

On Political Theatre

To begin with the obvious: the playwright writes plays. He chooses plays as his way of speaking. If he could speak more clearly in a lecture, he would lecture; if polemic suited him, he'd be a journalist. But he chooses the theatre as the most subtle and complex way of addressing an audience he can find. Because of that, I used to turn down all invitations to speak in public, because I didn't want an audience to hear the tone of my voice. I don't like the idea that they can get a hand-down version of my plays sitting in a lecture hall and sizing me up. In the theatre I am saying complex and difficult things. I do not want them reduced by either my views on the world, or, more importantly, the audience's idea of my views. I want no preconceptions. I don't want, 'Oh, of course Hare is a well-known anti-vivisectionist, that's why there's that scene where the dog is disembowelled'. I want the dog cut up and the audience deciding for themselves if they like the sight or not. The first lesson the playwright learns is that he is not going to be able to control an audience's reactions anyway; if he writes an eloquent play about the sufferings of the Jews in the Warsaw Ghetto there is always going to be someone in the audience who comes out completely satisfied with the evening, saying at last someone's had the guts to say it, those Nazis knew what they were about. As you can't control people's reactions to your plays, your duty is also not to reduce people's reactions, not to give them easy handles with which they can pigeon-hole you, and come to comfortable terms with what you are saying.

So why, then, am I changing tack and beginning to try and speak a little in public about the theatre? It is partly because I have been trying in the last few months to put my ear to the ground and find out what a particular section of my audience is thinking and feeling; but it is also for other and very pressing reasons which I hope will become clear as I go on.

I'd like to start with a story which has always taken my breath away, from Hardy's incomparable novel *Jude the Obscure*. The young mother, homeless in Oxford, living in appalling poverty with a family she cannot possibly support, puts her head in her hands, and says in the presence of her eldest boy, 'O, it is better if we had never been born'. Later that day she goes upstairs.

At the back of the door were fixed two hooks for hanging garments, and from these the forms of [her] two youngest children were suspended, by a piece of box-cord round each of their necks, while from a nail a few yards off the body of little Jude was hanging in a similar manner. An overturned chair was near the eldest boy, and his glazed eyes were slanted into the room; but those of the girl and the baby were closed.

I always think this is the ultimate cautionary tale for playwrights. That someone will actually take you at your word. That you will whip yourself up into a fine frenzy of dramatic writing on stage, have your superbly played heroine step harrowingly to the front of the stage and cry out in despair, 'It is better that we had never been born,' and there will in fact be an answering shot from the back of the stalls and one of the customers will slump down dead having committed the sin of assuming that the playwright means what he says.

For this is an austere and demanding medium. It is a place where the playwright's ultimate sincerity and good faith is going to be tested and judged in a way that no other medium demands. As soon as a word is spoken on stage it is tested. As soon as a line is put into the reconstruction of a particular event, it will be judged. In this way the theatre is the exact opposite art to journalism; the bad journalist throws off a series of casual and half-baked propositions, ill-considered, dashed-off, entertainment pieces to put forward a point of view which may or may not amuse, which may or may not be lasting, which may or may not be true; but were he once to hear those same words spoken out loud in a theatre he would begin to feel that terrible chill of being collectively judged and what had seemed light and trenchant and witty would suddenly seem flip and arch and silly.

Judgement. Judgement is at the heart of the theatre. A man steps forward and informs the audience of his intention to lifelong fidelity to his wife, while his hand, even as he speaks, drifts at random to the body of another woman. The most basic dramatic situation you can imagine; the gap between what he says and what we see him to be opens up, and in that gap we see something that makes theatre unique: that it exposes the difference between what a man says and what he does. That is why nothing on stage is so exciting as a great lie; why *Brassneck* never recovers as a play after its greatest liar is killed off at the end of the first act.

I would suggest crudely that one of the reasons for the theatre's possible authority, and for its recent general drift towards politics, is its unique suitability to illustrating an age in which men's ideals and men's practice bear no relation to each other; in which the public profession of, for example, socialism has often been reduced by the passage of history to wearying personal fetish, or even chronic personality disorder. The theatre is the best way of showing the gap between what is said and what is seen to be done, and that is why, ragged and gap-toothed as it is, it has still a far healthier potential than some of the other, poorer, abandoned arts.

To explain what I mean I should tell you of a conversation I once had with a famous satirist of the early sixties who has been pushed further and further into the margin of the culture, later and later into the reaches of the night on BBC2, or Radio Solent, or wherever they still finally let him practise his art. He said, 'I don't understand why every day I feel my own increasing irrelevance to the country I am meant to be satirizing.' I suggested it is because satire depends upon ignorance. It is based on the proposition, 'If only you knew.' Thus the satirist can rail, 'If only you knew that Eden was on benzedrine throughout the Suez crisis, stoned out of his head and fancy-free; if only you knew that the crippled, stroke-raddled Churchill dribbled and farted in Cabinet for two years after a debilitating stroke, and nobody dared remove him; if only you knew that Cabinet Ministers sleep with tarts, that Tory MPs liaise with crooked architects and bent off-shore bankers: if only you knew.' But finally after his railing, the satirist may find that the audience replies, 'Well, we do know now; and we don't believe it will ever change. And knowing may well not affect what we think.'

This is the first stage of what I think Marxists call 'raising consciousness'; a worthy aim and yet . . . consciousness has been raised in this country for a good many years now and we seem further from radical political change than at any time in my life. The traditional function of the radical artist – 'Look at those Borgias; look at this bureaucracy' – has been undermined. We have looked. We have seen. We have known. And we have not changed. A pervasive cynicism paralyses public life. And the once-active, early sixties' satirist is left on the street corner, peddling pathetic grubby little scraps of sketch and song – Callaghan's love life? Roy Jenkins' taste for claret . . .

And so we must ask, against this background, what can the playwright accomplish that the satirist cannot? What tools does he have that the satirist lacks?

The first question a political playwright addresses himself to is: why is it that in advanced industrial societies the record of revolutionary activity is so very miserable, so very, very low? The urban proletariat in this country knows better than we ever can that they are selling their labour to capital; many of them know far better than we of the degradations of capitalism. Of the wretched and the inadequate housing into which many of them are born; of the grotesque, ever worsening imbalance in the educational system whereby the chances of progress to examinability even at 'O' level, even at CSE level, are still ludicrously low; of the functional and enslaving work they are going to have to do; of the lack of control they are going to suffer at their own workplace. Of all these things they know far more than we, and, most importantly, they are familiar with socialist ideas which see their sufferings as part of a soluble political pattern.

Worse, we have lived through a time of economic depression, which classically in Marxist theory is supposed to throw up those critical moments at which the proletariat may seize power. And yet, in my own estimate, European countries have been more unstable during times of affluence than times of depression. It is hard to believe in the historical inevitability of something which has so frequently not happened, or rather, often been nearest to happening in places and circumstances furthest away from those predicted by the man who first suggested it.

Confronted by this apparent stasis, the English writer is inclined to answer with a stasis of his own, to sigh and imagine

4

that the dialectic has completely packed in, or rather got stuck in some deep rift from which he cannot jump it out. And so he begins to lose faith in the possibility of movement at all. Compare this with a post-revolutionary society, like China, where the dialectic is actually seen to mean something in people's lives. In the play *Fanshen* it is dynamic. Political practice answers to theory and yet modifies it; the party answers to the people and is modified by it. The fight is for political structures which answer people's needs; and people themselves are changed by living out theoretical ideas. It is a story of change and progress.

Must it always be, however, that Marxist drama set in Europe reflects the state of revolutionary politics with an answering sluggishness of its own? By this, I mean, that sinking of the heart when you go to a political play and find that the author really believes that certain questions have been answered even before the play has begun. Why do we so often have to endure the demeaning repetition of slogans which are seen not as transitional aids to understanding, but as ultimate solutions to men's problems? Why the insulting insistence in so much political theatre that a few gimcrack mottoes of the Left will sort out the deep problems of reaction in modern England? Why the urge to caricature? Why the deadly stiffness of limb? Brecht uncoils the great sleeping length of his mind to give us, in everything but the greatest of his writing, exactly that impression, the god-like feeling that the questions have been answered before the play has begun. Even his idea of irony is unsufferably coy. He parades it, he hangs it out to dry as if it were proof of the broadness of his mind. It should not need such demonstration.

I do understand the thinking. The Marxist playwright working in a fairly hostile medium, feels that his first job is to declare his allegiance, to show his hand if you like. He thinks that because the play itself is part of the class struggle, he must first say which side he is on and make that clear, before he proceeds to lay out the ideas of the play as fairly as he may. To me this approach is rubbish, it insults the audience's intelligence; more important it insults their experience; most important it is also a fundamental misunderstanding of what a play is. A play is not actors, a play is not a text; a play is what happens between the stage and the audience. A play is a performance. So if a play is to be a weapon in the class struggle, then that weapon is not going to be the things you are saying; it is the interaction of what you are saying and what the audience is thinking. The play is in the air. The woman in the balcony who yelled out during the famous performance of *Othello*, 'Can't you see what he's going to do, you stupid black fool?' expressed the life of that play better than any writer I ever knew; and understood the nature of performance better than the slaves of Marxist fashion.

I think this fact, that we are dealing, all of us, actors, writers, directors, with something we cannot calibrate because it is in the air and nowhere else, accounts for the fact that theatre is often bound up in mysticism and why it is known throughout the Western world as a palace of boredom. Is there any boredom like boredom in the theatre? Is there anything as grey, as soul-rotting, as nerve-tearing, as being bored in the theatre, or as facing the bleak statistical likelihood that you will be bored in the theatre for 99 per cent of the time you spend there? I can sleep anywhere on earth, haystack, bus, railway station; I have slept soundly with mortar bombs landing eight hundred yards away, yet I cannot sleep in the theatre. This I put down to the fact that I cannot bear to sleep when so many of my fellow human beings are in such intolerable pain around me; not only my comrades in the audience, but also my colleagues on stage. For if theatre is judgement, it is also failure. It is failing, and failing, and failing.

I think that it is in some way to avoid this uncomfortable fact that dramatists have lately taken to brandishing their political credentials as frequently as possible throughout their work, and that political theatre groups have indulged in such appalling overkill, in some way to stave off failure with an audience; to flaunt your sincerity, to assert and re-assert a simple scaffolding of belief in order not to face the real and unpredictable dangers of a genuinely live performance is all a way of not being judged. It is understandable, but it is wrong. It is in no way as craven as the scaffolding you will find in West End theatres, the repeated reassurances to the audience that narrow lives are the only lives worth leading; nor in my mind is it in any way as poisonous as the upper-middle-brow, intellectual comedies which have become the snob fashion of the day, meretricious structures full of brand references to ideas at which people laugh in order to prove that they have heard of them; the pianola of chic which tinkles night and day in Shaftesbury Avenue, and which is thought to be real music in the smart Sunday papers. The English theatre loves the joker, the detached observer, the man who stands outside; no wonder, faced with this ubiquity of tat, that political theatre tends to be strident and unthinking, not in its attitude to its content, but in its distrust of the essential nature of performance itself.

Historically it is hard for a serious playwright to be confident. History has not behaved in the way that was asked of it; and the medium itself in which we work has chronic doubts about its own audibility. Bronowski hectors from a corner of a tenement slum; while the Queen settles down on Fridays to watch *It Ain't Half Hot Mum*. The airways are saturated with conflicting messages. All a playwright can do is promise to speak only when he has something to say; but when he speaks, what special role can he assume?

For five years I have been writing history plays. I try to show the English their history. I write tribal pieces, trying to show how people behaved on this island, off the continental shelf, in this century. How this Empire vanished, how these ideals died. Reading Angus Calder's *The People's War* changed all my thinking as a writer; an account of the Second World War through the eyes of ordinary people, it attempts a complete alternative history to the phony and corrupting history I was taught at school. Howard Brenton and I attempted in *Brassneck* to write what I have no doubt Calder would still write far better than we, an imagined subsequent volume *The People's Peace*, as seen, in our case, through the lives of the pretty bourgeoisie, builders, solicitors, brewers, politicians, the masonic gang who carve up provincial England. It was my first step into the past. When I first wrote, I wrote in the present day, I believed in a purely contemporary drama; so as I headed backwards, I worried I was avoiding the real difficulties of the day. It took me time to realize that the reason was, if you write about now, just today and nothing else, then you seem to be confronting only stasis, but if you begin to describe the undulations of history, if you write plays that cover passages of time, then you begin to find a sense of movement, of social change, if you like; and the facile

7

hopelessness that comes from confronting the day and only the day, the room and only the room, begins to disappear and in its place the writer can offer a record of movement and change.

You will see what I am arguing. The Marxist writer spends a great deal of time rebuking societies for not behaving in the way that he expected them to; but also, furious because change is not taking the form he would like it to, he denigrates or ignores the real changes which have taken place in the last thirty years. A great empire falls apart, offering, as it collapses, a last great wash of wealth through this country, unearned, unpaid for, a shudder of plenty, which has dissolved so many of the rules which kept the game in order; while intellectuals grope wildly for an answer, any answer to the moral challenge of collectivism, the citizens have spent and spent, after the war in time of wealth, but recently in a time of encroaching impoverishment. We are living through a great, groaning, yawling festival of change – but because this is England it is not always seen on the streets. In my view it is seen in the extraordinary intensity of people's personal despair, and it is to that despair that as a historical writer I choose to address myself time and time again: in *Teeth 'n' Smiles*, in *Knuckle*, in *Plenty*.

I feel exactly as Tom Wolfe does in a marvellous account of his opportunities as a writer:

About the time I came to New York ... the most serious novelists abandoned the richest terrain of the novel: namely, society, the social tableau, manners and morals, the whole business of the 'way we live now'. There is no novelist who captures the sixties in America or even in New York in the same sense that Thackeray was the chronicler of London in the 1840s and Balzac was the chronicler of Paris and all of France ... That was marvellous for journalists, I tell you that. The sixties were one of the most extraordinary decades in American history in terms of manners and morals. Manners and morals *were* history in the sixties. I couldn't believe the scene I saw spread out before me. But what really amazed me as a writer I had it practically all to myself ... As fast as I could possibly do it, I was turning out articles on this amazing spectacle I saw bubbling and screaming right there ... and all the while I knew that some enterprising novelist was going to come along and *do* the whole marvellous scene in one gigantic bold stroke. It was so ready, so ripe – beckoning ... and it never happened.

8

I can't tell you how accurately that expresses a feeling I have always had as a playwright and which I know colleagues have experienced, that sense that the greater part of the culture is simply looking at the wrong things. I became a writer by default, to fill in the gaps, to work on the areas of the fresco which were simply ignored, or appropriated for the shallowest purposes: rock music, black propaganda, gun-selling, diplomacy. And yet I cannot believe to this day that a more talented writer will not come along and *do* the whole scene. In common with other writers who look with their own eyes, I have been abused in the newspapers for being hysterical, strident and obscene, when all I was doing was observing the passing scene, its stridency, its hysteria, its obscenity, and trying to put it in a historical context which the literary community seems pathologically incapable of contemplating. In *Teeth 'n' Smiles* a girl chooses to go to prison because it will give her an experience of suffering which is bound in her eyes to be more worthwhile than the life she could lead outside: not one English critic could bring himself to mention this central event in the play, its plausibility, its implications. It was beyond their scope to engage with such an idea. And yet, how many people here have close friends who have taken control of their own lives, only to destroy them?

We are drawing close, I think, to what I hope a playwright can do. He can put people's sufferings in a historical context; and by doing that, he can help to explain their pain. But what I mean by history will not be the mechanized absolving force theorists would like it to be; it will be those strange uneasy factors that make a place here and nowhere else, make a time now and no other time. A theatre which is exclusively personal, just a place of private psychology, is inclined to self-indulgence; a theatre which is just social is inclined to unreality, to the impatient blindness I've talked about today. Yeats said, out of our quarrel with others, we make rhetoric, while out of our quarrel with ourselves, we make poetry. I value both, and value the theatre as a place where both are given weight.

I write love stories. Most of my plays are that. Over and over again I have written about romantic love, because it never goes away. And the view of the world it provides, the dislocation it offers, is the most intense experience that many people know on earth.

And I write comedy because . . . such ideas as the one I have just uttered make me laugh.

And I write about politics because the challenge of communism, in however debased and ugly a form, is to ask whether the criteria by which we have been brought up are right; whether what each of us experiences uniquely really is what makes us valuable; whether every man should really be his own cocktail; or whether our criteria could and should be collective, and if they were, whether we would be any happier. However absolute the sufferings of men in the totalitarian Soviet countries, however decadent the current life of the West, the fact is that this question has only just been asked, and we have not even the first hundredth of an answer. To give up now would be death.

I said at the beginning that I have chosen to speak, in part simply to find out, to put my ear to the ground. And I must tell you what I find in universities. I find a generation who are cowed, who seem to have given up on the possibility of change, who seem to think that most of the experiments you could make with the human spirit are likely to be doomed or at any rate highly embarrassing. There is a demeaning nostalgia for the radicalism of the late sixties, people wanting to know exactly what the Vietnam marches were like. To me it would be sad if a whole generation's lives were shaped by the fact that a belief in change had fallen temporarily out of fashion; in Tom Wolfe's terms, it would be sad if this historical period had no chronicler.

Our lives must be refreshed with images which are not official, not approved; that break what George Orwell called 'the Geneva conventions of the mind'. These images may come on television, something of a poisoned well in my view, because of its preference for censoring its own best work, or simply banning it; or they may come in this unique arena of judgement, the theatre.

I find it strange to theorize. Mostly theatre is hard work and nothing else. It is no coincidence that some of the British theatre's loudest theorists are notoriously incompetent inside a rehearsal room. It is a different kind of work. The patterns that I've made today in my own work and talking about others are purely retrospective, just the afterbirth; the wonder of performance is – you will always be surprised. The short, angry, sandy-haired, squat playwright turns out to write plays which *you* experience as slow, langorous, relaxed and elegant: the great night you had in the theatre two years ago turns out upon rereading to be a piece of stinking fish. I would wish it no other way.

An old American vaudevillian of the thirties drank his career away, fell into universal disfavour, but was finally found and put into an old people's home in California by a kindly producer who had once worked with him many years before. Visiting the old actor on his deathbed, the producer said, 'You are facing death. Is it as people describe? Is there a final sense of reassurance, a feeling of resignation, that sense of letting go that writers tell us consoles the dying?' 'Not at all,' said the comic, 'on the contrary. Death is none of those things that I was promised. It is ugly and fierce and degrading and violent. It is hard,' he said, 'hard as playing comedy.' All I would add is, not as hard as writing it.

SLAG

For Margaret

First performed at the Hampstead Theatre Club, London, on 6th April 1970, with the following cast:

JOANNE	Rosemary McHale
ELISE	Marty Cruickshank
ANN	Diane Fletcher

Designed by John Halle
Directed by Roger Hendricks-Simon

JOANNE (23)
ELISE (26)
ANN (32)

Scene 1: Common Room. Summer
Scene 2: Cricket Pitch. Summer
Scene 3: Bathroom. Summer
Scene 4: Common Room. Same Day
Scene 5: Bedroom. Autumn
Scene 6: Common Room. January

The play is written deliberately with as few stage and acting instructions as possible. Blackouts should be instant, gaps between scenes brief, and scenery minimal.

SCENE ONE

Common Room. They are standing formally with hands raised.

JOANNE: I, Joanne.

ELISE: I, Elise.

ANN: I, Ann.

JOANNE: Do solemnly promise.

ELISE ⎱
ANN ⎰ : Do solemnly promise.

JOANNE: For as long as I know Elise and Ann.

ELISE: For as long as I know Joanne and Ann.

ANN: For as long as I know Joanne and Elise.

JOANNE: To abstain from all forms and varieties of sexual intercourse.

ELISE ⎱
ANN ⎰ : All forms and varieties of sexual intercourse.

JOANNE: To keep my body intact in order to register my protest against the way our society is run by men for men whose aim is the subjugation of the female and the enslavement of the working woman.

ELISE ⎱
ANN ⎰ : The working woman.

JOANNE: All forms of sex I therefore deny myself in order to work towards the establishment of a truly socialist society. (ANN *breaks away*.)

ANN: Oh, come on.

JOANNE: What?

ANN: I've come along with you so far, but . . . socialist society!

JOANNE: All right, you may dissent at this point, but the essential commitment is made. All sex I deny.

ANN: Can we not drop the subject now once and for all?

ELISE: No one's going to test our determination anyway.

JOANNE: Is there any coffee?

ANN: No. No one's going to be much deprived.

ELISE: It's not as if we ever saw men except parents, and it's very unlikely we'll ever see any more of those.

ANN: It wasn't really that bad.

JOANNE: It was a disaster.

(*Exit* ELISE.)

ANN: They were a little conscious of the lack of numbers. Who wouldn't be? A chill in the air of Great Hall.

JOANNE: The singing of the Internationale should have warmed them up.

ANN: That was a singularly silly gesture on your part. Nobody knew the tune anyway. But your stupidity at least managed to unite them. We've been through the very worst that we can know, and now it'll be time to rebuild.

JOANNE: When Robinson Crusoe landed on a desert island, his first instinct was to create a perfect embryo of the society he had escaped from.

ANN: Thank you, Joanne, but can we leave politics out of this? We will build a new sort of school where what people feel for people will be the basis of their relationships. No politics.

JOANNE: In Bunuel's version—1952, I think, anyway his Mexican period, the part of Robinson Crusoe was played by . . .

(*Re-enter* ELISE.)

ELISE: Coast's clear. They've gone.

JOANNE: The part of Crusoe was played by . . .

ELISE: For Christ's sake shut up.

ANN: Let's not talk like that.

JOANNE: You started it.

ANN: What's the point?

JOANNE: She was getting at me.

ANN: Divided we fall.

(ANN *resumes chalking in the coloured parts of the blackboard.* ELISE *starts knitting.*)

ELISE: I've nearly finished another bootee. Its little feet are going to look so sweet.

ANN: Lovely.

JOANNE: All you need now is a fuck.

(JOANNE *picks up* Sight and Sound.)

ELISE: I'm sitting here and often I stop and think perhaps I've
seen my very last man.

ANN: Tradesmen.

ELISE: I mean real men. I can't quite grasp what that means.
Ann, Joanne, imagine it.

JOANNE: Tremendous.

ELISE: No more men.

JOANNE: The ideal.

ANN: We're perfectly well used to it. I've been two years
without now and I tell you I feel better.

ELISE: You don't look any better.

ANN: I eat better.

ELISE: Repulsive.

(JOANNE *goes to the window where something has caught her
attention. She screams out.*)

ANN: I've taken off weight and I don't have my skin trouble any
longer.

JOANNE: Stop buggering about, you vile little child.

ANN: I don't doubt, Elise, that men will some time reappear in
your life.

JOANNE: That's better.

ANN: And you will be happy. But until then we must spend the
time creatively.

ELISE: Hurrah.

ANN: We will build a new Brackenhurst.

JOANNE: When Robinson Crusoe landed on a desert island his
first instinct . . .

ANN: Well what would you do?

JOANNE: Do as you like. You're in charge.

ANN: You find it so easy to criticize. What would you do?

JOANNE: I don't know.

ANN: Really? Elise?

ELISE: What?

ANN: Do I have to do all the thinking?

ELISE: Mm.

JOANNE (*back at window*): Take that thing out of your mouth.
    (*A bell rings incredibly loud.*)

ANN: There's no time to be lost.

JOANNE: Incidentally, I'm fed up with my room.

ANN: Your room will be seen to.

JOANNE: When I was a projectionist . . .

ELISE: We don't want to know.

JOANNE: Do you know the last film I saw?

ELISE: *Touch of Evil*, Orson Welles, 1957.

JOANNE: Stupid to claim it's a great film, but it does contain
    the most wonderful camera-work.

ELISE: The last film I saw was *Look at Life*.

ANN: I haven't been for years.

ELISE: Called *Loads on Roads*.

JOANNE: That's late 68 *Look at Life*. Not a very great period at
    all. Very facile camera-work.

ELISE: I enjoyed it.

JOANNE: Crap.

ELISE: I thought it assured.

JOANNE: I thought it crap.

ELISE: I had a really good time.

JOANNE: What are you trying to get at?

ANN: And I never saw it.

ELISE: You'd have liked it, Ann.

JOANNE: What are you trying to prove?

ANN: Girls, my girls.

JOANNE (*faintly*): Oh yes.
    (ANN *gets up, throws the chalk into the air. The bell rings
    again. Yells across the room out of the window.*)

ANN: Get into class.

JOANNE: Who's teaching?

ELISE: I am.

ANN: Why aren't you in there?

ELISE: I've given them reading. I put that bossy one in charge.

ANN: Is that the sign of a good schoolteacher?

ELISE: We're appalling schoolteachers.

ANN: Come, come.

JOANNE: Are you going to teach?

ELISE: No.

JOANNE: I think I will, then.

(*Exit* JOANNE.)

ANN: I won't have that said.

ELISE: Why have we only got eight pupils then?

ANN: Eleven paid.

ELISE: Eight stayed.

ANN: The eight are very happy.

ELISE: Freaks.

ANN: You're as responsible as anyone.

ELISE: Agreed.

ANN: Though not as responsible as her.

ELISE: She's not harming anyone.

ANN: She's harming my girls. My beautiful girls. I'm
sentimental perhaps but I do think girls should be spared
her sort of nonsense.

ELISE: It does them good.

ANN: Stop expressing your opinions. They don't help.

ELISE: Leave off.

ANN: You're such a hopeless person. As a person. Don't you
wish anything for yourself?

ELISE: In the words of Isadora Duncan, I would like to be
remembered as a great dancer but I fear I will only be
remembered as a good bang.

(*Bell rings yet more insistently.*)

That's all. The whole thing can probably be blamed on
some childhood vitamin deficiency. Or a great rush of air to
my legs that sucks men to me. I'm chilly.

ANN: It is chilly.

ELISE: Stop staring at me.

ANN: Window.

(ELISE *shuts the window.*)

Do you think things are very far gone?

ELISE: Of course.

ANN: The parents were not impressed. What do you think of Joanne's plans?

ELISE: Ridiculous.

ANN: She's renamed her study the Women's Liberation Work. She says she's teaching dialectics this week instead of gym.

ELISE: You'll have to fight back.

ANN: What do you think of my plans?

ELISE: Hopelessly naïve.

ANN: I like the idea of a new cricket pavilion.

ELISE: Hopeless optimism.

ANN: I'd like a new row of baths.

ELISE: Hopeless incompetence.

ANN: They're currently filthy.

ELISE: The girls tell me they find it exciting to smoke cigarettes in their baths, the height of decadence.

ANN: I'd prefer you didn't talk about the girls smoking in front of me.

ELISE: You know they smoke.

ANN: I do not know they smoke. I don't know that at all. And if they do, Elise, I want it reported to me properly, not slipped into our conversation by subterfuge. I'm only trying my best.

(*No response.*)

There are sixteen too many milk bottles coming every day. This has been going on for nine days. There are 144 spare bottles of milk in various shades of cheese.

ELISE: Joanne is domestic science.

ANN: Joanne is.

ELISE: She's a constant reproach.

ANN: I've told her.

ELISE: I told her to love life. If you come to Brackenhurst unused, you are sure to be unused for life.

ANN: It's not that bad. Fancy a game?

ELISE: Thank you, no.

ANN: Just because you always lose.

(ANN *is bouncing a ping-pong ball on her bat.*)

ELISE: I lose at all the games I play from ping-pong upwards and at Brackenhurst as there's nothing else to do it makes for a very fine time.

(ANN *starts thwacking the ball hard against the back wall and leaping and grunting to return it*.)

ANN: And that. And that. And that.

ELISE: If the Governors see fit to close the school, we'll all be out of a job.

ANN: And that.

ELISE: Are they all relations of yours?

ANN: Mostly.

ELISE: Look at this dress. Do you think it suits me?

(ANN *stops ping-ponging*. ELISE *walks manneredly round the room, head high, legs in a straight line*.)

ANN: I've seen it so often I can't tell.

ELISE: I should have been a model. I would have shown clothes to advantage. I would have loved it. I should have been an actress.

  "Thou know'st the mask of night is on my face
    Else would a maiden blush bepaint my cheek
    For that which thou has't heard me speak tonight."
Acting. That was Acting.

(ANN *has returned to her blackboard*.)

(*Loud and black*.) O Desdemona!

ANN: Look, I think it's all in, come and see.

ELISE: Where? It looks very nice.

ANN: It's taken me four hours that. The children need colour to help them learn.

ELISE: Why don't you get rid of Joanne?

ANN: I am responsible as much to my staff as to the children in my care. I have to think on everyone's behalf.

(*Enter* JOANNE.)

You're meant to be teaching. Why have you left?

JOANNE: I got bored. Your children are so stupid. I was reading Schopenhauer at 10 but this lot can't manage an alphabet.

ANN: Who's looking after them?

JOANNE: I left that bossy one in charge—Lucrecia Bourgeois as I

23

call her. She's loving it.

ANN: You're the worst of the lot.

JOANNE: There's a dog, incidentally, crapping on your tennis courts.

(*Exit* ANN *fast to tennis courts.*)

You were talking about me.

ELISE: Rubbish.

JOANNE: You changed the subject.

ELISE: I bet there's nothing on the courts.

JOANNE: Flabby cow. The jerk. Go and look.

ELISE: Doesn't bother me.

JOANNE: Flabby cow.

ELISE: Child.

JOANNE: Tit. Withered tit.

(*Enter* ANN.)

ELISE: Well?

ANN: There's nothing there.

JOANNE: You've hardly looked.

ANN: I've looked enough.

JOANNE: The dog's probably gone by now but I doubt if the crap will have fled.

ANN: I've looked once.

JOANNE: Take a proper look.

ANN: No.

JOANNE: Do you want to warp my development or something?

ANN: O.K.

(*Exit* ANN.)

ELISE: What's out there?

JOANNE: If she can't see it, that's her problem.

ELISE: Invention.

JOANNE: In a situation like this, anything is possible. The ascendant triumph of the mind. The battle pitched in heaven and in hell.

ELISE: You mean there's nothing out there?

JOANNE: You must allow for things beyond your understanding.

ELISE: You mean there's nothing out there.

JOANNE: The inner eye.

ELISE: You don't impress me with these antics and you only lose the sympathy of Ann.

JOANNE: The revolutionary consciousness—my own—admits of no limitation to possible fields of vision. The world is infinite. As soon as anything may be said to have revolutionary essence, it may be said to exist.

ELISE: Do dogs' stools have revolutionary essence?

JOANNE: The case of the dogshit is marginal and particular.

(ANN *is back*.)

ANN: What is the point of all this? You send me hunting. . . . I really don't understand you.

JOANNE: There are things about you I dislike.

ANN: Let's simply talk about it.

JOANNE: It's there if you look for it.

ANN: I don't know.

JOANNE: This is a woman's world.

(ANN *and* ELISE *reel*.)

ELISE: Again!

ANN: Nothing to do with it.

JOANNE: I'm sick of you stamping about like a man gone wrong.

ELISE: So what?

JOANNE: If men reappear, if we ever see men again at Brackenhurst, they will have to be fey imitations of women to make any impact at all. Let me tell you this——

ELISE: Again.

JOANNE: No, really, listen. Brackenhurst inches the world forward. Brackenhurst is sexual purity. Brackenhurst is the community of women. Nothing is pointed, nothing perverts.

ELISE: She's off her tiny tits.

ANN: Politics again. I've told you about politics.

JOANNE: I'm talking about women being women.

ELISE: There are some things a woman doesn't talk about.

JOANNE: Yes?

ELISE: And her rights are one.

ANN: Her rights is one.

JOANNE: I'm talking about women being really women, being different from men.

25

ANN: When I edited my school magazine, we made the rule you could write about anything you wanted except sex, religion and politics. I've tried to stick to that rule in life.

JOANNE: And the dog's crap?

ANN: The original point.

JOANNE: Yes.

ANN: Wasn't there. You don't have any respect at all.

JOANNE: It was there.

ANN: There are old-fashioned values and discipline is one.

JOANNE: Please look again.

ANN: If you people wash away the old-fashioned values, what happens to the old-fashioned people who happen to believe in them.

ELISE: You're not old-fashioned.

ANN: There are people riding on the back of those values. You can't shoot the horse away from under them.

ELISE: It doesn't make sense.

JOANNE: I've long since lost track.

ANN: If I can't discipline my staff into abandoning superficial left-wing feminist nonsense——

JOANNE: The point of the conversation. . . .

ELISE (*to* ANN): You don't *have* any values.

JOANNE: I'm trying to get through to you.

ANN: You're just using me.

JOANNE: Forget it.
        (*Pause.*)

ANN: It's not there. I've combed the ground.

JOANNE: Thank you.

ELISE: How did we get into this conversation?

JOANNE: Forget it.
        (JOANNE *goes to pour out a scotch. Pause.*)

ANN: Feminist nonsense.

JOANNE: You've never listened, how do you know?
        (*Pause.*)

ANN: In three weeks the chairman of the governors comes to inspect and we're far from ready.

ELISE: We ought to have something special to show her.

ANN: Let's paint the hall.

JOANNE: Are you determined to ignore me?

ANN: Oh, shut up.

JOANNE: I won't be ignored.

ELISE: Does she know there are only eight pupils?

ANN: Everyone knows.

ELISE: Could we keep it from her? Does she know we've lost the Royal child?

ANN: Everyone knows.

JOANNE: It left a damn sight better off.

ANN: It hardly profited from the particular trick you taught it.

JOANNE: Everyone should know.

ANN: What you taught that child was not on the syllabus. It was not royal either.

JOANNE: Royal children are just the same as any others. They should know how to masturbate. It's instinctive.

ANN: If it's instinctive, you didn't need to induce it.

JOANNE: I did not demonstrate, nor did I make any physical gesture of demonstration. I lent it some elementary literature.

ANN: Put about by your bloody feminists.

JOANNE: Masturbation is the only form of sexual expression left to the authentic woman.

ANN: I don't see the value of the act.

JOANNE: There are three of us here. For five hundred, five thousand, five million years, the inferior sex, the sex used, used for their sex: the fingers of the nation sidling for the clit, fingers of power and of government. At Brackenhurst there are only women. Brackenhurst is a new way of life.

ELISE: Brackenhurst has everything but men.

JOANNE: Exactly. Brackenhurst inches the world forward. Here at least is a pure ideal. No men.

ANN: There are no men here because they might savage the children. It's nothing to do with sexual abstinence.

ELISE: I'm a normal sort of woman.

ANN: I want this to be a tight-knit community.

ELISE: I am normal.

JOANNE: This is the battle-ground of the future. From the start there were those who said marry, infiltrate, get in there, and a different crowd who argued—separate, the divorce is total. It's between intercourse or isolation. I favour isolation. After black power, woman power.

(*Sound of children off has grown audible. Rowdy cheers as if they could hear what* JOANNE *was saying and approved.*)

ANN: Disorder!

(ANN *stomps to the common-room door, yells out.*)

If I catch anyone talking, I'll have them on oats and water for a week.

(*Silence.* ANN *closes the door very slowly.*)

ELISE: That bossy one can't keep order.

ANN: All I care about is that you lost us our best pupil.

JOANNE: The child had asked to be taken away long before it wanked itself off.

ANN: Don't be so vulgar.

JOANNE: I read the letter it wrote a week before it left. It said mummy the dormitory walls are wet and I want out of this hole.

ANN: Cruel. Really.

(JOANNE *pours out another scotch.*)

ELISE: She was peculiarly our own.

JOANNE: She paid the fees.

ANN: Her mother paid.

JOANNE: Her mother was a fool.

ANN: Her mother was a queen.

ELISE: Her father was a bit odd.

JOANNE: Her father was the queen. He's the only one I admire in this whole rotten business.

ELISE: It was your fault.

JOANNE: I hate children anyway.

ELISE: They sense that.

JOANNE: They hate me.

ANN: They think you're working class.

JOANNE: I am working class.

ELISE: Cheltenham's only member of the working class.

JOANNE: It doesn't mean I'm not.

ANN: No more politics. I've had enough.

ELISE: If you're working class, I'm Brigitte Bardot.

JOANNE: We're all in the same frig.

ELISE: And other platitudes.

JOANNE: Will you stop getting at me?

ELISE: I won't let you rest until . . .

JOANNE: Ann, will you tell your assistant to shut up, I'm taking
   to drink.

   (*Another scotch.*)

ANN: Elise, shut up——

ELISE: Don't do what she says.

JOANNE: Have you checked recently for the revolutionary turd?

ANN: Of course I have.

   (*Another scotch.*)

JOANNE: Then now I'd like you to look for that leak on the roof.

ELISE: You don't know there's anything there.

JOANNE: If my bedroom walls are wet, it's a good bet to hunt on
   the roof for the reason.

ANN: You should refer it to the Building Maintenance
   Committee.

JOANNE: We are the committee.

ELISE: We're not in session.

JOANNE: I'm for your going up.

ELISE: I'm against it.

ANN: I'm chairman.

JOANNE: Which means you have to vote for. Chairman always
   does.

ANN: Very well, I see I shall have to go, but if this is another of
   your damnfool tricks . . .

ELISE: She's having you on.

JOANNE: I would never . . .

ANN: Getting me up on the roof.

JOANNE: Up, up and to the roo-oof.

ELISE: It's undemocratic.

ANN: I'll do it to keep the peace. I'll do anything to make you
   happy.

(*Exit* ANN *to roof.*)

ELISE: You've no right to upset her.

JOANNE: Let her face facts.

ELISE: Women's Liberation Workshop!

JOANNE: She's spent her whole life pretending she's a man.
Deserves what's coming to her.

ELISE: She's just a dear, sweet middle-class girl. Like us all.

JOANNE: No such thing as middle-class. In a capitalist economy,
there are only two functions—labour and the organization
of labour. People often refer to something called a middle-
class which suffers mythically from a middle-class morality
but there's no such thing. There's the controllers and the
controlled.

ELISE: You don't believe that.

JOANNE: I do.

ELISE: And which category do Cheltenham girls fit into?

JOANNE: That's nothing to do with it. All women are controlled.
It's no longer a matter of birth. There's a new system of
privilege based on intelligence—or rather a certain sort of
acquisitive masculine intelligence that will bend in any
direction to smother alternatives. In this society where an
active, probing, hopeful intelligence is the sign of being a
good bloke, women are valued for one thing—their
reproductive facility. They bang like shithouse doors. The
alternative society that we create may be black or it may be
crippled or it may, let's hope, be female—but it is an
alternative. There'll be no moral judgments, or processes of
consultation, or export drives, or balance of payments.
There is independence of mind and body. The alternative
cannot be defined.

ELISE: Why not?

JOANNE: By escaping definition it escapes parody and defeat.
Brackenhurst is the first real experiment in all-female living.

ELISE: And this is it? This is it?

JOANNE: Yes.

ELISE: This is all-female living? This is the revolution?

JOANNE: Yes.

ELISE: What we've got now?

JOANNE: Yes.

ELISE: I'd rather not.

JOANNE: It's only in embryo. We've scarcely begun. I anticipate communal female living on a massive scale—independence of thought among teachers and pupils. I've already begun. I've told the children that you and Ann haven't yet grasped the concept. I teach them to despise Ann because she wants to make Brackenhurst like other societies.

ELISE: What about me?

JOANNE: I tell them you're immature because you still want to give your cunt to capitalism.

ELISE: I've never thought of it that way.

JOANNE: Do.

ELISE: I never could. Men are just men to me and there it is.
(ANN *goes flying down outside the window and lands unseen with a thump.*)
My God!
(ELISE *makes to dash across the room to the window.*
JOANNE *grabs at her and stops her getting there.*)
She's hurt herself.

JOANNE: Leave her.

ELISE: She's fallen off the roof.

JOANNE: Don't help her, for God's sake, we want a crisis.

ELISE: Let go of me.
(JOANNE *forces* ELISE *on to the ground and sits on top of her.*)

JOANNE: Any intermediate action that serves to reinforce the status quo rather than to restructure the whole system must by very definition be wrong.

ELISE: Get fucking off me.

JOANNE: The present situation must be allowed to develop to a crisis point in order to emphasize to all the needs for the complete overall destruction of the present scheme of things. Let her lie there a bit.
(ELISE *forces* JOANNE *off her and rushes up.*)

ELISE: Fucking maniac.

JOANNE: Liberty! Equality! Sisterhood!

31

(ELISE *rushes to the window, opens it.*)

ELISE: Are you all right?

ANN: Slight fall. Nothing at all.

(ANNE *is seen to get up, completely unscathed. Climbs in the window.*)

Foot must have slipped.

ELISE: Let me get you a drink.

ANN: Please don't bother.

(ANN *rubs her ankle, but seems unbruised.*)

I was stretching for the drainpipe when my foot slipped.

ELISE: You could have been hurt.

ANN: I'm pretty tough. I'll go back up.

(ANN *gets up to go out.*)

ELISE: You can't go up now.

ANN: Why not?

ELISE: You've just had a fall.

JOANNE: Finish the job.

ANN: I'll find out what's up there.

JOANNE: Did you find anything?

ELISE: You can't go up again right after falling down. It's very dangerous.

ANN: Nonsense.

ELISE: You can't possibly go back.

ANN: I promise you it's O.K.

ELISE (*vehement*): I forbid you.

ANN: Elise.

ELISE (*still vehement*): There's nothing wrong with the pipe. Stay where you are.

ANN: Really, I can't deal with both your tempers.

ELISE: What are you going up for? Her?

ANN: I said I'd have a look.

ELISE: Her bedroom walls are perfectly dry. I've felt them. Do you know what she's just told me? Do you know what she tells the children?

(JOANNE *goes and pours another drink.*)

ANN: I can imagine.

ELISE: I wouldn't repeat the things she says about us.

ANN: She's free to say what she likes. She's a member of my staff.

JOANNE: Are you going up on the roof or not?

ANN: Of course.

JOANNE: You'd better go up before it's dark.

ELISE: Don't you dare.

ANN: What?

ELISE: I suppose you believe this stuff about how she's miserable at night.

ANN: I'd do the same for you.

ELISE: Kiss my foot.

ANN: Huh.

JOANNE: Let's get on. It must be lovely on the roof.

ANN: I'm bound to protect her.

ELISE: I accept that, Ann, and will you lick my big toe?

ANN: Don't be so silly. Ha Ha.

ELISE: Cut my toenails with your teeth.

ANN: Don't be so silly.

ELISE: Cut my toes.

ANN: Please let's be friends.

ELISE: Toes.

JOANNE: Isn't that sunset beautiful?

ELISE: Put my toes in your mouth.

ANN: Out of sheer embarrassment.

ELISE: Go on.

ANN: You don't . . .

ELISE: Go on.

JOANNE: Isn't that the most beautiful sunset?

ANN: Come.

ELISE: Ann.

ANN: Elise.

ELISE: Do what you say.

(ANN *kneels down and bites the nail off* ELISE's *toe.*)
Fantastic.

(ANN *bounds back and away, smiling.*)

JOANNE: A girl could almost be happy.

ELISE: Now lick.

ANN: Come.

ELISE: Lick my toes.

(ANN *licks* ELISE's *toes*.)

JOANNE: Absurd. Ludicrous. Are we meant to take that seriously?

ANN: That was nothing.

(ANN *gets up*.)

JOANNE: Why can't people think of anything else when they think of women?

ANN: That proved nothing.

JOANNE: They think of sex.

ANN: It doesn't mean anything, Elise. It's quite without significance.

ELISE: Now do it again but with more tact.

JOANNE: Lick a toe with tact.

ELISE: Again.

JOANNE: How can you lick a toe with tact?

ELISE: Don't be difficult.

ANN: Tact isn't in it.

ELISE: Don't be difficult.

(ANN *licks again*.)

Exactly.

ANN: Absolutely.

JOANNE: Fucking ridiculous.

ANN: It just felt good.

(JOANNE *is pouring out another drink*.)

I'll have a drink, Joanne.

JOANNE: Get it yourself.

ANN: I take it from you now, Joanne, but I'm hard put to take it when the girls are around.

JOANNE: Some kind of imaginative gleam in me upsets you.

(*Exit* ELISE *quietly at this line*.)

ANN: I have some status here.

JOANNE: You know I'm an artist.

ANN: I know.

(ANN *goes to get a drink*.)

JOANNE: Not the kind of artist that actually has anything to do

with art. I wouldn't touch it eeurch. Culture eeurch. But an
artist in the way I am. I want gold cherubs blowing
trumpets over my bed and an ivory bathtub to wash in.

ANN: Anything.

JOANNE: Not dripping polystyrene.

ANN: It's tiled over to keep it warm.

JOANNE: It gives me hay fever. I trip daily over those stringy
raffia mats on the slippery path to the bathroom, where the
basin is slimy with a coat of old toothpaste, other peoples'
spittings of toothpaste and saliva. In this state I fall
downstairs to teach eight benighted little sods what—you
change the time-table so often I'm doing woodwork when
I should be teaching chemistry. I want out of it, my love.

ANN: There's nothing I can do.

JOANNE: I'm determined to leave.

ANN: Of course.

(JOANNE *gets two drinks, one for* ANN.)

JOANNE: Here at Brackenhurst, a distinctive sound. The heavy
breathing that means nothing is happening. At Brackenhurst
nothing ever happens. The tedium is quite a challenge, quite
an experience. The distinctive English sight of nothing
happening and nothing going to happen.

ANN: Nothing ever happens at Brackenhurst.

JOANNE: What was the point of that game with the toes?

ANN: That was Elise's idea.

JOANNE: Ah.

(*From the nearby classroom,* sound of children singing The
Lord is my Shepherd *in agonized treble.*)

ANN: Elise is teaching again. She has the knack of making them
happy. She's a superior teacher. When the governors come,
I'll expect you to behave. I'll expect you to be a positive
person.

JOANNE: You're poisoning me.

ANN: I'm quite without malice.

JOANNE: I've had stomach cramps all week. There's poison in
my food.

ANN: You must complain to the kitchens.

JOANNE: You are the kitchens.

(*Music stops.*)

ANN: You're a child and you're lucky to be here, and it's only because Elise and I love you and look after you that you are able to face life at all, and it's only because we want you to be happy that we protect you. You're a parasite and depend on us, and every night I pray for you, and I'd maybe like you to be somewhat grateful.

JOANNE: My arse.

ANN: You're a schizophrenic, Joanne.

JOANNE: Cow, flabby cow.

ANN: The doctor said you ought to be told.

JOANNE: Sodden flabby cow.

ANN: I'm tired of having to love you.

JOANNE: I'm sick of your motherly concern.

ANN: Schizophrenic garbage.

JOANNE: Cow.

(*Blackout on the last word.*)

During the scene change: The Lord is my Shepherd.

Brackenhurst playing-fields. Bright day. Glare. ANN *and* ELISE *are lounging in deckchairs, with a high wire fence behind them. They watch the game intensely. Immediately the lights come up they clap.*

ANN: Very good.

ELISE: Good.

ANN: Very good.

ELISE: Shot.

ANN: She's got a lovely cover drive.

ELISE: Shot.

ANN: Don't let her catch you. Run, for God's sake, run.

(*Sounds of the game very low.*)

ELISE: She's all right.

ANN: She will not play off her back foot. She will not move

36

on to it.

ELISE: I've told her often enough.

ANN: I've told her again and again.

ELISE: The visitors are good. They're undeniably good.

ANN: Doesn't it make you glad to be alive? What is it Wordsworth says?

ELISE: Dunno.

ANN: Ah.

(*Enter* JOANNE *dressed in white*.)

JOANNE: God, it's hot.

ANN: It's hot or it's cold, you always complain.

JOANNE: It's a man's game anyway, it's quite wrong for women to play it at all.

ANN: They're not a match for our first eleven.

JOANNE: What eleven? There *are* only eight.

ANN: Seven. Another dropped out this morning. The chauffeur came to remove her.

ELISE (*gets up*): I can't see why we're so bad at this business.

ANN: We're not bad.

(JOANNE *takes* ELISE's *seat*.)

ELISE: I know I'm not very clever and, Joanne, you're controversial, Ann, you're a little scaring to the young, but we're no worse than most.

ANN: D'you think Benenden has this trouble?

ELISE: They seem to hold on to their pupils.

ANN: You think we're doing something wrong?

ELISE: There seems to be something missing. The schizophrenic's got my chair.

JOANNE: It's mine.

ELISE: We're rather short on facilities.

ANN: Oh well done. What a good shot. That was good. I still say a pavilion. That's where we fall down. Everyone should get a prize on Sports Day—things like that. Class tells.

ELISE: Men in the dormitories.

ANN: Elise.

ELISE: I am pornography.

ANN: I am cricket.

(*They laugh.*)

JOANNE: I want to go and see a film. Take your filthy seat.

(ELISE *takes* JOANNE'*s seat.*)

ANN: The bus went hours ago and there's not one back today.

JOANNE: I'll go tomorrow.

ANN: No bus tomorrow because it's Thursday.

JOANNE: I'm walking tomorrow.

ANN: It's eighteen miles.

JOANNE: I'll cycle.

ANN: The tyres are flat.

JOANNE: I want to see a fucking film.

ANN: Don't swear.

ELISE: Shot.

JOANNE: I'm sick of looking at things live. I want to see them second hand.

ANN: When D. H. Lawrence went to the cinema for the first time he found it so—vulgar—he vomited.

JOANNE: You mean old snipcock.

ELISE: Joanne.

ANN: Lawrence was the most wonderful man of our age.

JOANNE: Lawrence never got over his amazement that the bits slotted together.

ANN: Lawrence loved truth and beauty. Stop this filthy talk.

(*Pause.*)

Stupid girl has run herself out.

(*They clap.*)

ELISE: Well played.

ANN: Good innings.

ELISE: Well done.

ANN: Very good.

ELISE: How ugly she is.

JOANNE: She can't help that.

ELISE: Never said she could.

JOANNE: Why pick on me all the time?

(JOANNE *gets up and walks off towards the returning batswoman offstage.*)

I say, Sarah.

38

(*Exit* JOANNE.)

ANN: Now.

(ELISE *replaces her own chair with an old deckchair she gets from the fence and sits down in another spot with her original chair.*)

ELISE: There.

ANN: That one?

ELISE: It'll do what's required. I prepared it.

ANN: It's hardly fair to her.

ELISE: Don't weaken now.

ANN: Excellent. I have very high hopes of this joke.

ELISE: This is awfully good fun.

ANN: Who is it now?

(ELISE *points.*)

Oh, it's her. She won't score anything.

ELISE: I hate her.

ANN: She's not much.

(JOANNE *enters.*)

JOANNE: I said well done to that girl and she said that was no compliment coming from me as I hate cricket.

ELISE: True.

JOANNE: I get easily upset.

(JOANNE *sits in the chair. It collapses.*)

ELISE: Hurrah, hurrah.

ANN: She fell right into it.

JOANNE: What imagination.

ELISE: Don't be sarky. You fell right into it.

JOANNE: Imaginative.

ELISE: Don't try and get out of it. You fell for it.

JOANNE: I'm suffering, damn you.

ANN: Don't take it so seriously.

ELISE: Have a little fun.

JOANNE: Doesn't anyone realize how much I suffer?

ANN: We can see.

ELISE: So can the whole school. All seven.

JOANNE: You will not take me seriously.

ELISE: No.

JOANNE: Isn't there a time to stop joking and——

ELISE: No.

JOANNE: You shun me, the girls shun me.

ANN: You're making a ridiculous exhibition of yourself. Shut up and sit down.

JOANNE: What have you got against me?

ELISE: Relax.

ANN: You think we persecute you.

JOANNE: You poison my food.

ANN: You think everyone hates you.

JOANNE: It's a pathetically ineffective way of poisoning anyone to put arsenic in their food, because it starts coming out in their hair. Look.

(JOANNE *gets up, shakes her head down and runs her fingers through her hair.*)

ELISE: Dandruff.

JOANNE: Arsenic.

ANN: We love you.

JOANNE: You collapse my deckchair.

ELISE: Joke.

JOANNE: It's not just you, it's the girls.

ANN: You think everyone is against you.

JOANNE: Let me make myself clear. I didn't come here to be liked. I came for different reasons and it wasn't to entertain you or fartarse on your behalf. I was wrong to be sidetracked. I'm tough as leather as the children say—they hate me. O.K. What I set out to do was educate this mob to be themselves. I'm here to teach isolation so I resent the fact I have to mix with you at all. I want every child to know that it's a girl and different for being a girl and better for being a girl. I want a separate culture. I want a different way of life. We're too far gone to want anything but everything—all the way out. I want a self-sufficient child. I want an alternative to everything men are. I left everything I loved, I haven't been to the cinema for I don't know how long, to come to Brackenhust, to work in a community that was feminine by necessity and make it feminine by choice.

—

You should want to be women. And I found—what did I
find—Elise whose idea of the sexual revolution is to open
her legs and say AAAAAH and Ann—what can I say? And
a combined ability that keeps a tenuous grasp on just seven
children. I'll teach them all they need and I don't care if
you hate me for it.

ELISE: It's gone right past square leg.

ANN: Oh well hit.

ELISE: And you teach them—sleight of hand.

ANN: Not that incident again.

ELISE: You teach them dexterity with the Mum rollette.

JOANNE: What a squalid mind you have.

ANN: Let me tell you something, Joanne, that I ought to have
told you a long time ago.

JOANNE: What's that?

ANN: No, I can't be bothered.

JOANNE: You have nothing to tell me.

ANN: I'm putting you in charge of the School Corps.

JOANNE: Over my dead body.

ANN: If necessary. I'm appointing you Sergeant Major. It's a
position of some responsibility. At Brackenhurst we control
the minds of the young. We have the influence to shape
their lives. I have listened to you for some time now,
Joanne. I've heard your views on power, responsibility,
education, the British Press, constitutional monarchy, the
race to the moon, the emancipation of women, Lord
Thomson, the Archbishop of Canterbury, cricket, dancing,
smoking and masturbation and I'm glad having listened to
judge your opinions pure balls and your mind irretrievably
shallow.

ELISE: That's strongly put.

ANN: I'm so tired of the political mind.

(JOANNE *breaks away fast to the back*.)

JOANNE: Where's the gap in this bloody thing?

(JOANNE *darts back and forth, gives up trying to find a gap,
throws herself up on to the wire instead.* ANN *gets up*.)

ANN: Come back here.

JOANNE: I'm getting out.

    (JOANNE *clambers up towards the top.* ANN *pursues, catches her leg, pulls at it, brings her to the ground.* JOANNE *up on her feet launches at* ANN; ANN *throws her over her shoulder to the ground. Helps her up, leads her forward.*)

ANN: Karate specialist, you see. Simple skill worth knowing.

    (JOANNE *is sat down gently.*)

JOANNE: You hurt me.

ANN: Everyone tries a breakout at one time or another.

ELISE: The third mistress always tries.

JOANNE: You've let them go before.

ANN: The mistresses, not the girls.

ELISE: The girls are easier to catch.

ANN: One girl reached the village but the uniform gave her away.

ELISE: I thought this was meant to be the ideal community.

JOANNE: If we are to be grouped together for some social purpose . . .

ELISE: Social theory.

JOANNE: But this is a repressive . . .

ANN: You are hardly likely to get any farther than anyone before you.

JOANNE: Masculine . . .

ELISE: Not on those legs!

JOANNE: Does no one listen to anything I say?

ELISE: No.

JOANNE: I feel victimized.

ANN: This school . . .

JOANNE: Don't bother to go on.

ANN: This school . . .

JOANNE: Don't bother to go on.

ANN: This school . . .

JOANNE: I don't want to hear. We don't want to hear.

ANN: This school . . .

JOANNE: Don't finish that sentence.

ANN: This school . . .

JOANNE: I won't let you.

ANN: This school . . .

JOANNE: You're not to.

ANN: This school . . .

> (*Pause. Surprise.*)
> This school has some standards to keep up. And I will murder to maintain them.
> (*Pause.*)

JOANNE: I think that sums up things pretty well. From now on war.

> (JOANNE *tries minimally to break again, but* ANN *is on her feet almost before she moves.*)
> Vicious.
> (JOANNE *edges back towards* ANN's *old chair, which she moves away from the other two.* ANN *is left without one.*)

ANN: Education should be lethal. I think of teaching as a knife.

JOANNE: Vicious.

ANN: We must be very careful what they hear and see. The sight of you, Joanne, is therapeutic. They thank God they're not like you.

ELISE: It's true.

ANN: I use you in my social adaptability classes. Some of the girls have very advanced theories about you.

JOANNE: Such as.

ANN: I use you as an example of the modern woman.

JOANNE: What about her?

ELISE: Me?

JOANNE: Permissiveness.

ELISE: I wish it was.

JOANNE: Debauchery, love of body. Isn't she in your classes?

ANN: Elise is the Assistant Headmistress.

JOANNE: That's not what it says on the lavatory wall.

ANN: It is really of no consequence. You and I know that, Joanne. We are above such things. I look at Elise.

ELISE: Don't bother with me.

ANN: And pity that pathetic dependence on the body.

JOANNE: Pathetic.

ELISE: I'm just backward.

43

ANN: You shudder she's so retarded.

ELISE: I'm just backward, I like cricket and sex.

ANN: Cricket, my God.

(ANN *runs out to the front of the stage, peers out. Sigh of relief. Claps.*)

I completely forgot.

ELISE: Shot.

ANN: Very good.

JOANNE: Nothing has changed.

ELISE: Excellent.

ANN: Excellent. Doesn't it make you glad to be alive? After all your bickering and complaint? It's criminal not to enjoy yourself. I'm so sorry for you, my love.

JOANNE: Forget it.

ANN: But I must ask you to do your duty now. That dreadful woman is signalling which means you must go out and umpire.

JOANNE: I hate it.

ANN: It's your turn.

JOANNE: I make all the wrong decisions. Everyone gets so angry with me.

ANN: Quite right. It makes for a game of chance. Better by far for the character.

ELISE: I'm always fair.

ANN: I always try to throw in some errors of judgment to spite all those frightful girls who are all skill and no charm.

ELISE: They think it's favouritism.

ANN: I'll do your umpiring for you, Joanne, if you'll do my shower duty in return.

JOANNE: Thank you.

(*Exit* ANN.)

JOANNE: All right, tell me now.

ELISE: Do you really want to know?

JOANNE: She trusts you, doesn't she?

ELISE: She believes I love Brackenhurst.

44

JOANNE: It's all a bit improbable.

ELISE: I don't know the details but I can tell you this much. There are no men at Brackenhurst.

JOANNE: Tradesmen.

ELISE: Let's not get political. Tradesmen aren't real men. Who comes here? A few corn and meat merchants, hardly virile, hardly material for Ann. But . . . she is definitely having an affair with the butcher.

JOANNE: The butcher!

ELISE: She says he has capable hands. I'd call them murderous. Real butcher's hands with black hairs on the finger joints— they attract her.

JOANNE: How disgusting it all is.

ELISE: She thinks of him a lot. He's called Haskins.

JOANNE: There's an alliance, a union?

ELISE: Of course.

JOANNE: Intercourse on some, on several occasions?

ELISE: Of course.

JOANNE: The pig.

ELISE: Ann told me he was an *energetic* man.

JOANNE: Things are definitely happening.

ELISE: Oh yes.

(*Pause.*)

JOANNE: I knew that it would all come out.

ELISE: She's a woman of character.

JOANNE: I can see her across the field. Look, look. Everything other people would have wanted her to be. I daren't be too rude for fear you won't like me.

ELISE: It's all too far gone for that.

JOANNE: I feel silly.

ELISE: It's never stopped you before.

JOANNE: You don't like me anyway.

ELISE: I do.

JOANNE: She's capable, lovable, would even be a good mother to a child. She's a fool because she wants to be, like so many old people.

ELISE: She's 32.

JOANNE: She's old. Why do they all choose to be like that?
The trouble with Ann—
ELISE: Tell me the trouble with Ann.
JOANNE: The trouble with Ann—
ELISE: The trouble with Ann is the trouble with most people.
Her life stopped at the age of 18.
(*Minor uproar on the field.*)
What's happening?
JOANNE: Hard to say. I think Ann called a no-ball some time
after one of our lot was caught.
ELISE: Typical decision.
JOANNE: We must never accept things, never give in.
ELISE: What use is Ann to you?
JOANNE: No use. What's the time?
ELISE: Tea time.
JOANNE: I haven't worked everything out yet. You must
remember I have survived an English education. To have
any plan of action at the end of an English education is a
triumph.
ELISE: But you don't have a plan for Ann?
JOANNE: Brackenhurst is a pure ideal, pure idealism. I had a
dream last night. It concerned you. Would you like to hear
it?
ELISE: No.
JOANNE: I'll tell you.
ELISE: I should think it was a ballet dancer in flames or a snake
in a custard pie.
JOANNE: Not quite. This was the dream. You were about to have
a child, and the rest of us—there were a lot of us—
gathered round a table and waited for you to give birth. You
were not much inflated, simply we knew you were pregnant.
You didn't look it. We knew it in the way you can be sure
in dreams. You suddenly asked to be excused, to slip out
for a few moments, but I protested. I took an active part
because I felt involved which is unusual. I felt so strongly,
not towards you, but about you. I wanted to *see* you have
the child. You lay down on the table and the first animal

46

came out. There was some discussion among us as to
who should have the first bite, but a man interrupted
and ate your first child which was a chicken. The second
was a fish and I had some. You lay on the table and
the wet animals came regularly from you. And we all
ate.

ELISE: You really are a fraud.

JOANNE: It's true.

ELISE: You muck around stamping about in our lives.

JOANNE: I'm just trying to help.

ELISE: Listen, help yourself.

JOANNE: How?

ELISE: Ann's changed. She's gone weak in the heart from knowing
Haskins . . . He's your man.

JOANNE: I want to get at her somehow.

ELISE: Use the butcher.

JOANNE: Yes.

ELISE: The butcher's knife. Look, they're coming in.
(*Applause.*)

JOANNE: It looks like *Accident*. Joseph Losey, 1967. The great
Dirk Bogarde.

ELISE: In for tea.

JOANNE: They look so fucking happy.

ELISE: Rah! Rah!
(*Enter* ANN *in a white coat.*)

ANN: Smashing game.
(*Blackout end of scene.*)

During the scene change Helen Shapiro sings Walking back to
Happiness.

SCENE THREE

A row of baths in a white-tiled room. ELISE *alone. She dances a*

47

few steps of her Walking Back to Brackenhurst *routine in complete silence but with facial expression. Runs suddenly to behind a tiled shower wall. Enter* JOANNE. *A bucket falls on her head. Pain. She jumps up and down once or twice holding her head, hopping ludicrously. Turns. Sees* ELISE.

JOANNE: A bucket just fell on my head.

ELISE: No sense of humour.

JOANNE: Tit.

ELISE: I didn't do it.

JOANNE: Bloody Ann did it. They're out to get me. Last night the chandelier that's over my bed crashed down as I was getting in. It's getting so I daren't move.

ELISE: It's all your imagination.

JOANNE: It was a vow we all took, remember? And it was inherent in the vow that we'd all love each other a little more.

ELISE: It wasn't specified.

JOANNE: And we will stick to that?

ELISE: Yes.

JOANNE: And there will be a little more—love.

ELISE: Give me a hand.

JOANNE: I've a yoyo here I want to mend.

ELISE: Eh, lass.

JOANNE: It's not running properly.

ELISE: Thou wer't born idle and thou shal't cum to nowt.

JOANNE: That's very good.

ELISE: It should be. I was born there.

JOANNE: You come from the North?

ELISE: Of course.

JOANNE: I never knew. Was your father a miner?

ELISE: No.

JOANNE: Not the other side, not a millowner?

ELISE: Of course not.

JOANNE: And were you poor?

ELISE: Very.

JOANNE: And did you eat chip butties and go to chapel?

ELISE: Incessantly.

48

JOANNE: Oh, Elise I never guessed you were working class. Why's your name Elise?

ELISE: They mis-spelt Elsie on the birth certificate.

JOANNE: And when you were young was it all day trips to Bingley and Huddersfield and Salford and Leeds? Is that how it really was? I see it so clearly. Did your parents fuck loudly in upstairs rooms?

ELISE: The only person who fucked was my sister. She married early and they came to live with us in the room next door to me. And at nights before I really knew what was happening, she used to cry out suddenly when she reached her orgasm—"Eh, by gum."

JOANNE: How splendid!

ELISE: It was wonderful. I used to lie there and imagine what it would be like to have a real vaginal orgasm.

JOANNE: No such thing.

ELISE: There is.

JOANNE: Isn't.

ELISE: Is.

JOANNE: All orgasms are the same in the female. The idea that there are two kinds has been put about by oppressive males determined to deny women their rightful clitoral pleasures.

ELISE: Nonsense.

JOANNE: It's true. Men have consistently attempted to down-grade the clitoris. They claim it is just a withered penis. What arrogance! A withered penis! The clitoris has been scientifically established as having the greatest concentration of sensory nerve endings of any part of a human body, male or female. More than this.

ELISE: There's more?

JOANNE: It has also, inch for inch, measure for measure, a far greater erectile capacity than the comparatively dull, insensitive, numb male organ.

ELISE: Is that really true?

JOANNE: The satisfaction of the female is correspondingly greater than that of the male. The penis is a poor blunt

49

instrument beside the sensitivity of the delicate amazing
clitoris.

ELISE: Are you a virgin?

JOANNE: Of course.

ELISE: Then you don't know what you're talking about.

JOANNE: You don't have to have felt a penis to know these
things. You can make your mind up perfectly adequately
from descriptions and drawings.

ELISE: Help me clean the baths.

JOANNE: No.

ELISE: There's an inspection in half an hour. As soon as the
Greek dancing's over. And I've got my song to rehearse.

JOANNE (*sitting*): Now give us a song!

ELISE: Do you want to see?

JOANNE: Please.

ELISE: For the Governors of Brackenhurst a song, in the modern
idiom.

JOANNE: Come on.

ELISE: Give us a chance.

> Walking back to Brackenhurst
> Ump a o ye ye
> Had enough of loneliness
> Ump a o ye ye
> Brackenhurst's the place for me
> It's the only place to be.

(ELISE *re-practises getting the dance right that goes with it.*)
How was it?

JOANNE: Dreadful.

ELISE: Why?

JOANNE: What does it mean? It doesn't mean anything.

ELISE: I've always wanted to entertain. I'm going to try showbiz
when I get out.

JOANNE (*up*): Is it easy to do that walk?

ELISE: Nothing simpler.

JOANNE ⎫ (*together*): Walking Back to Brackenhurst
ELISE ⎭ Ump a o ye ye
Had enough of loneliness

Ump a o ye ye
Brackenhurst's the place for me
It's the only place to be.

JOANNE: I'm coming along.

ELISE: Very good.

JOANNE (*singing*): *I'm Singing in the Rain*. Gene Kelly. 1951. I never thought to have any talent. Look, I'll show you how to do the Gene Kelly.

(*She dances, rather slowly, but with some beauty.*)

ELISE: I've got work to do.

JOANNE (*snatching the brush*): Let someone else do the work.

ELISE: Give me that. I've got to do it.

JOANNE: Why?

ELISE: Ann told me to.

JOANNE: So?

ELISE: I'll report you.

JOANNE: What do you think you're doing, Elise, obeying her?

(*They process round with* ELISE *trying to get the brush.*)

Are you really going to spend your entire life imagining penises of amazing thrust and magnitude—phantom penises—alternately fucking and obeying, laying down under men whatever they say? Lying down under Ann?

ELISE: Give me the brush.

JOANNE: Use your claws. And counting your shares? You see, I've found out about the shares in Shell Oil and ICI and Marks and Spencer and——

ELISE: Good shares!

JOANNE: Class traitor—a working-class girl with shares in Dow Chemicals. A very good share the napalm share as long as the war holds. Supply and demand—very much a seller's market nowadays in napalm.

ELISE: I'm putting it aside for my old age.

(JOANNE *tosses her the brush.*)

JOANNE: Quite so.

(ELISE *sets to work cleaning one bath while filling another with water.*)

ELISE: You've been hunting through my papers.

JOANNE: I'm fascinated by your private life. I find it studded with young bucks.

ELISE: You have read everything in my room.

JOANNE: Everything. If we're to live together, make this community work then we must know everything about each other, so we're strong in each other.

ELISE: Not much strength in my things.

JOANNE: I don't know.

ELISE: Quite the opposite. I don't like you hunting about, trying to make me political.

JOANNE: Make you? We're all political. We're in politics up to our eyeballs, in the shit, God help us.

(JOANNE *throws Ajax over the floor as she speaks.*)

ELISE: What's that for? Help me scrub.

JOANNE: No.

ELISE: Ann'll see to you. Wait till I tell her. What is that for?

JOANNE: It's for Ann to clean. Principles of guerrilla warfare. I am fighting back where least expected.

(ANN *enters in Greek costume.*)

ANN: Did you grease the bottoms of the Greek dancers' shoes?

ELISE: Did she do that?

JOANNE: Not saying.

ANN: They're falling about like skittles in there. I'm going to have a word or two to say. Free form and bodily expression it's meant to be, and you've got them tumbling about showing their knickers in front of the Governors.
Clean up that mess on the floor, Joanne. If you won't help, then you'll have to go.

JOANNE: Suits me.

ANN: Are these chairs not done, Elise, mercy, and the Governors not five minutes away?

JOANNE: From where I'm standing I can see the butcher calling at the door. He's knocked twice and looks like giving up.

ANN: I'll go down and speak to him.

JOANNE: I think it's a delivery, I'll see to it.

ANN: Please, I can manage.

JOANNE: I am Domestic Science, I can go.

ANN: I am Kitchens, I will.

JOANNE: The Governors are waiting for you in the Hall.

ANN: Out of my way.

JOANNE: Let me.

ANN: Quick or he'll go.

JOANNE: Exactly. Back to the Greek dancing.

ANN: I want to see the butcher.

(*She gets by.*)

JOANNE: There's nothing between his legs you couldn't find
elsewhere.

ANN: Vulgar. Heartless Child.

JOANNE: So?

ANN: You're fired.

(ANN *rushes out.* JOANNE *yells after her.*)

JOANNE: If a lascivious and debauched headmistress can't
even . . .

(ELISE *drudges on.* JOANNE *turns back.*)

I'm out of it. She's just let me go. And there's a Warner
Brothers Retrospective at the National Film Theatre and I
just couldn't be happier.

ELISE: What about our community?

JOANNE: The mistake of any doctrinal group is to render itself
monolithic. In other words, intercourse or isolation? I'm
leaving. I must take my practical experience of a feminist
community—Brackenhurst—to my sisters in the outside
world. Who can benefit from what I learnt here.

ELISE: She won't let you go.

JOANNE: To show women everywhere they don't have to lie
down for anyone.

ELISE: You haven't done anything here. You haven't gone one
inch towards helping any woman here.

JOANNE: I've got that woman on the run. This place'll never
give off that dreadful masculine chill again. Look, she's
chasing the butcher down the drive.

ELISE: You've closed the whole place down.

JOANNE: Well, that's good, isn't it? Are you going to run that

bath all day? Dawn. An empty street. A delicatessen.
Goldstein's delicatessen. A scrap of paper blowing down
the cardboard street. A streetlight still lit. Two boys dressed
in something like tweed and urchin caps, sly as hell
with shining faces. A brick, a window, they throw it
through, hands into the cooked meat counter but the
alarm's gone and we're on our way into another Warner
Brother's Retrospective season.

(ELISE *has turned the bath off.* ANN *has entered.* JOANNE
continues to fanfare the Retrospective.)

ANN: You know I don't mind about all the troubles, Joanne,
that have set you aside from the rest of us, your being an
artist and therefore different. But the point must be made.
You live in a world of your own, and you must control
your fantasies.

(ANN *throws her a leg of lamb.* JOANNE *catches it.*)

You are Domestic Science.

JOANNE: You sacked me.

ANN: That remains to be seen.

JOANNE: I'm dismissed. (*Threatening with the joint.*) I promise
you.

ANN: We need you far too much.

ELISE: Far too much.

ANN: There's no need for that now, Elise. The Governors have
gone.

ELISE: What about my song?

ANN: Keep it for another time.

ELISE: My song.

ANN: There are very few governors left. A few more governors
than pupils in fact, but not very many all the same.

(ANN *has been standing at the back. She drops to her knees.*)

God, why I allow it I will never know.

JOANNE (*gently*): Let me go. There are only five pupils. You
don't need three teachers.

ANN: Where would you go?

JOANNE: I'd work in the cinema again.

ANN: You couldn't cope, it's become terribly hard work. They

54

have seventy-millimetre equipment. That's man's work.

JOANNE: There's no ready reason . . .

ANN (*no longer resigned but really angry*): You're as much sold
on this place as the rest of us. (*Recovering.*) Isn't she, Elise?

ELISE: Yes.

JOANNE: Why do you want me to stay?

ANN: Because we love you.

JOANNE: Why do you love me?

ANN: Because you're you. You're my testament to Brackenhurst,
I remember the Princess said to me——

JOANNE: Snob.

ANN: The Princess said—"Why employ somebody with such a
feeble grasp of reality." She meant you. "Your Highness,"
I replied, "here we care." And her Highness answered and
I was very moved by this, "Perhaps in the kingdom of the
mind the sane are mad and the mad sane." Such a way she
said it. And they say royalty aren't intellectuals. They
aren't in the way you are, Joanne: neurotic and miserable,
trying to make us all sad.

JOANNE: She still took her kid away.

ANN: You drive everyone away. The Governors fled so fast you
might have thought the house was on fire. Your feminist
appeals strike no chord in women and simply repel men.

JOANNE: Good. It was a real disappointment to me when you
gave in. Chastity was something of a passion of mine. To
have held off for so long, Ann, and then to give in to the
butcher—a fine man, a working man, an artisan, certainly.
But not the man you deserve, through no fault of
his own a victim, poor sod, one of the sodding people.

ANN: I'm a cumbersome performer. I don't count myself very
much. I haven't laid bare great golden fields of happiness
I'd care to tell you about. I don't have simple sexual needs.
No one who teaches at Brackenhurst does. We're all in the
Freud and underpant class. The men I've known leave soon
afterwards. But my experience of men is what makes me a
woman.

JOANNE: How grotesque.

ANN: Grotesque it may be to you whose experience of sex is the Brackenhurst changing-rooms in among the brassieres, but to those of us——

ELISE: Do keep it down——

ANN: You're on my side.

(JOANNE *leaps on to the end of the bath facing the audience.*)

JOANNE: All my suffering! I shall crop my hair like Joan of Arc. Dreyer 1926.

(*She falls face downwards into the water, comes up.*)

Extravagant gesture.

(*But* ANN *is over at the side of the tub and speaks at once.*)

ANN: While you're there, Joanne, listen.

(ELISE *takes* JOANNE'S *other arm and they support her head over the edge of the end of the bath.*)

The world is not divided into two. The bad and the good and the women and the men. Do you understand that? Do you understand?

JOANNE: I don't believe it.

(ANN *and* ELISE *duck her head and hold it under the water.*)

ANN: Can you hear me?

(ANN *and* ELISE *lift her head out.*)

All right, do you feel better? You've caused a lot of trouble with your views. Let's get this straight. I am a woman and I'm inferior to men. The woman's place is below, beneath and under men.

JOANNE: It's not.

(ANN *and* ELISE *duck her head and hold it under the water.*)

ANN: I will fight to the death for my right to be inferior. Inferiority is a privilege I wish to preserve. I don't want to be equal. And I don't want my girls equal. And I don't want a socialist community.

(ANN *and* ELISE *lift her head out.*)

JOANNE: Now it comes out.

(ANN *pushes her down repeatedly and hard into the water.*)

ANN: See what I want? See what I want?

ELISE: Leave her alone.

ANN: I'm losing my pupils, my governors, my school, my

self-respect.

ELISE: Leave her alone. Let's go for a drink.

(ANN *lets go of* JOANNE. ANN *and* ELISE *leave*.)

ANN (*as they go*): Yesterday she handed all the girls a jar of Vaseline.

(*Exeunt*.)

(JOANNE *gets dripping out of the bath*.)

JOANNE: Very good, excellent.

(*Blackout end of scene*.)

During the scene change: Henry Mancini.

SCENE FOUR

Common Room. ANN *and* ELISE *are at opposite ends of the room, well dressed. They're pissed, but elevated not slurring.*

ANN: Drink?

ELISE: You can take me out tonight.

(ANN *goes to get a drink*.)

With the present shortage of men you may take me out.

ANN: Thank you.

ELISE: Don't be shy.

ANN: What would you like?

ELISE: Scotch.

ANN: Go mad and have a Campari.

ELISE: I'll have a scotch.

ANN: My first. . . .

ELISE: What? Go on, say.

ANN (*mumbling*): Lovely dress.

ELISE: Thank you.

ANN: Lovely.

ELISE: Huh huh.

ANN: You've got the figure for it too. So slim.

ELISE: Flat-chested. I've always had small breasts.

ANN: I didn't imagine they'd shrunk.
(*Remark is unreasonably funny. They laugh.*)
Oh very good. So far very good.
ELISE: It doesn't convince me for a moment. I feel exceedingly foolish. I'd never laugh at a joke like that.
ANN: I was perfectly well in there.
ELISE: It's not a bit realistic.
ANN: I wish I had your breasts.
ELISE: You're welcome to them.
ANN: I don't know what it is people like about big breasts.
ELISE: Don't be absurd. Absurd. Have you ever talked like, a man would fly if you said that.
ANN: Who's the man?
ELISE: You are.
ANN: So?
ELISE: So. . . .
ANN: I make the rules.
ELISE: You can't have it both ways. Are you a man?
ANN: I'm the bloody man.
ELISE: Then no breasts. Breasts are out. You may comment on mine but you may not refer to your own.
ANN: I knew when I first met you that here was someone very warm, very responsive, who would understand the troubles —in my life immediately.
ELISE: A great improvement. Certainly. . . .
ANN: A lot of people want the physical thing.
ELISE: That's my experience.
ANN: But when somebody special——
ELISE: Absolutely the same thing with me.
ANN: Then there is an immediate—I want a word.
ELISE: Rapport——
ANN: Rapport——
ELISE: Yes?
ANN: It's going to be more than physical. Though of course it may be physical as well.
ELISE: As well. Of course.
ANN: It will in fact be better for the physical thing will be based

on something real.

ELISE: That's tremendously exciting.

ANN: It will be based on our respect for each others' minds.

ELISE: Rather than our bodies.

ANN: You know.

ELISE: I know.

ANN: Don't you think we have something?

ELISE: Ann, I've no sooner sat down than——

ANN: I don't mean to rush you.

(JOANNE *enters unseen at the back of the stage, but they realize.*)

ELISE: And in front of Joanne.

(ANN *and* ELISE *burst out laughing.*)

There've been others, Ann.

ANN: I know.

ELISE: Oh I don't mean others physically, though there have been others—physically. I mean I'm not young enough to imagine. . . . Let's say I've woken up more times than I've been to bed. I'm not young enough to think things will ever be different.

ANN: I don't want to crowd you out.

ELISE: No.

ANN: I mean it.

ELISE: Yes.

ANN: No I mean——

ELISE: Listen.

ANN: Yes.

ELISE: We'll have a go.

JOANNE: Is this a private game or can anyone join in?

ELISE: It is for two players.

ANN: Elise and I.

ELISE: Love is not a game. The love of a man——

ANN: Here played by me——

ELISE: For a woman——

ANN: Elise——

ELISE: Is the yolk of the cosmic egg. The good bit.

JOANNE: I see you're going to be foolish all night.

59

ELISE: I've come from the graveyard where my father is buried into the light of a room where a man sits and waits not attending the service, not invited. His room has white walls and enough books to go round and—oh—he has I cannot describe it he has wise eyes and is peaceful and well liked and contented in the evening, and can forget, is able to forget.

ANN: I'm walking with a dog across a hillside and can see the farm where he is mending a barn door at which he is hopeless, as he is at most practical things, but I keep it in me that I don't think he's very good at things, as he is nice and as he is a bit soulful.

JOANNE: I'm lying with my legs open being licked off by a dog. He is brave and nice and has wise eyes.

ANN: Your hair's all wet.

JOANNE: I fell in the bath.

ANN: I hope it taught you a lesson.

ELISE: Describe his prick.

ANN: Uncircumcized.

JOANNE: You've got slovenly minds and worse bodies and why I should expend this energy on you I don't know. What's wrong is not the system but that you poor cheap victims of the thing should absurdly see yourself as winners.

ELISE: There's something in what she says.

ANN: I admire her for saying it.

ELISE: She's certainly got guts.

ANN: And a hell of a way with words.

ELISE: You've got to admire her.

ANN: Now shut up.

ELISE: How long's his prick?

ANN: Never measured it. Too satisfied to care.

JOANNE: If the length of a man's penis were the measure of his worth then life would fall very easily into place.

ELISE: At my husband's school—

JOANNE: Your what? Your husband?

ELISE: I am married, you know.

JOANNE: I never knew that.

ANN: Roger.

JOANNE: You're married? And you persist in this fantasy that marriage is good and men were made for women?

ELISE: Like falling off a horse. You get back on again.

JOANNE: My God!

ELISE: You carry on. I've still got his shares. If the facts of all this depress you, let's stop now rather than carry on. Roger meant lots to me more than you could guess from the transcript of the divorce proceedings which is in itself an unsung opera.

ANN: If the memory of him obtrudes into our lovemaking.

ELISE: We must go on.

ANN: Is Joanne in the way?

ELISE: Leave her.

JOANNE: Babylonian whore.

ANN: If when I feel you you can feel no pain.

ELISE: Relax.

ANN: Can we make it? Over the years and past the debris into the rosetrees and the valley.

ELISE: Over the hollihocks and the chrysanthemums into the waterfall and the clearing past the breakfasts and the crying and the——

ANN: Rosetrees.

ELISE: Past the rosetrees into a clearing. Help me into the clearing.

ANN: Can we make it?

ELISE (*loud and black*): O Desdemona! (*Loud but not black.*) Heaven forfend that I, to whom thou hast entrusted love, here, here on this teeming soil, that hast our meeting here entrusted to the earth, should, with mine own hand, pluck my dagger from my side, and with deliberate stealth make to plunder that which I have made my own.

ANN: Hush sweet Ophelia, let not the ardour of thy love thy temper overthrow.

ELISE: If we settled in advance for less than what we wanted, admitted from the start it was impossible to do the thing properly, would that be more satisfactory?

61

ANN: No.

ELISE: Is there a way, could there be a way of starting a relationship that wasn't going to end in confusion and turning away at parties to avoid the eye of the person who knew you.

ANN: Maybe someone whose balls you've played with while they were asleep.

ELISE: Is there a way of coming to them and looking them in the eye and being honest and free?

ANN: If I took you, if I took you inside me——

ELISE: Other way round.

ANN: Sorry, if you took me inside you, would you wonder if I cried suddenly at night or fled to London or forgot a meeting.

ELISE: How can I tell you what an affair with a woman like me would be like? I'm flirtatious, horribly romantic and unreliable.

ANN: And as a man, I'm prone to sudden anger, like a lion in the way I am.

ELISE: I'm like a cheetah.

ANN: I'm like a lion.

ELISE: I'm like a gnu.

ANN: I'm like a hippopotamus.

ELISE: If there were some way of expressing to you directly the likelihood, the probability of disaster, then you might back away and say you didn't want to get hurt.

ANN: If you could see as I do the hope of the world lying in women being different from men, I've always put them on a pedestal—they're kinder and better able to cope.

ELISE: In this whirligig.

ANN: In this vortex.

ELISE: In this whirligig there are no masters. There is man. There is woman.

ANN: There is desert.

ELISE: Desert?

ANN: Against the elements, man, woman.

ELISE: There is desert. I wish it were possible. What do you think?

JOANNE: I think you're nuts and we've been through this before.

ELISE: But this time a real relationship——

JOANNE: The number of times I've heard you say you were a gnu and Ann respond with the unlikely information that she's a hippopotamus are really beyond counting. If it ever came to anything, I wouldn't mind, but the evening drags on until the gnu turns to the hippopotamus and says shall we watch News at Ten?

ELISE: There ought to be a way of starting a relationship as you mean to go on. What happens now?

ANN: I don't know. You've done more of this than I have.

ELISE: That's not a very nice thing to say.

ANN: I'm sorry. I didn't mean it.

ELISE: Forget it.

ANN: Elise, let it be now.

ELISE: Are you ready?

ANN: I can't wait.

ELISE: I'm so scared at this stage.

ANN: This is an inevitable stage. Think of it as expression.

(ANN *and* ELISE *confront.*)

Elise.

(ANN *puts her hand on* ELISE'*s breast.*)

JOANNE: Stop.

(*The interjection is routine.* ANN *and* ELISE *ignore it.*)

Stop.

ANN: Why?

JOANNE: In front of me.

ANN: Undress.

(ANN *steps back.* ELISE *turns away from* JOANNE *towards* ANN *and takes off the top of her dress. Her breasts are bare.*)
Incredible.

(ELISE *turns round to* JOANNE, *turning her back on the audience, lets the top drop to the floor. Pause.* JOANNE *faints.*)

(*Blackout as she goes down. End of scene.*)

SCENE FIVE

Two beds, side by side, but not touching. JOANNE *is sitting up in one reading* Sight and Sound. ELISE *is buried invisibly deep in the other.*

JOANNE: "The lyric fluency of Ozu is the nearest the Japanese cinema gets to Chekhov." Discuss.

(ELISE *grumbles in her sleep.*)

"Lee Marvin represents not just capitalist man in a state of repressed aggression, but the entire weltanschauung of contemporary American life." Oh yes.

(ELISE *turns again.*)

ELISE: What time is it?

JOANNE: Five.

ELISE: Morning?

JOANNE: Afternoon.

ELISE: What's happening?

JOANNE: Ann is teaching chemistry. I am reading drivel. Are you feeling any better?

ELISE: No.

(ELISE *comes up from under the covers, goes over to the mirror.*)

JOANNE: "Donald Duck's dribblings of premature ejaculation symbolize the failure of Western man. . . ."

(ELISE *is looking at herself hard in the mirror and interrupts.*)

ELISE: Can you see anything?

JOANNE: No.

ELISE: It's coming all right. I have a sudden passion for pineapple. I'd really love a slice of pineapple.

JOANNE: Yesterday it's prunes, today it's pineapple. You don't fool anybody.

64

ELISE: Won't anyone believe me?

(ELISE *exercises. Left hand to right foot, right hand to left foot.*)

JOANNE: You'll damage the little bastard.

ELISE: Give it a lively ride.

(ELISE *starts running on the spot.*)

(*Singing as she runs*): We are from Roedean
                    Good girls are we
                    We take care of our virginity
                    And again and again
                    And again and again
                    Right Up Roedean School
                    Up School Up School

(*As* ELISE *sings,* JOANNE *draws the curtains and winter afternoon light pours into the dark room.*)

I'll make the little bastard glad he was born.

JOANNE: You're so sure it's a boy.

ELISE: I want a boy. You believe me then.

JOANNE: I think it shows great imagination.

ELISE: You believe it exists.

JOANNE: I think it's the most wonderful thing.

(ELISE *goes back to bed.*)

ELISE: I don't want to do myself damage.

JOANNE: Of course not.

(JOANNE *tucks her in.*)

I still say you've been screwed.

ELISE: And I say I haven't.

JOANNE: It doesn't happen like that.

ELISE: It happened this time.

JOANNE: You can't be pregnant if you haven't been laid. It's never happened before.

ELISE: Once.

JOANNE: That doesn't count.

ELISE: I may have a Messiah.

JOANNE: You'll never convince me. It was a vow, a vow mutually agreed. No men. Pure feminism, pure love. Brackenhurst inches the world forward. You agreed.

ELISE: I never agreed.

JOANNE (*throwing away* 'Sight and Sound'): I won't read this rubbish. It was agreed between us that it was possible to create a society of women. That was fine. As long as no one betrayed the ideal, I tolerated dissent. But then Brackenhurst fell apart. Brackenhurst is pure feminism. Brackenhurst inches the world forward. The falling apart was in this manner: Ann laid, Haskins responsible, retribution strangely transferred to you.

ELISE: She got the fun, I got the baby. She and I were very close.

JOANNE: Exactly.

ELISE: You don't resent us loving each other?

JOANNE: You're not in love. It is a conspiracy.

ELISE: There was very little else around.

JOANNE: I am very little else, I suppose.

ELISE: You're not really mature. And you seem to provide yourself with all the loving you need.

JOANNE: Brackenhurst inches the world forward. I've taken to smoking.

(JOANNE *lights a cigarette.*)

ELISE: Not the only sign of decay.

JOANNE: My hair's falling out with arsenic poisoning and my nails have gone soft.

ELISE: It's all fantasy.

JOANNE: You thinking yourself pregnant and me thinking myself dead.

ELISE: Murdered.

JOANNE: Yes.

ELISE: Why should she want to kill you?

JOANNE: Why does she keep me here?

ELISE: You're her pupil, really. You're the only one now, apart from that one downstairs.

JOANNE: I always knew Bossy Lucrecia would outlive the rest.

ELISE: Ann has made her Head Girl.

JOANNE: As she's the only one, it's not much of an honour.

ELISE: Symbolic.

(ELISE *takes out her knitting from under the covers.*)

JOANNE: Ugh, motherhood suits you. How can you?

ELISE: What?

JOANNE: Knit. Aren't you ashamed? Doesn't it mean anything to be cast in a forever and always role of the most blatant submission?

ELISE: I like it.

JOANNE: Have you never wanted to change?

ELISE: Women have babies.

JOANNE: So?

ELISE: It's biological. They dive for the breast.

JOANNE: But the care of babies? Is that all you look forward to?

ELISE: I spent the first half of my life on my back. I want something to show for it.

JOANNE: But the two should be connected. Years of indulgence —nothing. Then you stop and suddenly you're pregnant. Now you'll spend the rest of your life tending a kid while life happens around you.

ELISE: Nothing ever happens at Brackenhurst.

JOANNE: I don't mean Brackenhurst, I mean the world.

ELISE: Brackenhurst inches the world forward, Brackenhurst . . .

JOANNE: All right. That can't be all you want.

ELISE: My mother was a Communist. She had three houses, a large private income, a couple of scarcely literate novelist lovers and a small pink card that said she was a member of the Communist Party. My father had very little to do with her apart from their initial union, a policy he was wise to maintain for all his thirty-seven years. Spent mostly as a schoolteacher before his early death when a gold crucifix suspended from the ceiling of Chartres Cathedral fell on his head. Hence my hatred of religion. And of teaching. So I wasn't very political from the start. My mother's money was in patent medicine. My father's heart was in culture. Which is probably why I'm sick of watching you two fight it out. I've never seen the need to get that worked up.

JOANNE: I thought you were working class.

ELISE: I never said so. I shall devote my life to rearing children.

JOANNE: It soon won't be necessary. This might interest you.
(JOANNE *has picked up a book from the side of her bed*.)
There are 46 chromosomes in each human cell. Did you
know that? In each cell. Of these 46, two are the sex
chromosomes, determining sex. Now both sexes have in
common one X chromosome, and in the woman the other
sex chromosome is an X as well. Whereas in the man it's a
Y. The woman is XX, the man XY. That Y is an impurity,
a biological accident that is being slowly eradicated by
natural development, which is working towards the purest
form. Pure XX—female as we call it today.

ELISE: Babies?

JOANNE: Some other method.

ELISE: A better method?

JOANNE (*mocking*): Who knows?

ELISE: And will there still be love?

JOANNE: If you want it.

ELISE: Pleasures of the body?

JOANNE: Pleasures of the mind.

ELISE: I don't want your evolution.

JOANNE: No choice.

ELISE: And will we ever be happy?

JOANNE: Don't be trivial.

ELISE: I don't call it—ow, it kicked.
(ELISE *shoots up to the top of the bed*.)

JOANNE: Impossible.

ELISE: I felt it.

JOANNE: I believe you felt it, but I don't believe it kicked. Taste
this.

ELISE: What is it?
(JOANNE *holds up a transparent bag of white stuff*.)

JOANNE: This is my mashed potato. We had it for lunch, I'd like
you to try some. It's poisoned.

ELISE: Eugh, it's vile.

JOANNE: Taste some, titface.
(ELISE *puts a finger in, scoops, and gingerly tastes*.)

ELISE: Mashed potato.

JOANNE: I said.

ELISE: I think it's very good.

JOANNE: Are you getting that bitter taste—acid tinge?

ELISE: No. How did you get it?

JOANNE: I scooped it off the plate when Ann wasn't looking. It's blatantly poisoned. I have to get rid of it.

(JOANNE *throws it expertly out the window.*)

There's quite a pile out there, but no one ever notices. I wouldn't tell anyone but you.

ELISE: There's no one else to tell.

JOANNE: True.

ELISE: We ought to see more people.

JOANNE: I've suddenly seen what's dogged me all along. Ann is the father of your child.

ELISE: Hardly.

JOANNE: The X chromosome ascends.

ELISE: Ha ha.

JOANNE: I've been thinking all day about your story and there's one thing missing. Where's the man?

ELISE: Do you think I like being abnormal?

JOANNE: It's biologically possible Ann is the father.

ELISE: When it first happened I was hell's ashamed. Who wants a baby and not know how?

JOANNE: It's obviously Ann's.

ELISE: You agree it exists.

JOANNE: I've changed my theory to fit the facts.

ELISE: How could Ann have done it?

JOANNE: You remember that night?

ELISE: I'm not asking when, I'm asking how.

JOANNE: What was that business about, the night I fainted? The night you did your act in front of me?

ELISE: Oh. Joke.

(*Pause.*)

JOANNE: This child's not going to do what you want. It won't get you out of here. It is incestuous offspring of this place.

ELISE: It is the hope I have of happiness.

JOANNE: I'm sorry for you then. I'm changing for supper.

(JOANNE *goes behind the screen*.)

ELISE: There's no need to dress behind there.

JOANNE: Doesn't matter.

ELISE: I wouldn't be embarrassed to see your body.

JOANNE: Please.

ELISE: I'd quite like it.

JOANNE: I don't want to be watched all the time.

ELISE: There's no need to be so prudish.

JOANNE: I am not a prude. I just——

ELISE: What?

JOANNE: For Christ's sake leave me alone.

ELISE: Body body body body body.

JOANNE: AAAAH!

(*Silence*. JOANNE *still behind the screen*.)

ELISE: Joanne. Joanne, are you all right? Are you O.K. in there?
(ELISE *gets out of bed, goes towards the screen, passing the mirror, so she stops a second, stands sideways, looks to see if she's any fatter, pats her stomach, goes on, stops*.)
Joanne.
(ELISE *goes behind the screen, as* JOANNE *comes round the front unseen, creeping round to the very front, sits down on the floor*.)
Joanne.

JOANNE: And your child will very probably be stillborn.
(ELISE *comes out from behind the screen*.)

ELISE: You worried me.

JOANNE: Not really.

ELISE: If I have a boy I'll call it Joseph, but if it's a girl Joanne.

JOANNE: Ha ha.

ELISE: I mean it. You don't know how much I love you.

JOANNE: Elise, will you please be quiet?

ELISE: You don't know how easy you are to upset. You're a joy.
(*Enter* ANN.)

ANN (*coming fast through*): Lucrecia's chemistry is definitely improving.
(ANN *goes immediately behind the screen*.)

JOANNE: Daddy!

ANN (*from behind the screen*): Are you any better, Elise?

ELISE: I'm sure I'm pregnant.

(ANN *comes out with a hypodermic needle with a little bottle of liquid on the end.*)

ANN: I'm giving everyone flu injections this year to prevent the school grinding to a halt.

(ANN *holds the needle up to the light and pulls back the plunger.*)

JOANNE: Don't bring that thing near me.

ELISE: Nor me. In my condition it'll upset nature's balance.

ANN (*pointing to a pile of sheets in the corner of the room*): Joanne, I told you.

JOANNE: Very well.

ANN (*smiling*): Lucrecia——

(*Exit* ANN.)

(JOANNE *moves round to* ELISE's *bed.*)

JOANNE: Out of bed, earthmother, I've got to change your sheets.

ELISE: Do you think she's murdering our last pupil?

JOANNE: Pump her full of vitamins to keep her breathing, more like.

(JOANNE *is changing the sheets on* ELISE's *bed.* ELISE *has gone to lie on the third [vacant] bed.*)

Get off that bed, heffalump.

ELISE: Why?

JOANNE (*moving to stand at the top of it*): It's mine.

ELISE: Pardon. (*Moves to centre bed.*)

(JOANNE *goes back to changing the sheets on* ELISE's *bed.*)

I wonder if things will be better next term.

JOANNE: They'll never get better. There'll be no change. We could be shitting gold bricks here and no one would come to sweep up the dung after us. People don't like Brackenhurst. It's like all the other useless institutions— schools, ministries, theatres, museums, post offices—people will go a long way to avoid them. Look at those lawns and flowerbeds and fountains. Nobody wants to go where people gather. Who wants it?

71

ELISE: There's mud on my slippers, Joanne. On my slippers, mud.

(*Enter* ANN, *with a spent hypodermic. Heads behind screen to replace it.*)

Ann, there's mud on my slippers.

ANN: Well, Sherlock, tell me what you think.

ELISE: I haven't been out of the house in them. (*Picking some off.*) Look.

(JOANNE *is by now at work on the centre bed.*)

Joanne, did you borrow my slippers for your agricultural class?

JOANNE: Of course not. I mean, yes.

ANN: No, you mean yes?

JOANNE: I admit it, yes.

ELISE: You planted vegetables in my slippers.

JOANNE: Not in them. Wearing them. That's how the mud got on them, sorry.

ELISE: The pom-poms will wilt if you get them wet.

JOANNE: It's all in the past.

(ANN *has joined* JOANNE *working on centre bed. Pause.*)

ANN: You're cheerful, Joanne.

JOANNE: I'm sorry, does that spoil the atmosphere?

ANN: Not at all.

(*Pause.*)

ELISE: There's a trail of mud in fact right across the room.

JOANNE: It leads from the vegetable patch to your bed.

ELISE: Not that way it doesn't.

JOANNE: I'll do this bed, while you finish that.

(JOANNE *is over at the third bed, taking with her all the dirty sheets which she puts down by the side of the bed.*)

ANN: I'll help.

JOANNE: It's O.K.

ANN: Don't put those dirty sheets on the floor.

JOANNE: They're dirty.

ANN: No need to make them dirtier.

(*To avoid* ANN *picking them up,* JOANNE *chucks them over to* ELISE, *who is back on her own bed.*)

JOANNE: You look after them.

ELISE (*opening them out*): They're incredibly dirty.

JOANNE (*moving to the far side*): I'll do this side.

ELISE: Joanne, have you been growing vegetables in your bed?

JOANNE: No.

ANN: No you mean yes?

JOANNE: No I mean no.

ELISE: Well the world must be fighting its way through the floor.
(ANN *is by now at the bottom of the bed. She lifts up the bed,
there's a muddy blanket underneath which she casts aside,
then lifts up the floor. Reveals hole, shovel, etc.*)

ANN: You're tunnelling your way out.

JOANNE: *The Great Escape*, John Sturges, 1963.

ANN: You've ruined my parquet floor in your malicious
attempt to escape.

JOANNE: I thought I'd get away with it.

ANN: You thought I wouldn't notice great piles of earth you've
been throwing out the window.

JOANNE: I've been trying to mix it with the soil.

ANN: What about the great white patches of cold mashed
potato, then?

JOANNE: That's poisonous potato. You can see the plants have
died out there.

ANN: The plants have suffocated under the weight of garbage
you pour on to them.

JOANNE: It was the only place to put it.

ANN: What were you doing in the first place?

JOANNE: I wanted out.

ANN: You could have come and spoken to me. I would have
listened.

JOANNE: I know.

ANN: Quiet, wait till you're spoken to. Expectavi orationem
mihi vero querelam adduxisti.
(ANN *moves to the downstage table and sits down.* JOANNE
shrugs at the Latin.)

JOANNE: Look how far I got, look how near I was to getting out.

ANN (*taking up her writing-pad*): I knew all the time.

JOANNE: Like that dog. You know about that.

ANN: It's your fault walking in the grounds at night.

JOANNE: You didn't tell me you starved the thing. I was the first meat it had seen in weeks.

ANN: Alsatians can go for long periods without food.

JOANNE: Just see how near I was.

(ELISE *is knitting again.*)

ELISE: Second bootee finito. Leggings now.

ANN (*holding up the letter she's written*): "Dear Mum, How are you? It's been a long time since I've written but we've been terribly busy this term—always like this in the Christmas term. I've hardly had time to sit down. What can I tell you about Brackenhurst?" (*Starts writing.*)

JOANNE: I thought the hols were very quiet. Through the summer months I dug so gently into the earth, towards great peacefulness, great rest.

ANN: "These are not days, mother, in which private education is much valued. I sometimes feel we are out of step with this generation. It is a constant struggle to keep in tune with new ideas. However, a new cricket pavilion will go some way . . .". (*She returns to writing.*)

JOANNE: I'm giving myself a time limit. If I'm not out of here by the time that child is born, I'll kill myself.

ELISE: Agreed.

ANN: "How is father? How is his face? Joanne and Elise send you their love. They are a constant source of help to me."

JOANNE: I'm going to be sick. (*She rushes out.*)

ANN: "We have Mrs. Reginald Maudling coming for speech day next year. Rather a catch. Love, Ann." Elise, you remember mother?

(*Re-enter* JOANNE.)

JOANNE: Poisoner.

ANN: What?

JOANNE: You're poisoning me.

ANN: How do you know?

JOANNE: Aesophogal pain, vomiting, bloody diarrhoea with traces of mucus, weakness, jaundice, restlessness, headache,

74

dizziness, chills, cramps, irritability, paralysis, polyneuritis, anesthesias, paresthesias, hyperceratosis of the palm and soles of the feet, cirrhosis of the liver, nausea, abdominal cramps, salivation, chronic nephritis in the cardiovascular system, dependent edema, cardiac-failure.

ANN: Remedy?

(JOANNE *holds up a small bottle in her hand.*)

JOANNE: Dimercaprol. Complete recovery six months.

(*Blackout. End of Scene Five.*)

SCENE SIX

The Common Room, devastated in the cause of slipper hockey. A large table with a blackboard at the back covered in scores. ELISE *is umpiring at the back. All three are wearing tennis skirts.*

ANN: The hockey championships of Brackenhurst.

JOANNE: This is serious.

ANN: The serious championship.

JOANNE: We need a fourth.

ELISE: I'm no good anyway, I'd as soon give up.

JOANNE: Certainly not. This is to the death.

ELISE: I can scarcely get across the pitch. I'm so far gone.

JOANNE: And here at Brackenhurst the tension is well nigh unbearable, with three prima donnas of the hockey circuit ranged in claw to claw fighting. Ann:

ANN: Precision great maturity skill wonderful effortlessness.

JOANNE: Joanne:

ANN: Brute power brilliant aim marvellous speed.

JOANNE: Elise:

ANN: The odd fluke shot relieving general hopelessness.

ELISE: Thank you.

JOANNE: It would be much better if we had a fourth.

ELISE: Man.

(*A brief violent rally between* ANN *and* JOANNE.)

ANN (*crying out*): Vigour and dash.

JOANNE (*slamming*): Con brio.

ANN: My goal.

JOANNE: That was practice. We hadn't started properly.

ANN: That was not warming up. That was game. Elise?

ELISE: Wasn't watching.

JOANNE: That's right. Opt out.

> (JOANNE *whips off her cardigan very fast and we see her arms for the first time which are covered in scars and tattoos.*)

ANN: What.

ELISE: Tattoos!

JOANNE: The criminal sisterhood: tattoos.

ANN: And scars.

JOANNE: I cut my wrists.

> (JOANNE *hits viciously,* ANN *rushes for it but misses. Leaves it.*)

ANN: When?

JOANNE: Some months ago.

ANN: What happened ?

JOANNE: Nothing. You've heard of haemophiliacs, well I'm a haemophobiac, couldn't keep the wretched stuff flowing. Come on, serve.

ANN: The tattoos.

JOANNE: Everyone has them.

ANN: Who?

JOANNE: In Holloway.

ANN: In Holloway!

JOANNE: The prisoners tattoo their girl-friends' names on their arms; but when they get out their pimps are angry because they say it drives off custom.

ANN: Let me see. (*Reads* JOANNE'*s arm.*) Ann. Elise.

JOANNE: Leave me alone. (*She breaks away.*)

ANN: You've tattooed our names on your arm.

JOANNE: I'm taking a penalty. My pimp'll be angry when I get out.

ELISE: Five minutes' time.

ANN: Plenty can still happen.

ELISE: We'll know in five minutes.

JOANNE: We've sat through this vast vacation waiting for damned anybody to enrol, face it, nobody's coming.

ANN: Give it time. We are teachers first and foremost, you and I, plain strength it would be wrong to misapply.

ELISE: Five minutes and the term starts.

(JOANNE *hits the slipper but* ANN *catches it with her hand.*)

ANN: Unlock the doors.

JOANNE: Hardly any point. We know already.

ANN: That's not true.

JOANNE: I think we'll be able to control the flow.

ANN: You're really back on form.

ELISE: She got her confidence back.

JOANNE: I do feel secure.

ELISE: Do I chalk up that last goal or not?

ANN: Let her have it.

JOANNE (*bowing*): Madame.

ANN: Bully.

JOANNE: I don't want to keep you from your duties, my dear.

(ANN *puts down her stick.*)

ANN: I call it poor sportsmanship when you needle insidiously and scratch at subjects that are nothing to do with the game in hand.

JOANNE: We're only playing to pass the time, thanks to your scholastic success. We should be out on cocoa duty in the normal way of things, or lugging trunks up abandoned staircases to the dorm, instead of staging the international championship of all time.

ANN: We know why Brackenhurst has hit a poor patch. One person teaching knife throwing, jewbaiting, guerrilla antics and sexual self-help has sharply influenced enrolment figures.

JOANNE: Fire me.

ANN: Quite. Service.

(ANN *serves and the ball is way out of line.*)

JOANNE: Your own goal.

(ANN *lays down her bat and stalks out.*)

Mark up that point, Elise.

ELISE: To you?

JOANNE: To me. She's mad. Give me the slipper.

(ELISE *lumberingly serves.* JOANNE *scores effortlessly.* ELISE *trundles to get it, almost falls.*)

You look really ugly today. Ugly in some special way falling over yourself for that little thing.

(*The bell rings incredibly loud.*)

She's gone completely off her head.

(ANN's *voice comes over the loudspeakers.*)

ANN (*off*): Testing, testing 1-2-3-4-5——.

ELISE: It works.

JOANNE: Four weeks' work and it had better.

ANN (*off*): Testing. Report immediately to your headmistress. Do not collect two hundred pounds, do not pass go.

(JOANNE *makes huge gestures of insanity and gabbles.*)

(*Sings—off.*) What the world needs now is love, sweet love.

JOANNE: Give me another.

(JOANNE *wins casually.*)

No fun with you. Look at your horrible body.

ELISE: My stomach is in a way very beautiful.

JOANNE: It would need a woman to fancy you. You really look revolting.

ELISE: Doesn't matter, you used to say, what women look like. Physical appearance was a snare, something men had invented to grade off women.

JOANNE: One day—all women—are going to be equal.

ELISE: It's not so much that women aren't equal. It's more that they're ugly.

ANN (*sings—off*): What the world needs now is love, sweet love.

JOANNE: Give over.

ELISE: When I first learnt I was pregnant and I didn't go to a doctor by the way, just stopped getting the curse and watched myself inflate, then I felt the joy of a way to leave Brackenhurst. Now I've had the bugger in my womb so long I feel I've lugged it from here to Singapore.

JOANNE: There are times when I feel I've suffered so much that the world has just got to move over and yield.

(*An enormous hymn comes flooding over the speakers, with the voices of 400 schoolgirls raised in song.*)
(*Shouting through the din.*) Where's it coming from?

ELISE: It's her.
(*Enter* ANN *her hands raised as if at the head of a religious procession.* JOANNE *dashes out,* ANN *bows slightly, smilingly at* ELISE. *The music ends very suddenly, the plug ripped out and* JOANNE'S *voice comes over the speakers.*)

JOANNE (*off*): The revolutionary party has seized control of the radio station and therefore declares the revolution complete. End of revolution.
(*The speakers go dead.*)

ANN: There's no one. Not even Lucrecia. There are no pupils.
(*Enter* JOANNE.)
Congratulations on your revolution.
(JOANNE *seizes the hockey stick.*)

JOANNE: Total annihilation.

ANN: Very well.
(*They take up their stances but*)

JOANNE: Enough.
(*They both immediately relax.*)
The experiment must be counted a flop. The fight began on a real pretext—we wanted the hearts and minds of our pupils. I was to set up a feminist community. The result is the first feminist birth.

ANN: That's not the way I saw it.

JOANNE: The wrists I cut in summer several times. We have credentials of our suffering—all of us.

ELISE: My baby.
(ANN *drops to her knees and puts her ear on* ELISE'S *stomach.*)

ANN: Is that the little baby? Ooh. Diddums. Can I come out now, Auntie? No you can't—not for a month or two. Oh he's crying.

ELISE: He wants a little peace. Joanne, lock the doors.
(*Exit* JOANNE.)

ANN: Is he crying? Ooh. Are you sad?

79

ELISE: It wasn't worth waiting through the vac.

ANN: We held on.

ELISE: Really it was just delay.

ANN: What do you do now?

ELISE: Find a father.

ANN: Elise.

ELISE: It's well enough for you. You have a man.

ANN: I never knew Haskins. I pretended.

ELISE: But you said.

ANN: Think I'd sleep with a tradesman? I've got some pride left.

ELISE: Virility attracted you.

ANN: I just wanted to annoy her.

ELISE: While you were poisoning her.

ANN: Yes.

ELISE: This is not the way women speak together, it's not the way they live. It doesn't ring true.

ANN: The slow sprinkling of arsenic seemed as humane a way as possible. I've not thought Joanne evil or depraved. Wayward more like and needing me.

(*Enter* JOANNE.)

JOANNE: So I can go now?

ELISE (*with real, unparalled enthusiasm*): I just want to say to you, Joanne, I think you're bloody marvellous and your generation is more bloody marvellous than any before it. And if ever I want a friend for life, I'll want you.

JOANNE: Women are going to be free one day to behave as they choose. We're only so far fledglings on this earth.

ANN: Break it up.

ELISE: There was no virgin birth. There are simply declining standards in private education and that is all.

(*Exit* ELISE.)

JOANNE: Private schools were always like this. We're not unusual.

ANN: I know what you feel. We've all been brought up to be sold out and pitied and scorned and screwed and abused. She's right. So what?

JOANNE: So?

ANN: Well, exactly.

JOANNE: Why are the workers silent, Ann? Why does the revolution land with such a sigh? Twenty-five years the war is over, and everyone trying to get the workers to respond. And they won't. Where are the working women? Lulled by romantic love and getting home to cook the dinner.

ANN: I was weaned on R. A. Butler and the Beveridge report, so I don't know what you're talking about.

JOANNE: Why have half the world, the women, vowed never to fight, to be slow to anger, not to destroy the world?

(JOANNE *starts moving the furniture*.)

ANN: If you'd ever had anything but some generalized complaint I could sympathize. But you don't even know what you want. Some unstated alternative that evaporates like your breath on the air.

JOANNE: Help pack these away.

ANN: Those are good chairs you're manhandling. What are you doing?

JOANNE: Historic evolution. The end of Brackenhurst. *Citizen Kane*. Orson Welles. 1942.

ANN: I've no intention.

JOANNE: This is the end of it.

(JOANNE *takes a machine-gun out of the furniture at the back.* ANN *is facing downstage and can't see* JOANNE, *who has put on a Negro mask*.)

ANN: Please don't leave me. Please.

(ANN *turns and sees the pointed machine-gun*.)

JOANNE: After the revolution, retribution.

(*Enter* ELISE *with her bike*.)

ELISE: Look what I've been hiding in the wine cellar.

JOANNE: Get out the way.

(ELISE, *excited, throws down the bike, runs to cower behind* JOANNE.)

(*To* ANN.) Don't move.

ELISE: See my bike. I'll be in Gloucestershire by dawn.

JOANNE: Shut up.

ELISE: Down the M1, pausing only for childbirth at an all-night caff.

JOANNE: Shut up. This is my revolution.

(JOANNE *starts walking downstage to* ANN.)

ANN: Don't think I can't take a joke, Joanne.

ELISE: Give it to her, give it to her, Joanne.

ANN: I just——

ELISE: Let her have it.

JOANNE: Shall I?

ELISE: Yes.

JOANNE: Yes?

ELISE: Yes.

(JOANNE *fires the gun, which is a toy; it goes phut-phut-phut*.)

You're joking.

JOANNE: No. (*Embraces* ANN.)

ELISE: Some gladiators you turned out to be. I've spent the last year watching you two throw each other round like Indian clubs.

JOANNE: We're all just sorry school is closing down.

ELISE: Why?

JOANNE: We're all just sorry.

ELISE: There's nothing in our lives that's worth redeeming, take my word for it. We're teachers and that's all, and you two are good teachers because there's nothing in your lives that doesn't constitute a lesson. And while you've been talking the children have left. You've lived so long on other people's behalf you've ceased to recognize yourselves. There's nothing here worth keeping and certainly nothing holds us together. My bike. (*Exit.*)

ANN: Elise.

JOANNE: Let her be.

ANN: Your fault.

JOANNE: Yours.

ANN: Look what you've done to her.

JOANNE: If women are ever to be strong, they've got to be strong. . . .

ANN: Jo-jo.

JOANNE: And lighthearted. She is right.

ANN: This school worked for a long time before you came and it can work again.

JOANNE: Sure.

ANN: We can make it work. Circulate Burke's Peerage for new pupils. Build up towards next term.

JOANNE: She is right.

(*Re-enter* ELISE. *Her stomach is quite flat.*)

ELISE: It's gone. There was a great wet fart and it had gone.

(*They shift from foot to foot, half-gesture, walk in small circles about the stage. Chronic unease, suspension, restlessness. Half a minute passes in silence.*)

JOANNE (*raising her arms*): Well then——

(*Instant blackout.*)

THE GREAT EXHIBITION

for Tony

LEAR: . . . Is man no more than this? Consider him well. . . . Thou art the thing itself; unaccommodated man is no more but such a poor, bare, forked animal as thou art. Off, off, you lendings! Come, unbutton here.

[*Tearing off his clothes*]

FOOL: Prithee, Nuncle, be contented, 'tis a naughty night to swim in. . . .

SHAKESPEARE, *King Lear*

The Distribution of Private Property: Percentage of total net private capital in relation to percentage of total population.

	1911/13	*1924/30*	*1936*	*1951/56*	*1960*
Top 1%	65½	59½	56	43	42
Top 5%	86	82½	81	68	75
Top 10%	90	89½	88	79	83
Top 20%	—	96	94	89	—

The Great Exhibition was first presented by Michael Codron at the Hampstead Theatre Club on 28th February 1972, with the following cast:

HAMMETT	David Warner
ABEL	Neil Wilson
MAUD	Penelope Wilton
JERRY	John Gregg
CLOUGH	Philip Ross
A WOMAN	Di Trevis
CATRIONA	Carolyn Seymour

Designed by Saul Radomsky
Directed by Richard Eyre

Act I: PUBLIC LIFE   Friday 4 p.m.
                      Friday 7 p.m.
                      Saturday 1 a.m.

Act II: PRIVATE LIFE Thursday 6.30 p.m

ACT I

Public Life

A few beats of some pompous orchestral music played very loud. House lights to darkness, and CURTAIN *up in darkness. Then a single spotlight comes up on a naked woman.* HAMMETT *speaks unseen in the dark.*

HAMMETT: There ain't nothin' I ain't seen.
   (*The woman turns round.*)
   Nothin' I ain't done.
   (*The spot goes out. In the darkness you hear a door open and* HAMMETT *saying "Come in." Then the Lights flick up to show a study/sitting-room, with a door at the back leading to a small hallway and one door downstage, which leads to the bathroom. A comfortable room with a chaotic big desk, a sofa, a trolley of drink, and a lot of books. It should preferably be boxed in. A large built-in cupboard is at the back next to the main door.* HAMMETT *is a half-bald, ugly, slug-like pedantic thirty-three-year-old. He's beckoning in a large man in a trenchcoat and pork pie hat,* ABEL, *who looks round the room.*)
ABEL: The usual problem?
HAMMETT: Yes. My wife.
   (ABEL *nods slightly. Then he picks up a rather weary-looking cannabis plant from the sidetable and walks across to* HAMMETT.)
ABEL: Grow your own, do you?
HAMMETT: Yes, the natural thing, you know. I distrust the commercial product. You don't know where it's been.
ABEL: Yes.
HAMMETT: If you keep it near a radiator in slightly moist soil,

you can get a very reasonable whatsit—trip. Feel—
(*He leads* ABEL's *hand to feel the soil.*)
Just moist.

ABEL: Right.

(HAMMETT *takes the plant and smiles at it.*)

HAMMETT: I believe it flowers in the summer. An added bonus.
Unfortunately, moving in my circles I get very little chance
to smoke.

ABEL: What do you do?

HAMMETT: I'm a Labour M.P.

(ABEL *sits down.*)

I think you look splendid in that costume.

ABEL: Thank you.

HAMMETT: Bogart crossed with Scotland Yard.

(*Sneer from* ABEL.)

Well——

ABEL: Tell me——

HAMMETT: I suppose I imagine—quite without evidence—that
my wife is unfaithful to me, and I imagine that you are the
man to find out.

ABEL: How did you pick on me?

HAMMETT: Your name comes alphabetically first in the Yellow
Pages.

ABEL (*nodding*): That's why I changed my name to Abel. Used
to be Wilson. I never got any work. Same in the army——

HAMMETT (*smiles*): Yes.

ABEL: What does your wife do?

HAMMETT: She's a casting director. In the theatre.

ABEL: Have you talked about adultery?

HAMMETT: No.

ABEL: What makes you think how you do?

HAMMETT: I. I, er, really don't want to be interrogated about this.
I'd rather just employ you. I find the whole process morti-
fyingly embarrassing anyway, and I don't want to make it
worse. I'm very fond of her——

ABEL: Well——

HAMMETT: Very fond of her.

ABEL (*winks*): We can fix that.

HAMMETT: I'm sure.

ABEL: You're at the dirty end of a dirty trade, Mr. Hammett. Smashing protection gangs, thugging up students, nosing badgers out—that's the clean and easy work. It balances out. Divorce is different. It's more emotional.

HAMMETT (*nods, stands up*): Thank you.

ABEL: You're really not going to tell me any more?

HAMMETT: No.

ABEL: I like it.

(*They shake hands.* HAMMETT *leads* ABEL *out of the door. A moment later he dances back on with Astaire's elegance, singing.*)

HAMMETT: I wanna be kissed by you.

By you and nobody else but you.

(*Instant* BLACKOUT. *A three-second pause. Then the* LIGHT UP *again. No longer full daylight. Seven o'clock.* HAMMETT *is hiding behind the door. At once* MAUD *comes in, in a coat and trouser suit with a load of parcels she takes down to a chair downstage. She is thirty, very beautiful in a model's way, but unlike a model, slightly fat. Her beauty overflows.* HAMMETT, *unseen, takes a single creepy step forward.*)

Hello, angelcake.

MAUD: I knew you were there, you horrible little man.

HAMMETT: My chicken, how are you?

MAUD: Fine.

(*She falls into the chair. He moves round the room drawing the heavy curtains.*)

It smells in here.

HAMMETT: Like damask roses.

MAUD: What have you been doing?

HAMMETT: I've been forging a letter to the Prime Minister. It's from the Gay Liberation Front. It says, "We're right behind you, Ted."

MAUD: Back in politics.

HAMMETT: Of a kind. (*Turns.*) And you?

MAUD (*gets up*): I was pestered all morning by a man called Campoli. Campoli and his three magic balls.

HAMMETT: What was the trick?

MAUD: He ate them. Those three great beautiful golden shimmering globes into the air—and—

(MAUD *mimes a juggler, throwing one up especially hard, then sticking out her tongue and catching it and gobbling it up.*)

—went down like jellied eels.

HAMMETT: Good trick.

MAUD: Couldn't use him, though. Not in *King Lear*.

(*She kicks off her shoes and starts to undress.*)

HAMMETT: What then?

MAUD: Then made a few foolhardy decisions, randomly slotted the wrong actors into the wrong roles, had a jolly good laugh about it and headed home.

HAMMETT: Poor old actors.

MAUD: It's their chosen profession. Dressing-gown.

(HAMMETT *goes at once to the downstage door and unhooks the gown.*)

They choose to do it. Prance about and exhibit themselves. Ridiculous.

HAMMETT: Ridiculous.

MAUD: It is.

(HAMMETT *stands waiting obedient as she gets down to her underwear.*)

And too many after too few jobs. Like pigs nuzzling for the teat. It's humiliating to watch them. I'm sometimes sickened by my own job.

(MAUD *gets into the offered gown.*)

HAMMETT: You poor thing.

MAUD: Well, you feel sorry for them, having to be nice to me.

(MAUD *laughs delightedly at the thought and goes into the bathroom.*)

HAMMETT: Yes.

MAUD (*off*): What's for supper?

HAMMETT: I ate it.

MAUD (*off*): It's only seven o'clock.

HAMMETT: I ate yours as well.

MAUD (*off*): You're disgusting.

(HAMMETT *wanders round the room picking up the clothes she has thrown down.*)

HAMMETT: You get mightily hungry sitting here all day and a spam fritter comes as something of a relief.

MAUD (*coming back in*): You don't have to sit there all day. Since the prophet went into the wilderness six weeks ago, he seems to have thought of nothing but food.

HAMMETT: Food's all I've got left.

MAUD: If this was a real retreat, you'd be totally self-denying.

HAMMETT (*her clothes draped over him*): I sat down at the age of twenty-one and I thought I'm going to need some enthusiasms to get me to the grave. And I chose three. Food, sex and socialism. And look at me now.

(MAUD *not amused.*)

I was only trying to make you laugh.

MAUD: You don't make me laugh. You depress me.

HAMMETT (*taking a dart from the dartboard*): Look—I get up in the morning and I get out the dartboard. When you've gone to work I ask myself how many people am I going to have to talk to today? I throw the dart. (*He throws the dart.*) Ah. What I call a bull's-eye.

MAUD: How many?

HAMMETT: One.

MAUD: How many did you score this morning?

HAMMETT: Nineteen.

(MAUD *looks at him.*)

I know. I've been in despair all day. I've rung Directory Enquiries eleven times to try and bump up my total. But I always get the same girl. Doesn't count.

MAUD: And who else?

HAMMETT (*pause*): Just you.

(HAMMETT *turns round to get the dart out of the board and* MAUD *goes out again.*)

Listen——

(HAMMETT *turns and finds her gone.*)

I'm only bloody talking to you.

MAUD (*off*): Talk.

HAMMETT: It really doesn't matter.

MAUD (*reappearing*): Charlie.

93

HAMMETT: Yes.

MAUD: Do I love you?

(HAMMETT *shrugs. Embarrassment.*)

Of course I don't.

HAMMETT: Hey ho.

MAUD: No, really.

HAMMETT: Really.

MAUD: I woke up this morning and I thought I really do not love you. I just thought eeeeugh.

HAMMETT: Great.

MAUD: It's nothing you've done.

HAMMETT: So it's eight years married, no sign of any upset and then——

(HAMMETT *snaps a finger.*)

MAUD: You can have a divorce if you want.

HAMMETT: Fuck off.

(*Pause.*)

MAUD: Charlie——

HAMMETT: We've had some good times, eh, Maud? Eh? Icky koochie and his froo-froo?

MAUD: The language is repulsive to me. Charlie.

HAMMETT: Well, whose icky fucking koochie was it? Yours.

MAUD: Yours. Your language has always been obscene or sentimental. One or the other.

(HAMMETT *sits.*)

Please. I've always loved you. Not foolishly or to excess. But loved you. Then I wake up this morning really just this morning, and I can't understand how I got where I am. My love. And next to me, you're just a hairy white lump——

HAMMETT: Thank you.

MAUD: I'm trying to explain. Where was I?

HAMMETT: You'd got to the great white lump.

MAUD: Yes. And there it was. That's how the day began. And when I came round to getting home, I did feel dread. And I come in and find you freaking badly behind the door——

HAMMETT: I was hiding.

MAUD: Are you frightened of me?

(HAMMETT *shakes his head violently.*)

94

These last six weeks have been pretty spectacular. You seem
to be deserting your old life with all the flourish of the
British leaving India. So I thought I'd contribute. Well,
what with honesty the new house style——

HAMMETT: That's not quite how I see it.

MAUD: Vigorous reassessment and so on. You in retreat, me in
despair. Please don't eat your fingers.

HAMMETT: I'm sorry.

MAUD: Always gnawing at yourself.

HAMMETT: Don't criticize me, Maud. I've been a good wife to
you, everything you could want.

MAUD: You're sorry for yourself.

HAMMETT: I'm not. I'm just riddled with guilt. If someone got
up and said Martin Borman is in this room, I'd get up and
yell it's me.

MAUD: My dear. I've always thought you a bit weak. But I'd
always felt rather responsible.

HAMMETT: Ah.

MAUD (*clipping on her bathcap*): But now I'd like to live for a bit
without making excuses for anyone.
   (*Pause.*)

HAMMETT: Feel better?

MAUD: Yes, thank you.
   (*Pause.*)
   (*Smiles*): There.
   (MAUD *walks rather briskly out of the backstage door. At once*
   ABEL *steps out of the cupboard next to the main door.*)

ABEL (*deadpan*): Boo.

HAMMETT (*turning*): Shit.

ABEL (*holding a tape recorder up in the right palm*): It all looks
fairly cut and dried to me.

HAMMETT: Get out of there.

ABEL: I'm meant to be following the lady.

HAMMETT: Not here.

ABEL: Everywhere. If the discussion takes the turn I'm expecting,
I'd be very grateful if you could co-operate by addressing
your fruitier remarks more in the direction of the cupboard.
These things have rather a low range.

HAMMETT: I couldn't possibly.

ABEL: I'm getting the gist anyway.

(ABEL *closes himself in the cupboard as the main door opens and* MAUD *comes in spooning at a pot of yoghurt.*)

MAUD: Tell me what you think, Charlie. Come and sit down.

(HAMMETT *stands still, smiles.* MAUD *sits on the sofa.*)

HAMMETT: I— (*Gestures.*)

MAUD: Come and suck at the nipple of my eternal fount.

(HAMMETT *throws an agonized glance at the cupboard, then goes and sits next to her.*)

HAMMETT: Nothing to say.

MAUD: Koochie.

(*Pause.*)

HAMMETT: Nothing to say.

MAUD: I'm used to your silences. As a kind of superiority. Waiting for me to winkle you out. Well, I won't. I've driven this relationship along like some clapped out nag and cart for eight years, and I'm sick of whipping.

HAMMETT (*getting up, moderate*): Yes, I see that.

MAUD (*histrionically*): Whipping, do you hear me, whipping?

HAMMETT: Very funny.

MAUD: And there weren't even any coffee beans left.

HAMMETT: I ate them.

MAUD: Coffee beans?

HAMMETT (*pointing*): Bad breath.

MAUD: I would tell you if you had bad breath.

HAMMETT: Just what you wouldn't. You'd like to watch people dropping infected around me and never let me know. Watch me lose my friends.

MAUD: You don't have any friends.

HAMMETT: Allies.

MAUD: You never knew anyone. Never liked anyone except me, never thought or cared for anyone.

HAMMETT: I can't afford to start thinking of other people as people, it would make life far too complicated.

(*Slap on the end of his epigram he bangs twice on the cupboard door that leads to* ABEL.)

Are you unfaithful? Two bangs yes, one bang no.

MAUD: What?

HAMMETT: Never mind. Don't tell me. I suppose you're going to the theatre tonight?

MAUD: Just as usual.

HAMMETT: What is it?

MAUD: La Mama Nairobi.

HAMMETT: Bung-ho.

MAUD: They're meant to be very good.

(HAMMETT *holds up his hands as if he'd never tried to deny it*.) Fantastic bodies.

HAMMETT: Ah well, then——

MAUD: Do you want to come? Last moments. I'd better leave tonight.

HAMMETT: I don't think I want to spend the last fading seconds of my marriage at a performance by the African *avant-garde*.

MAUD: Very physical.

HAMMETT: I think I'll spend the evening stuffing a duck.

(HAMMETT *puts her discarded yoghurt pot in the waste-paper basket*.)

MAUD: Can I tell you something?

HAMMETT: No.

MAUD: You've been for eight years my only contact with the real world. Isn't that laughable?

HAMMETT: Very.

MAUD: I've always said there are two kinds of people. Human beings and actors. I work all day with actors, and watch them in the evening. They're all right, I suppose, a broody sort of cattle who respond to the goad, obsessed with themselves, as well we know, but not quite—people. Right?

HAMMETT (*quietly*): Yes.

MAUD: And you were meant to be among people. Right?

HAMMETT: Yes.

MAUD: That was your job. But you don't care about it any more.

(HAMMETT *nods*.)

So——

(HAMMETT *nods harder to cut off her logic. A light bulb on* HAMMETT's *desk starts flashing on and off regularly*.)

Telephone.

HAMMETT (*vaguely*): Leave it.

MAUD: It might be for me.

HAMMETT: Please leave it.

(MAUD *gets up*.)

MAUD: We can't.

HAMMETT: It's no effort.

(*They both watch it for a moment or two*. HAMMETT *completely dead between the eyes*.)

MAUD: How can you just leave it there like that?

HAMMETT (*shrugging*): Easy. When I'm alone I cover it with a biscuit box. (*Doing so*.) There. I'm working now on a letter-box for the front door that will burst into flames twice a day and incinerate the contents.

MAUD: I like letters.

HAMMETT: You practically eat your mail for breakfast. I've never understood it.

MAUD: You never have. You pimple.

HAMMETT: With your porridge oats.

MAUD: I'd better pack.

HAMMETT: What ghastly people we are, Maud.

(MAUD *laughs, then goes into the bathroom*.)

Who's leaving who, anyway?

(MAUD *comes back in with a suitcase*.)

MAUD: I'm leaving you.

HAMMETT: So it's possible just to wake up and decide you don't love me.

MAUD: It's true.

HAMMETT: What made you decide?

MAUD: Nothing. It's unconscious. (*Going out again*.) It was nice to know someone outside the theatre.

HAMMETT: No longer nice.

MAUD (*off*): No longer so far outside the theatre.

HAMMETT: No.

(MAUD *comes back in with some bathroom things for the case*. HAMMETT *stands well back*.)

I can't manage the business of people any longer. I never wanted to know anyone in the first place except you. You're all I ever wanted. One of the ideas of abandoning

98

my job was to get to know you again. As we so rarely meet.

MAUD (*standing over the suitcase*): Now you're in my hair all the time.

HAMMETT (*smiles*): Yes.

(*The doorbell rings.*)

Oh Jesus.

MAUD: You go.

HAMMETT: I can't face it. It's bound to be some kind of challenge in the form of a human being.

MAUD: Don't be stupid.

(*It rings again.*)

Remember you've got to make nineteen.

HAMMETT: Later. I'll go and shake hands with a rugby team.

MAUD: I'm not going in my dressing-gown.

HAMMETT: No.

(*It rings again.*)

As long as there's not going to be conversation. I don't mind thumbscrews or the Chinese water torture, as long as it's not to be conversation.

MAUD: Ah.

(MAUD *closes the suitcase and slings it aside. Then goes out.*
HAMMETT *goes to the cupboard and opens the door.*)

HAMMETT: You bastard.

(*He closes the door and goes into the bathroom.* MAUD *comes in, all over* JERRY, *a thirtyish Australian with very long fuzzy hair and steel glasses.*)

JERRY: I've been ringing like hours.

MAUD: Jerry. How super.

JERRY: How are you, darling?

MAUD: Fine. Fine.

JERRY: How's everything?

MAUD: Fine.

JERRY: Super.

MAUD: Fantastic.

JERRY: How great to see you.

MAUD: I'll er. Make some tea.

JERRY: Great.

(MAUD *goes out.* HAMMETT *slips at once silently back in the*

99

other door. JERRY *notices him.*)

(*Chilly*): How are you?

HAMMETT (*nods, pauses*): Fine.

(*They sit down.* JERRY *starts rolling a joint.*)

What are you up to these days?

JERRY: Oh, drifting, you know.

HAMMETT: Drifting.

JERRY: Yeah. It's the only way. To relax in the arms of nature. Just to roll the way the world tips, eh, Charlie?

(HAMMETT *smiles.*)

To trust the old cosmic rollmeover. Fantastic.

HAMMETT: You left the merchant bank then?

(JERRY *looks at him with loathing.*)

JERRY: And I hear you've forsaken the world.

HAMMETT: Hare Krishna, meditation. You know.

JERRY: Yeah. (*Offers joint.*) Smoke?

HAMMETT: No, thank you. To be honest I grow my own. (*He gets up to show him the plant.*) I plant it in John Innes Number One soil, and you see, on the bulldog clip I've fixed a 50 watt sunlamp which guarantees six hours of sunlight every day. It's a young plant, of course, but I think you'd like its flavour.

(MAUD *has come in.*)

MAUD: He doesn't actually smoke himself, of course.

HAMMETT: No.

MAUD: He vomits.

HAMMETT (*smiling*): Other people see flowers and colours when they smoke. I see schoolmasters and commissionaires. Nazi atrocities, that sort of thing.

MAUD: Hopeless.

HAMMETT: Question of metabolism. (*To* JERRY.) What do you see?

JERRY: Everything.

HAMMETT: Ah. I get the falling sensation everyone's so keen on, but it usually means my stomach is coming up to meet me.

MAUD: The tea will be boiled.

(MAUD *goes out.*)

HAMMETT (*thoughtful*): And like a child I'm scared of choking on my own bile. So much for marijuana. Are you going to the

100

theatre this evening as well?

JERRY: Not my scene.

HAMMETT: Nor mine.

JERRY: Dead medium.

HAMMETT: I used to love it when I was young. I loved great acting. And big actors. I'd have been bumboy to the lot of them given half the chance. Like Clara Bow. She lay down and received whole American football teams. I'd have done as much for the entire membership of the Garrick Club.

JERRY (*only interested in his joint*): Fantastic.

HAMMETT: Maud was an actress, will you believe it, the first professional I'd met. She'd been to a school where some plastered dike had taught her the golden rule of the theatre, which was—get out there and glitter. Good advice. Maud would run on the first six steps, come to a dead halt, wobble, flutter her eyelashes, hit an unnaturally high note as if calling a dog at eighty paces, lend a perfectly equal emphasis to every tortured syllable, and then smile at the end of each sentence. Smile and wobble. She was lovely. Best of all as Cordelia. The only smiling and wobbling Cordelia. I loved particularly the glazed expression the whole company had. Witch hazel painted on their eyeballs or something. But not just that. It was that they looked all the time into the distance, desperately avoiding each other's eyes, as if there was some danger that if two of them actually acknowledged each other some terrible kind of contact might happen and the whole performance be ruined. If an actor had the line, "Look into my eyes", you could actually see the shutters come down behind his eyeballs. The man who was playing Lear opposite Maud, and I mean dead opposite Maud, arrived at rehearsals with some charts under his arm. He then laid them out on the stage and retraced the very moves Sir Barry Jackson had used with the Birmingham Repertory Company in 1924. The moves turned out to have a kind of triangular zest. I loved it. It seemed to me at the time that the theatre put to good use could be the most sophisticated possible means of ignoring what people were actually like. (MAUD *enters with a tea-tray stacked with things.*)

MAUD: I hope hubby's not been boring.

HAMMETT: I am usually boring.

JERRY: He's been fascinating.

MAUD: Tea?

JERRY (*taking the cup*): Ta. (*Offering the joint.*) Tea?

MAUD: Ta.

(HAMMETT *has moved over to the desk and is snatching a look at the phone by lifting the biscuit tin for a few seconds, then putting it back. It's invariably flashing.*)

What were you talking about?

(HAMMETT *shrugs.*)

MAUD: Scotch to go with it?

JERRY: Yeah.

(MAUD *pours out three glasses of scotch and takes one to* HAMMETT.)

MAUD: And a glass of hot milk for you.

HAMMETT: Thank you.

(*He knocks back the scotch in one, then looks at* JERRY *and* MAUD *laying out their tea, scotch and pot.*)

You look like children with their chemistry sets.

MAUD: And there is cake.

JERRY: Cake!

(*They laugh.* JERRY *takes a bite, then shakes his head with a little howl.*)

We have lift-off.

HAMMETT: Do you remember how I doted on the theatre when we met?

MAUD: Blimey.

HAMMETT: My little nanky-pooh.

MAUD: Charlie.

HAMMETT: This sophisticate has forgotten all that part.

MAUD: I can't have appeared as nanky-pooh for nanky-pooh is a man.

HAMMETT: That is nevertheless how I remember you.

JERRY: Jesus.

HAMMETT: I was hardly into politics at the time. Trudging down to Aldermaston. What do you do when you get there? Trudge back. This time in lines. You brought a little gaiety, didn't you, dear?

(MAUD *just stares at him.*)

We moved on to rip up a regional seat of government. That's a place where old Tories go to die. After the bomb drops—remember the bomb?—it's down to the dugout and lashings of hot cocoa and discipline. Survival of the fittest —the fittest in this case being Harold Macmillan, Sir Alec Douglas-Home, Reginald Maudling and a little-known neuter from Broadstairs called Edward Heath. Poor chap. Anyway, Maud was with an actress of left-wing disposition. She had left-wing disposition like other people have smallpox. That's where we met. I wore a dufflecoat. Maud wore an expression of extreme distaste for the whole experience.

MAUD: Untrue.

HAMMETT: Don't worry. You were proved right in the end. The bomb never dropped. Here we are.

JERRY: Yeah. The actress and the bishop.

(HAMMETT *looks again at the flashing bulb under the tin.*)

MAUD: Jerry is, of course, lucky to find us here at all on a Friday evening. We always used to go to Sunderland at the weekend.

HAMMETT: My constituency.

MAUD: Has my husband shown you his good constituency member?

HAMMETT: Nothing wrong with Sunderland.

MAUD: But since he took the veil things have been much livelier here.

HAMMETT: This Amazon imagines that any politician is somehow not quite a person.

MAUD: More like a fucking zombie.

HAMMETT: There you are.

MAUD: And when it comes to people not being people you're one of the world's great experts. It's Charlie's belief that the stupider, drunker and more illiterate you are, the nearer you are to being a *real* person. It's the last great middle-class myth. Somewhere there are people more real than me.

HAMMETT: Happier than me.

MAUD: You remember the tribal superstition that somebody

photographed has had a bit taken away. Well, that's
Charlie's idea of public life. That by some incredible process
he's been cannibalized.

HAMMETT: I know what's happened.

MAUD: This man is one of the world's great performers. Give us
a puff.

(JERRY *hands her the joint.*)

HAMMETT: This stuff has no effect on her.

(HAMMETT *kneads his hands in the air round her head.*)
Inside her head it evaporates and disappears. It's never
absorbed. The tissues of her brain contract like an old lizard,
and won't let it in.

(MAUD *has deliberately dragged like a maniac and a huge cloud
of smoke goes up around her as he speaks.* JERRY *has taken out
a packet of Smarties from his pocket, and is pouring them on
to the tray.*)

JERRY: Smarty?

MAUD: Fantastic. (*She eats some.*) So it's only by sitting alone in
his room, squaring up to a spam fritter that he's able to keep
his diminishing personality intact.

HAMMETT: It's my integrity——

MAUD: Charlie's integrity always features in these conversations
with all the immediacy and glamour of the lost city of
Atlantis.

HAMMETT: Damn your cotton-picking poplin knickers.

MAUD: That's what he's really been trying to say. Bam your
pluckinkichen flugging jibbers.

HAMMETT: I——

MAUD (*to* JERRY): This stuff tastes more like cinnamon. What are
they—toy cigarettes?

JERRY (*dazed*): What?

HAMMETT (*pointing to* JERRY): For some people it's easy.

MAUD (*turning to* HAMMETT): What?

HAMMETT: Never mind.

MAUD: No, come on, what are we saying, Charlie?

HAMMETT: Almost nothing.

MAUD: Is your brain so completely eroded?

(*A sudden silence.* HAMMETT *is dumb.* MAUD *loses her thread.*)

Come on. Tell me. Please.

HAMMETT: I've handed out my life in small parcels and who ever gave me anything back?

(*The doorbell rings.* HAMMETT *goes quietly out and closes the door behind him. Pause.*)

MAUD: Fucking zombie.

(HAMMETT *comes back in with* CLOUGH, *a senior politician.*)
Who is it?

HAMMETT: It's the Home Secretary.

(JERRY *hastily stubs out his joint.*)

CLOUGH: Alas no longer.

HAMMETT: Home Secretary as was.

CLOUGH (*shaking hands*): Mrs. Hammett.

MAUD: John. Excuse me.

(*She goes out.*)

HAMMETT: And this is a friend from the banking world.

JERRY (*shakes hands, then backs out*): I think I'll just phase out.

(*Exits.*)

CLOUGH: Funny fella.

HAMMETT: He's a dying man.

CLOUGH: I'm sorry.

HAMMETT: He's got terminal acne.

(CLOUGH *sits down.*)
Can I get you anything?

(CLOUGH *puts up his hand.* HAMMETT *picks up the cannabis cake.*)
Perhaps you'd like a slice of—but you might not like it. Or a scotch?

(CLOUGH *puts up his hand again.*)
How are the chaps?

CLOUGH: In good heart. Charlie——

(HAMMETT *looks behind him as if he thought* CLOUGH *were addressing someone else.*)
I want a confidential talk. Are we alone?

HAMMETT: Apart from my private detective.

(HAMMETT *points to the cupboard.* CLOUGH *smiles uneasily.*)

CLOUGH: You never visit your constituency.

HAMMETT: No.

CLOUGH: Why not?

HAMMETT: It's a long way and when you get there it's a dump. And the people resent me because I'm not working class.

CLOUGH: They voted you in.

HAMMETT: They'd vote in Madame de Pompadour as long as she stood on the Labour ticket.

CLOUGH: You never attend Parliamentary debates.

HAMMETT: I'm disillusioned with Parliamentary democracy.

CLOUGH: You haven't answered our letters or spoken to anyone in the party for six weeks.

HAMMETT: I haven't stepped outside this house.

CLOUGH: What do you say?

HAMMETT: What is there to say?

(*Shuffle. Unease.*)

CLOUGH: Well——

HAMMETT: Even if the system worked, which it doesn't, would it be worth it? Not for the people, but for *us* would it be worth it?

CLOUGH: That's not important.

HAMMETT: Of course it's important. It's the only thing that is. If you live in a kindergarten, you end up behaving like a child. It's as simple as that. If you live in a rancorous, run-down, disillusioned, opportunist, self-important shack, you end up an M.P.

CLOUGH: Like you.

HAMMETT: Like me. Show me one M.P. who resembles a man. Not a pedant or a hypocrite or a mental cripple or a liar or an egomaniac or a performer or a fool, but a sort of well, let's say human being.

CLOUGH: It puts us in a tricky situation.

HAMMETT: You could say.

CLOUGH: The Labour Party encompasses a wide spectrum of views. Yours rather slip off the edge.

HAMMETT: By Jesus.

(CLOUGH *smiles again.*)

Not that my life is any better than yours. But I'm young enough to get out.

CLOUGH (*nods*): You could change your mind.

(*Pause.* CLOUGH *gets up.*)

Well——

(*They smile at each other.*)

HAMMETT: Sit down.

(CLOUGH *sits.*)

I thought you'd be sorry if I wanted to go.

CLOUGH: It's not a club any more. You're free. No reason why
dissidents shouldn't drop away.

(ABEL *comes silently out of the cupboard and slips out of the*
main door. CLOUGH *watches him go rather uneasily, but*
HAMMETT *doesn't notice him.* CLOUGH *frowns slightly.*)

HAMMETT: No.

CLOUGH: I know you won't go with banners streaming.

HAMMETT: Lord, no.

CLOUGH: Like Nye Bevan and his false teeth.

HAMMETT: A different kind of exit altogether. More a merging
into the background. Pass away in the night.

CLOUGH (*nods*): Good.

HAMMETT: I don't expect anyone to understand *my* reasons.

CLOUGH: I understand. I don't sympathize. I see it differently.
People are born, I've always thought, with a fundamental
nastiness—right—which they've got to work out in some
way. And if you choose, as we did, to go into the profession
of being nasty, which we call politics, then in an odd way
you've found a form of self-expression. And I believe you're
purified. Now look, take me. From the start I've always
thought of myself as a cunt. I knew it was in me, see? It
was there, like being born with a fist in your chest. But
how could I put that quality to use? How was I to fulfil
myself?

HAMMETT: As Home Secretary.

CLOUGH: Exactly.

HAMMETT: You did well.

CLOUGH: I know.

HAMMETT: You weren't a complete cunt.

CLOUGH: Thank you. But at nights I'm a kind of angel, Charlie.
My wife compares me with St. Francis of Assisi. She says
I've a natural ways with dogs. In the evening.

HAMMETT: A question.

CLOUGH: Yes.

HAMMETT: The Labour Party.

CLOUGH: Yes.

HAMMETT: Bit of a joke?

CLOUGH (*spreading his hands*): If that's what you think. You don't understand me. Psychology tells us—if we care to listen—that helping each other's only a form of perversion anyway. That doesn't worry me. For myself I've no interest in motivation, why people do things, or for that matter what they want to do. I'm simply interested in what they do, what they actually do. And whether it's good. And psychology being a notoriously half-fart science can't tell us that anyway.
So I don't let my motives get in the way. Do you understand?

HAMMETT: Absolutely.

CLOUGH: Well.

HAMMETT: I can't talk like you.

CLOUGH: I can't talk.

HAMMETT: I can't talk about what I believe in. I can talk about anything else. Eloquence should be reserved for things that don't matter. I went into socialism like other people go into medicine or the law. It was a profession. Half out of eloquence, half out of guilt. And as the eloquence got greater so did the guilt. (*Smiles.*) I could cut my tongue off.

CLOUGH: Smell of pot.

HAMMETT: My wife.

CLOUGH: You're a lucky man.

HAMMETT: Yes.

CLOUGH: So. May we choose ill health?

HAMMETT: As you wish.

CLOUGH: I think so. Couldn't serve your constituency through your long illness. Do you think?

HAMMETT: O.K.

CLOUGH: What illness?

HAMMETT: I've always fancied quinsy. I like the name.

CLOUGH: Quinsy it is. (*Gets up.*) Now I'll have to find you a successor. I'm sorry for you, Charlie. Really. (*Smiles.*) It all boils down to disadvantages of birth.

HAMMETT: Yes.

CLOUGH: Still we can't all be working class.

HAMMETT: No, I suppose breeding shows through in the end.

(*They laugh without enthusiasm.*)

CLOUGH: Good on you.

HAMMETT: Thank you.

CLOUGH: Keep your pecker.

(*They go to the door.*)

Do you think I could send you round to the Labour Party
psychiatrist? He's attached to Transport House.

(*Pause.* HAMMETT *gestures by putting up his hand in Socialist
salute.*)

HAMMETT: Che Guevara.

CLOUGH (*in response*): How's your father?

(HAMMETT *gestures to the door.* CLOUGH *opens it. As he is about
to step into the hall, a shriek and* MAUD, *without her clothes,
charges into him. She laughs. He puts up his hands as if
threatened by a bank robber, and stands aside.* MAUD *rushes
past them, then a moment later a naked* JERRY *slips sideways
by with a ludicrously polite "Excuse me".* HAMMETT *hasn't
gone into the hall but stands looking downstage.* CLOUGH *turns
back to the room, but sees* HAMMETT's *turned back and just
quietly makes for the front door, pausing to look right and left
as he goes for flying bodies. He goes out.* HAMMETT *moves
slightly forward.* ABEL *comes in and closes the door behind
him.*)

ABEL: You want a report?

HAMMETT (*not turning*): Ha ha.

ABEL: I'll make you a report. Your wife's being fucked by an
immigrant. Australian. When I say "fucked" I'm using it in
the loosest sense of the word.

(HAMMETT *sits down, still not looking at him.*)

Whatever name it has, it's happening vertically above you.
Or if you prefer, horizontally above you. Well, not a very
tricky case this one. The white heat of my professional know-
how had barely begun to glow before—well—he's got his
organ out and it's called proof conclusive.

(ABEL *sits down and peels a photograph off his Polaroid.*)
(*Handing the photo to* HAMMETT.) Have a photo. Ingenious. I
mean the camera.
(HAMMETT: *makes to hand it back.*)
Keep it. Plenty more. Give you something to yoyo over.
Not that the Ozzie gets me going. Spots all down his back
Spots and hairs.
HAMMETT: I wouldn't have wasted your time if . . .
ABEL: No.
HAMMETT: I honestly——
(HAMMETT *gets up, takes a frame from the desk, takes out a
studio portrait of* MAUD *and inserts his Polaroid picture in its
place. Then replaces the frame on his desk. Meanwhile they
talk.*)
You wouldn't credit my ignorance. We'd never talked about
divorce before.
ABEL: I sensed through the cupboard you were quite surprised.
HAMMETT: Yes.
ABEL: I've heard that kind of revelation before. I was under a
bed once when the news broke. Pandemonium.
HAMMETT: I think the Australian is an attempt to impress me.
ABEL: Bloke I knew had terrible trouble. Couldn't come.
(ABEL *gets up and puts two beer bottles down on the table in
front of him.*)
Wife tried everything. Tickled it with a feather, rubbed it
in lanolin, so on, so forth. Nothing. So she goes to the
doctor, explains the situation, he says feather, she says no,
it's been tried, he says—you can imagine—and so forth. He
said there's one foolproof method. Bang it over the end with a
bottle of beer. (*Flipping open one of the bottles.*) So she goes
home. That night he's trying as usual, having a spot of bother.
She waits till he's as near as he's ever going to get, pulls herself out, whips out a bottle of beer from behind her back
and WHAM——
(ABEL *suddenly bangs the opened bottle of beer on the top with
the unopened bottle. It comes spectacularly all over the table.*
HAMMETT *dives to clear up the foaming mess.* ABEL *wanders
away unamused.*)

Do you know what I find most amusing?

HAMMETT (*squeezing the cloth out of the window*): No.

ABEL: You might be my M.P. (*He laughs.*) The government and the people are miles apart.

HAMMETT: I know this.

ABEL: Do you know when I stopped voting Labour? When they started talking about "quality of life". I thought . . .

HAMMETT (*really vicious*): For Christ's sake I agree with you.

ABEL: All right.

(*Pause.* ABEL, *on hot bricks, wanders round to the desk and picks up the Polaroid photo.*)

Very nice piece of meat.

HAMMETT: Asked to describe Maud's body, I would hesitate but eventually plump for plump.

ABEL: Nice.

HAMMETT: On the march after Aldermaston, I was with a hawk-eyed Socialist with tight skin and small eyes. When she took her cardigan off her breasts hung like leather purses tied on to her rib-cage. Maud and I hid from her in the nuclear fall-out shelter, then slept together for the first time on the floor of the local primary school. The rain was running down the window, beating against the windows. You can't make love in a sleeping bag. When I woke in the morning she'd been elected Miss Aldermaston 1962, so I didn't see her that day. Except at a distance leading the Internationale. She did it superbly for one who didn't know the tune. She had all the irony of Raquel Welch in Vietnam. She was so ignorant it was marvellous. It was a state of grace. And in the following weeks I talked to her about socialism, and as I talked I became so convinced, it became so clear, that I decided to be a politician. My own eloquence, you see. The platform, the business of speaking it all delighted me. I courted Maud with public speeches. My actual proposal drew heavily on *Das Kapital*.

(ABEL *smiles.*)

She couldn't answer back. You're bored.

ABEL: No.

HAMMETT: I'm a bore.

III

(ABEL *makes a gesture of "if you say so".*)

I've never to this day spoken or argued out what I believed. My entry into politics was perfectly mistimed. I decided to be a politician about three days before the rest of the world became revolutionaries. Since then.

(*Pause.*)

Those who live by the word shall perish by the word.

ABEL (*puzzled*): I'm sure.

(MAUD *opens the door but doesn't step in at once. She's wearing a different dressing-gown and her hair is down and well combed.* HAMMETT *looks quickly, then turns away.* ABEL *stands up straight.*)

MAUD: My love. (*To* ABEL.) Hello.

(ABEL *nods awkwardly. Then hovers as he picks up a sealed beer bottle and moves towards the door.*)

ABEL: Keep this bottle about you. It's bound to come in handy. Remember: one thump.

(*He gestures a solid thump in the air, then gives it to* MAUD. *Goes out.*)

MAUD: Koochie. My love. I've abandoned La Mama. Thought we could have supper before I went. Grouse with spiced cherries.

HAMMETT: Great idea.

MAUD: With Jerry.

HAMMETT: Great.

MAUD: Stop us arguing. What did Cloughy want?

HAMMETT: Was that the first—intercourse—on the premises?

MAUD: It wasn't really intercourse.

HAMMETT: Oh.

MAUD: It was more like self-expression.

HAMMETT: In that case I'm not clear what you were trying to say.

MAUD (*laughs*): Charlie. When you're high, you don't need sex.

HAMMETT: I should get high.

MAUD: That's what I always say.

HAMMETT: I'm no fun, sugar blossom. You should leave me.

(JERRY *opens the door and comes in doing little exercises with his arms and legs to prove how wonderful he feels.*)

JERRY: Wow. Great. Weeooh. Zam zam. I could do with a beer.
   (MAUD *smiles at him, and is about to open a bottle.*)
   I mean, wait, hey, is that really tangerine gin? Fantastic. Not
   since Wogga Wogga.
MAUD: Have some.
   (JERRY *pours himself a large slug of tangerine gin.*)
JERRY: My God, it is. Nirvana. The fumes.
   (JERRY *puts it away, then turns to* HAMMETT.)
   People should be happy, yes?
HAMMETT: Yes.
   (JERRY *offers him a gin.*)
   No, thank you.
   (JERRY *gives it to* MAUD *who swallows it with indifference.*)
JERRY: I've never been so high since 1967. Do you remember?
   (MAUD *shakes her head.*)
HAMMETT: No.
JERRY: We were smashed out of our minds from breakfast time
   till the millenium. We thought it would never end. That was
   the summer of '67.
HAMMETT: '63 man myself.
JERRY: You despise my generation.
HAMMETT: No.
JERRY: You find my culture alien.
HAMMETT: Yes.
JERRY: You distrust the drug experience.
HAMMETT: Yes.
JERRY: I challenge you to prove that mari-mari-marijuana has
   any ded-d-d-d-deteriorating m-mental effects.
   (*He twitches twice and looks goofy.*)
HAMMETT: I think you're more or less the living proof.
JERRY: I'll smash your fucking face in.
   (HAMMETT *holds up his hands.*)
   It seemed possible—briefly—that the whole world was on a
   trip. That the whole cosmos had set sail. Can you imagine
   that?
HAMMETT: All too well.
JERRY: That was the summer of '67. Let me describe it to you.
HAMMETT: Please.

JERRY (*suddenly quite violent to* MAUD): Do *you* understand me?

MAUD: Yes.

JERRY: Do you understand me?

MAUD: I've said for Christ's sake.

JERRY: All right.

MAUD: Christ.

JERRY: You don't understand me. There was a moment, can I explain, there was a moment in—let's use the words we've got, shall we?—I've got to say *time*, right?——

MAUD: Yes——

JERRY: By "time" I mean something altogether more that I can't get the word for. There was a moment in time as we understand it, using linear time concepts, when the collective consciousness—right——?

MAUD: Yes——

JERRY: Was capable.

(HAMMETT *moves slightly in his chair behind* JERRY.)

Don't you come near me.

(HAMMETT *holds up his hands again.*)

Don't move. I know what you're doing.

(JERRY *turns slowly, anxiously back to* MAUD *as if threatened from behind by* HAMMETT.)

A moment when from a cellar in the Tottenham Court Road——

(*He swings round, but* HAMMETT *is sitting innocently still.*)

Came such vibrations that a truly international trip——

(JERRY *stops dead.*)

A moment of liberation . . . just a glimpse . . . a glimpse of infinite possibility of the collective.

(JERRY *points strange to his temples.*)

Consciousness.

HAMMETT (*encouraging him nervously*): Consciousness.

JERRY: Yes.

HAMMETT (*prompting*): Collective consciousness——

JERRY: The contact—between liberated minds, a real possibility of a community——

HAMMETT: Yes?

JERRY: Of the collective consciousness of a community——

HAMMETT: Keep coming, keep coming——

JERRY: Just fucking watch it.

(JERRY *leaps on to the chair* HAMMETT *is in, but* HAMMETT *is out from under him and across the room.* JERRY *picks up the pot plant by the leaf and swings the thing round so that the flowerpot flies off and cascades earth and brick round the room. He then screws the whole plant up in his hand, holds it out to* HAMMETT *in a gesture of defiance and stuffs it into his mouth.*)

I am going to see . . . I'm going to see the whole bloody thing.

(*There's silence as they watch, stunned, as he chews the whole plant. Pause. They hold still.*)

HAMMETT (*quietly*): What do you see? (*Gentle.*) Jerry?

(JERRY *just looks blank, then sits, then coughs nastily, and puts his hand to his mouth as he yanks out the green muck.*)

JERRY (*strangled*): Shit.

(*He then starts coughing and retching gently into his hand, just limp.*)

MAUD: What do we do?

(HAMMETT *goes to* JERRY's *side. He's curled like a foetus, spluttering.*)

HAMMETT: Take him to the bedroom.

(MAUD *takes the other arm. They lift the limp body up and drag it out of the room. Almost at once* MAUD *reappears and goes to* HAMMETT's *desk where she gets out a biscuit tin full of bottles of pills. Almost arbitrarily picks one bottle and runs out of the room. A couple of seconds later comes back in, pours a scotch, replaces the gin bottle.* HAMMETT *comes in, stands at the door.*)

He'd chewed the whole root.

MAUD: It's nasty.

HAMMETT: Yeah.

(MAUD *has another scotch at once.*)

MAUD: Have something from the armoury.

(HAMMETT *shakes his head.*)

That was disgusting.

HAMMETT: Yeah. I gave him a couple of mandrax. Sleeping pills. I don't know if he'll keep them down. And some aspirin. That lot should do him for a bit.

MAUD: .It should.

HAMMETT: I've had some odd experiences after sleeping with you, but it's never affected me that way.

MAUD: Charlie.

HAMMETT: I'm sorry.

MAUD: How do you think I feel?

HAMMETT: I haven't the slightest idea.

MAUD: I feel rotten.

HAMMETT: Oh.

MAUD: Poor Jerry. Poor sod.

HAMMETT: I've had a miserable day today. Froo-froo.

MAUD: You think if you come at me like some husband back from the office I'm going to forget what we talked about half an hour ago?

(HAMMETT *starts to collect the flowerpot pieces.* MAUD *has picked up the Polaroid photo in the frame.*)

What's this?

HAMMETT: Family snap.

(*He carries on picking up the bits. She stares at the photo and sits down, still looking.*)

MAUD: He's repulsive.

HAMMETT: Yes.

MAUD: Poor sod.

HAMMETT (*gets up from his knees*): It was quite by coincidence I'd employed a detective. I just wanted to know where you were.

MAUD: I wanted to leave you on one condition. That we didn't have to talk about it. I'd planned it during the three magic balls that I'd grease in on wheels, say do I love you and away. All in silence.

(JERRY *enters, staggering his way through the doorway.*)

JERRY: There are angels and they're talking to me.

(*He falls instantly flat on his face.*)

MAUD: For Christ's sake will you leave us alone?

(MAUD *goes across to the medicine tin and picks out a bottle, takes out some pills and stuffs them down* JERRY's *throat. Then stands over him and puts a toe into his stomach. He doesn't react.*)

I think he's all right now. Should we get a doctor, do you think, to pump him out?

HAMMETT: Not likely. He's been at this game so long he could swallow the whole pharmaceutical division of I.C.I. and still have room for tea and toast.

MAUD: I suppose.

HAMMETT: Bloke I knew took Guinness intravenously. Put some in a syringe and into his arm.

MAUD: What happened?

HAMMETT: He frothed a bit at the lips. Otherwise all right. Human body just won't give up.

(MAUD *laughs*.)

Bloke I knew. Never knew anybody but you. You were my excuse for not knowing anybody.

(MAUD *is packing*.)

You're packing.

MAUD: Yes.

HAMMETT: I really think it ought to be me. At least for a night or two.

MAUD: You don't have anywhere to go.

HAMMETT: I could go and sleep on the back benches.

MAUD: You ought to get back into circulation.

(HAMMETT *goes to his desk and unlocks the right-hand support compartment*.)

HAMMETT: You remember last year I tried to introduce a Private Member's Bill to lower the age of homosexual consent to sixteen.

(*He humps out a sack of letters and dumps it in the middle of the floor*.)

You know my views on homosexuals——

MAUD: They should have their balls cut off and be shipped out to Australia.

HAMMETT: Something like that. I don't give a damn as well you know. It just seemed reasonable——

(HAMMETT *picks out one empty brown envelope*.)

Smell that.

MAUD: Eeugh.

HAMMETT: That's shit. The postman used to bring my mail in

on the end of a pitchfork. And abuse.

(*He picks out one.*)

You are a . . . Your wife is . . . You should be . . . I collected them in the morning before you got up. That's what put me right off my mail.

MAUD (*reading*): They're horrible.

HAMMETT (*points*): The voice of England.

MAUD: These people are sick.

HAMMETT (*smiles*): Yes.

MAUD: Don't take it personally.

HAMMETT: No.

MAUD: I can't help you if you won't help yourself.

(HAMMETT *gets an old brown suitcase down from a high shelf.*)

That was my first real experience of Jerry and highly slimy it was.

(MAUD *points at the letters.*)

Why don't you throw those things out?

(HAMMETT *just stares at them.*)

HAMMETT: Do you know that dud detective Abel sat in a cupboard and recorded you saying that you didn't love me any more. I found that oddly—reassuring.

MAUD: Really?

HAMMETT: Puts the whole thing on a public footing. More or less a performance.

MAUD: And *he* photographed me?

HAMMETT: No doubt on cine film as well. In colour. With equipment for a slow-motion action replay. "Let's just watch the build-up to that great climax again, shall we, Jack?"

MAUD: Glad I didn't know.

(*Pause.* MAUD *is shovelling Smarties in fast now.*)

HAMMETT: I've been no use to you.

MAUD: At times.

HAMMETT: I've always resented your giving in so easily. In the first place. You needed so little encouragement. Taking your knickers off in that sleeping bag. But not just that. Agreeing to marry me so easily.

MAUD: What do you mean?

HAMMETT: It rather spoilt things for me when you agreed. I

expected fantastic difficulties.

MAUD: You wanted me to say no?

HAMMETT: I was rather disappointed you were in love with me. I'd hoped there was more to you than that. When I became a politician, "what a bore" I expected you to say.

MAUD: It was a bore.

HAMMETT: But you never said so.

MAUD: I thought you were boring.

HAMMETT: You didn't.

MAUD: I did.

HAMMETT: Oh Christ.

MAUD (*pause*): You seemed to me to be terribly dull. But I thought it must be my fault that I was missing something in you. That I couldn't at the time understand. Do you see?

HAMMETT: Yes.

MAUD: That's why you seemed such a smashing person to marry. Because you'd help me understand . . . why you were such a smashing person.

HAMMETT: Which I wasn't.

MAUD: As it turned out, no.

HAMMETT: We can safely say no.

MAUD: Wild goose chase.

(*Pause.*)

Koochie. If I made some saltimbocca alla romana would you eat any?

(HAMMETT *shakes his head.*)

It's not a Svengali situation. You didn't *make* me. So get your bloody fingers off.

(*They smile. She pulls a hair of his head off lovingly.*)

HAMMETT: Stop it.

MAUD: I thought through you I'd meet some *real* people. I mean real people. But in Sunderland they were rather aggressively real. They made a fetish of it. And you used to stand there, shifting foot to foot, worrying about your accent, and how can I get these real people to respect me? You weren't getting terribly close. Pints of black and tan jammed in our hands didn't fool anybody. The week-end felt like a penance for the life we led elsewhere. I never felt it necessary.

(HAMMETT *is deep in thought in his chair.*)

HAMMETT: I never like anybody. I just want them to like me.

MAUD: Socialism's a talent, like acting. No good trying if you haven't got it. My acting? You remember. Intellectually perfect. If I made a gesture—

(MAUD *makes a gesture.*)

—it was so clear—in my own mind. But it was a mile from what people actually saw.

(MAUD *makes a similar, but much more ham gesture.*)

I'd come on playing Juliet looking to all the world as if I was on week-end leave from the Red Army, but the interpretation—here—

(MAUD *points to her head.*)

—was superb. It's the same with socialism. The issues are so clear. You know so clearly what you think. Though I can't remember your ever being interested in doing anything. It was always what you were. I'm a socialist, Maud.

(MAUD *clicks her fingers in front of his face a couple of times, but he doesn't react. Pause.*)

You might at least argue when I say I'm leaving.

HAMMETT: It must be what I want.

MAUD (*decisively, to break the gloom*): I'm going to leave.

HAMMETT: My prerogative.

(*They both jump up.*)

It's my house and I'm going to leave it.

MAUD: I said it first, remember?

(*They both flip open their suitcases, side by side on the table.*)

HAMMETT: What the hell am I going to take, Maud?

MAUD: I'm taking a change of clothes.

HAMMETT: Change of clothes.

MAUD: Toothbrush——

HAMMETT: Toothpaste——

MAUD: Deodorant——

HAMMETT: Razor——

MAUD: And a good book.

HAMMETT: And that's what I'm getting away from, Mother.

(*He lifts the biscuit tin. The bulb is flashing underneath. He crashes the bottom of the tin on to the bulb smashing it into little pieces.*)

Leave me alone.

(*Now the light is broken the phone of course starts ringing.* HAMMETT *puts the phone into the biscuit tin, still ringing, and squirts the soda syphon on it for a few moments. It gurgles, then stops.*)

Now shut up.

MAUD: Histrionics.

HAMMETT: I just want to be left alone.

MAUD: Great.

HAMMETT: Fine.

MAUD: All right. You go. I'll stay here tonight and open a few windows. And tomorrow I'll be gone.

HAMMETT: Fine.

(HAMMETT *slams down the lid of his suitcase.*)

MAUD: The trick with the telephone was—(*thinks hard*)— pathetic.

(MAUD *drags* JERRY *out by the heels through the main door.* HAMMETT *opens his suitcase and throws in his picture of* MAUD *and* JERRY *together. He then puts on a dowdy brown mac.* MAUD *comes back in.*)

It gets tiring how one marriage partner is allowed to bag all the suffering. Suffering is so much your undisputed territory that no one else is allowed near.

(HAMMETT *closes the suitcase again.*)

If we haven't the chance to change our lives, to change everything in our lives, regularly and at will, then—there's no particular point, is there? That's what I've always thought. That's what you taught me.

(*Pause.*)

I'll make some cheese and mango chutney sandwiches if that's any help.

(HAMMETT *shakes his head. He turns upstage from the very front.*)

HAMMETT: Don't take yourself so seriously, Charlie.

(*The back wall of the set recedes and the two side pieces slide into the wings.* MAUD *goes out with the back of the set. The top*

*of the set is hoisted into the flies and the furniture in the middle
is either pulled back or lowered through traps. It's essential
that this should be a quite magical effect of the whole room
receding and flying apart as* HAMMETT *looks at it, darkening.
As the stuff flies away, he walks upstage into the newly created
bare stage, wearing a brown mac and carrying a suitcase.*

Clapham Common. HAMMETT *walks to the back of the
deserted stage. It's fairly dark with the occasional white light
sweeping dimly across the stage from car headlights. He walks
back down to the front of the stage, his lips moving as he talks
incomprehensibly to himself. On the end of a long pole three
brightly painted red-cheeked smiling dummies sweep across the
stage in an arc, their heads nodding loosely on their bodies.*
HAMMETT *stands quiet a moment and watches them go past. He
leaves his case downstage and walks a little quicker to a hiding-
place. From the top corner of the stage comes a* WOMAN,
middle-aged, well wrapped up with a scarf tied round her head.)

HAMMETT: Here.

(*The* WOMAN *stops.*)

Here. Would you like a treat?

(*The* WOMAN *is hypnotized.*)

WOMAN: Er.

HAMMETT: Can I show you something? I'll show you something
nice.

(HAMMETT, *facing upstage, exhibits himself to her.*)

(*Bowing slightly, gravely*): Madam.

(WOMAN *blank.*

*She stares at him, then looks at his face. After a long pause,
she walks rather tight-lipped and deliberately offstage. Not
running away, just asserting herself.* HAMMETT *turns after her.
As if after a huge effort he lets out an audible sigh. The dim*
LIGHT *fades down to* BLACKOUT.

A few seconds pause only. Then the LIGHTS *come up as
before, but now there is a bench downstage and in the far corner
a swing.* HAMMETT *is in a much more cheerful mood, and as the*
LIGHTS *appear he swings aside the two parts of his mackintosh
to reveal his trousers.*)

Ha ha. Take *that.*

(*He laughs at his mock assault. He whistles a little and tap dances a few steps on the ground. Then stops, crosses the stage silently and stands quite still. From the same corner as the* WOMAN, *comes* CATRIONA, *same age as* MAUD, *thin, blonde, smartly dressed, rather pinched-looking.* HAMMETT *moves across to intercept her with more confidence than before.*)

Here. Can I show you something?

CATRIONA (*pause*): No, thank you.

HAMMETT: Something nice.

CATRIONA: No, thank you.

(CATRIONA *stands, then moves on.* HAMMETT *stumbles after.*)

HAMMETT: Here, no, wait, hold on, let me *show* you.

CATRIONA (*rounding back*): As long as it's not going to take too long.

(HAMMETT *is taken aback. Pauses. Then exhibits himself rather shiftily to her.*)

HAMMETT: There.

CATRIONA: What, *that?*

HAMMETT: Yes.

CATRIONA: You must be joking.

(CATRIONA *laughs and walks on.*)

HAMMETT: For Christ's sake.

CATRIONA: The mac is good. That I will grant you. A real genuine wanker's mac. But the rest is so much malarkey.

HAMMETT: Thank you.

CATRIONA: Next time, zips. Zips are quicker. If you were half-way to being a real flasher, you'd know that.

(CATRIONA *moves on. He follows her offstage. The* LIGHTS *go out.*

A moment's darkness. The LIGHTS *up again. She comes in from the top. He intercepts her. She stops well short of him.*)

HAMMETT: I'm sorry.

CATRIONA: Listen, I walk across the Common every night. You get to see all sorts of things.

HAMMETT: Really?

CATRIONA: Yours doesn't compete. It's not in League Division Two. Not by South London standards. There are men round here who can tie reef knots.

(HAMMETT *smiles*.)

Listen, I've a big heart. You can have me here on the bench
if you want.

(HAMMETT *smiles*.)

No, seriously, if you want.

HAMMETT: I couldn't possibly.

CATRIONA: Then what were you flashing for? Eh, Horace? What
were you after?

HAMMETT: It's what I wanted to do.

CATRIONA: It can't be a——

(*Pause.* HAMMETT *is moving away*.)

Who flashed who?

HAMMETT: I flashed you.

CATRIONA: Right, my turn.

(HAMMETT *moves away*.)

No, come on. Flashing's fun. It's being flashed that's not
so terribly charming.

(HAMMETT *nods to concede the point. He sits down. She sits
down next to him. They smile at each other*.)

From early days you were drawn to places where bodies
were on show. Changing rooms, Turkish baths, these were
your regular haunts—you considered going into the medical
profession, embalming——

(HAMMETT *laughs*.)

Where did you go?

HAMMETT: Parliament.

(*They laugh happily together*.)

CATRIONA: Well, there you are.

HAMMETT: Point taken.

CATRIONA (*still smiling*): I recognize you now. You married my
best friend. I was at your wedding.

HAMMETT (*freezing over*): Small world.

(*A dreadful pause.* HAMMETT *goes up and walks away a bit.*
CATRIONA *bursts out laughing*.)

CATRIONA: I'm terribly sorry. Really. I won't tell Maud.

(*She laughs again*.)

HAMMETT: In the light I didn't recognize you. If I'd known you
were a friend of Maud's I wouldn't have dreamt of . . .

CATRIONA: Exhibiting yourself. No. Well, if I'd known you were Maud's husband, I wouldn't have dreamt of accepting.

HAMMETT: No.

CATRIONA: No.

(*Another pause.*)

You've separated?

(HAMMETT *nods vigorously.*)

I did tell her it was a disaster. We had the most frightful row in the powder room at the Connaught. I'd never met you really, but I told her that socialists were like socialism —they were a phase you went through when you were young.

HAMMETT: I find the whole business paralytically embarrassing and I'd rather we forgot it.

CATRIONA: She was Roy Rogers and I was the Cisco Kid. When we were young.

HAMMETT: I recognize you now.

CATRIONA: Waif-like, undernourished, you remember me.

HAMMETT: I do. You were against me.

CATRIONA: We were all against you. Nothing against grammar school chaps. Some of them are remarkably nice. But under pressure, out in Poona, up the jungle, where there's a crisis the grammar school chap trembles quite distinctively. But ten years on, who transpires on Clapham Common?

HAMMETT: The grammar school chap.

CATRIONA: Been at it long?

(HAMMETT *doesn't look at her.*)

Are you cold?

HAMMETT: Somewhat. I can't explain. Did you know Maud when she was young?

CATRIONA: Till she was twenty-one. We played together. We were chums.

HAMMETT: Everything that's good in us comes from our child-hood. Round about ten the rot sets in

CATRIONA: You're shivering.

HAMMETT: The English don't know that. They're obsessed with what happens after. Why can't they get over their adolescence?

CATRIONA: Pardon.

HAMMETT: Always talking about schools and colleges and dormitories, and hurry home for prep——

CATRIONA: Excuse me.

(CATRIONA *gets up.*)

HAMMETT: And my first fuck and homosexual fumblings and chronic misbehaviour on the football field——

(CATRIONA *walks away, trying to stop his flow, but he's away.*)

CATRIONA: Oi.

HAMMETT: It's some elaborate organized hypocrisy that every Englishman thinks his birthright, and a convenient way of henceforth pretending that he has lived some sort of life, any kind of life at all——

CATRIONA: Officer, take this man away——

HAMMETT: If we could just get over that, past that kind of relationship——

CATRIONA: He's been interfering with me.

(HAMMETT *gets up and takes account of her.*)

HAMMETT: I've been four years in Parliament, swept in, as they say, on the Labour landslide of '66. A lot of creepy-crawlies swept in on the froth of that wave. It's like a debating society, some ghastly boys' school, with the whole grotesque inhuman game of charades magnified and ritualized to the highest possible point of futility, the most elaborate conceivable way of not actually talking to each other, of not actually saying anything . . .

(CATRIONA *jumps up and down and applauds.*)

CATRIONA: Hurrah.

(HAMMETT *claps his hands.*)

HAMMETT: Hurrah. Hurrah.

CATRIONA: Great speech. It's a knock-out.

HAMMETT: As for you. You set the bloody cow against me.

CATRIONA: I did.

HAMMETT: From the start. I didn't have a chance.

CATRIONA: You didn't.

HAMMETT: What did you say?

CATRIONA: I said——

HAMMETT: That I was a bore.

CATRIONA (*pause*): Yes.

HAMMETT: I *am* a bore. But in my bath I'm Caruso.

CATRIONA: You've changed since then.

HAMMETT: Not really.

CATRIONA: You've gone bald.

HAMMETT: I'm not bald.

CATRIONA: You're bald.

HAMMETT: I have a disease called alopecia. Do you know it?

CATRIONA: No.

HAMMETT: Alopecia means that when I am unhappy my hair falls out. Hence my appearance. But when I stop worrying, and this is true, the hair begins to fight slowly back across the dome of my head like an advancing army of ants reclaiming old ground, until my hairline hits my forehead again and I'm covered like a young man. So people never recognize me when I'm happy. Not my best friends.

CATRIONA: Whoever they are.

HAMMETT (*looks at her rather sharply*): As you say.

CATRIONA (*explaining*): You were all alone at your wedding. Your side of the aisle was deserted. On the other side were sitting the gross battalions of the upper classes. I felt sorry for you.

HAMMETT: I was all right.

CATRIONA: When did you last have a head of hair?

HAMMETT (*smiles*): Ah. When I was ten. Do you suppose—I could ever be happy?

(CATRIONA *shakes her head.*)

I know. It's something to do with my personality. It seems such a rotten draw, so arbitrary. The personality I was lumbered with has proved quite inadequate for the job. I so resent being issued with the wrong equipment. It's like death. Death gives me no trouble at all. I couldn't care less about it. It's the other one I worry about—the one before. I can't get over the bloodiness of existing before I knew about it. It really balks me. I don't just mean my nine months in the womb—though they do depress me, they make me savage to think about, not just them, but the whole idea of the world spinning before I was born. It's the cosmic insolence of the thing that upsets me. Do you feel that?

127

CATRIONA: No.

HAMMETT: No. I shouldn't talk.

(*Pause.*)

What do you do?

CATRIONA: Mostly I'm just rich. Most of the time.

HAMMETT: Is that all?

CATRIONA: Sometimes I edit a magazine for teenage girls about cosmetics and men and abortions and things.

HAMMETT: Ah.

CATRIONA: Why were you flashing?

(HAMMETT *doesn't respond.*)

I talk to all the flashers here. I live on the posh side of the Common. They know me now. They don't even bother to get it out any longer. We take it as seen.

HAMMETT (*irritated*): All right.

CATRIONA: Does that upset you? Some people have a considerable sense of humour. Mind you, you have to, if you're going to go the whole hog and lower your trousers. You look pretty stupid one way and another. You were what I call a sneak-peeper, but the down-with-the-trousers-and-laugh-who-dares, they're the ones I really admire.

(*She laughs.*)

They look so stupid.

HAMMETT: Why do they do it?

CATRIONA: And others fail at the last moment. They say something like, "Hey, miss," and you say, "What?" They say "*miss*", "*what*", and they just say "never mind forget it". And they hurry away. Some won't even try me because I'm too young. They want to outrage really ugly old women, make them gape and stutter. I call them ideological flashers, because they want to embarrass the bourgeois. I'm a bad risk, truth to tell, I laugh too often like I did with you, and then I chase them about and challenge them. But they mostly like to talk.

HAMMETT: What about?

CATRIONA: Why should I tell you?

(*Pause.*)

Was I your first?

HAMMETT: No. There were fourteen before you. I've been at it half the night. A housewife and an older woman—but you won't understand——

CATRIONA: No?

HAMMETT: They weren't quite what I wanted!

(*He laughs.*)

Isn't that absurd?

CATRIONA: What did you want?

HAMMETT: Why should I tell you?

(*Pause.*)

CATRIONA: I could tell you weren't an original, you know. That mac was far too calculated, and the small brown case. You were acting the part, I'm afraid.

HAMMETT: I just wanted to express myself.

(*Pause.*)

CATRIONA (*very serious*): I mourn it really as a passing art. The element of surprise is draining away far too fast. We've seen it all before. Increasingly the flasher will apologize, touch his forehead, say I'm sorry this is very old hat, and will you forgive me for being unoriginal, but all the same, forgive me, let me show you—this. . . . There's nothing now left to hide. It's the flasher's dilemma. However suddenly he jumps, however deft his movements, however dark his expression, however innocent and lovely his victim, the likelihood is . . . she has seen it before. There is nothing left but the embrace.

(*Silence.*)

And to be touched.

(*Silence.*)

HAMMETT: It's not just that I'm boring, though I am, very boring, but that I'm a carrier as well. Boredom spreads round me like contagion. In perfectly cheerful rooms people begin to fidget and to fart. So not only am I not entertaining, also I am rarely entertained. I have to keep trying to catch groups of people off guard, slip in when they're not looking in the hope they haven't noticed I've arrived, so that for a few moments I can watch normal people smiling and amusing each other, before some scrupulous lout starts to sniff and turns to the door and notices me, and then—well —even if it were Oscar Wilde he'd say, sorry I can't actually remember the end of my story, I've got a terrible headache, and the epigram would just be left there hanging, like some blunted icicle. That's the effect I have. Have you noticed?

CATRIONA: I'd noticed you were boring.

HAMMETT: I'm spectacularly boring. I know something about it. It's not a matter of being funny—I can get my tongue round some pretty acute phrases, you know, jokes. It's just I make everyone uneasy. They can't relax. Parliament's the only place I've ever felt at home.

CATRIONA: They're all boring?

HAMMETT: They're all shell-shock victims, all life's walking wounded, putting a reasonable front on things. I go and gossip and feel at ease, and excuse myself by being rude about the place. What——

CATRIONA: Yes.

HAMMETT: I fear these events—this evening—what I fear—

CATRIONA: Yes.

HAMMETT: I fear tonight's the real beginning of my parliamentary career, not the end. The idea was—back there—if I can do this I can do anything.

(*Pause.*)

Smell the air.

CATRIONA: Eeeugh.

HAMMETT: You sound like Maud.

CATRIONA: Beg pardon.

HAMMETT: The ground I've trodden on for ten years has shifted away and I'm conscious of talking in the air. I can't even mouth the word "revolution" any longer. It sounds so limp and second-hand. Those of us who believed that the world would get better have been brought up short. The thing gets worse not just because of what happens, but because the weight of knowledge of what *ought* to happen gets greater. As things get more impossible they also get more obvious. As our needs get simpler, they get more unlikely to be fulfilled.

130

(*Pause.*)
Back there——

CATRIONA: Yes?

HAMMETT: Did I look a real twit, I mean, a real twit?

CATRIONA: Almost.

HAMMETT: What was wrong?

CATRIONA: You were diffident. It wasn't the full frontal flash.

HAMMETT: Flash me now.

(*They both get up.* CATRIONA *stands dead still a few yards away from* HAMMETT.)

CATRIONA (*perfectly still*): The eye doesn't waver. The hands are still. The trousers will fall like a guillotine. The mind contracts, your brain is like a stone. You look them in the eye. (*She steps forward and opens out her raincoat with superb inevitability. He puts his hands up as if dazzled at the radiance of her mock-flash.*) It's in the eyes. You have something to show. You have no doubts about its effects. There's no fanfare, no propaganda. You know it's going to work. You don't load the display with any emotion. You know what you're doing. (*Pause.*) You're flashing. (*Pause.*) You're flashing. (*With an immense rush Tara's theme from* Gone with the Wind *washes over the stage. With relief, they relax. He picks up his case, puts his arm round her and they go out. Unseen by them,* ABEL *walks briskly across the stage as the* CURTAIN *falls.* Gone with the Wind *rages on, well into the interval.*)

ACT II

Private Life

Six o'clock six days later in HAMMETT's *flat.* The Eton Boating Song *as the* LIGHTS *go down. And the* CURTAIN *rises.*

Same room but slummier. Clothes all over the floor and there are books, bricks and Coca-Cola bottles. HAMMETT *is dressed in a vest and pin-stripe trousers.* ABEL *is sitting opposite him at his desk.* HAMMETT *has a new level of deadly confidence.*

HAMMETT *is listening very intently.*

ABEL: Tuesday I tripped out on LSD.
> (ABEL *is thinking very hard.*)
> A wondrous psychedelia. It was like the cover of a gramophone record. Under the influence, ideas move. Can you understand that?
> (HAMMETT *shakes his head.*)
> Ideas have a life of their own. Very strange. I'd known about objects coming to life. But it's uncanny when ideas get up and start walking around.
> (*Pause. He's thinking as hard as he can.*)
> Cleaned me out, though. I felt good after. Once I'd had a few beers, I felt good.

HAMMETT: Who gave it you?

ABEL: Bloke I knew.
> (HAMMETT *lifts the lid of a laughing box briefly which is on his desk. It goes* "Ha Ha Ha".)

HAMMETT: She gave it you. (*Sudden*) Come on——

ABEL: Difficult case. V.v. difficult——

HAMMETT: You must know who he is——

132

ABEL (*getting notebook out, very fast*): Re Hammett. Adultery
　　wife of. Identification co-respondent of.

HAMMETT: The evidence.

　　(ABEL *gets out one photo and hands it over.*)

ABEL: That's it.

　　(HAMMETT *takes it.*)

ABEL: Christ it smells in here.

HAMMETT: Look at this.

ABEL: Sod me.

HAMMETT (*holding out the photo*): What are these?

ABEL (*surly*): Spots, I suppose.

HAMMETT: Spots. And?

ABEL (*nods*): Hairs.

HAMMETT: Spots and hairs.

ABEL: I should never have shown you the photographs.

HAMMETT: Do you think I'm stupid?

ABEL: I was more or less relying on it. The longer a job lasts the
　　more I stand to make. After a time most detective work
　　boils down to keeping the results secret from your employer.

HAMMETT: They live together?

　　(ABEL *nods.*)

HAMMETT: Uh huh——

　　(*Pause.*)

ABEL: When I was a boy—country childhood—we used to go to
　　the bathroom when the farmer was out to put straws up
　　frogs and then puff down them as hard as we could. The
　　frog inflated—eyes going round——

　　(ABEL *gestures.*)

　　Then whoof—went off like a landmine. Splattered all over
　　the walls. It smells like that in here.

HAMMETT: Does she know what I'm sleeping with?

ABEL: Certainly not.

HAMMETT: You haven't told her yet.

ABEL: I don't talk to her.

HAMMETT: No?

　　(*Pause.* HAMMETT *has his thumb on him.*)

ABEL: Well.

HAMMETT: Who tripped you out?

(ABEL *smiles*.)
You're being paid by both of us for peddling to each other
partial and inaccurate information about each other's
affairs.

ABEL: More or less.

HAMMETT: Nice to know she cares.

ABEL: I'm a card.

HAMMETT: Have I been——

ABEL: What?

HAMMETT: Have I been observed these last six days? In a sexual
sense?

ABEL: A bit.

HAMMETT: Which bit?

ABEL: At the beginning. You've seen it once you've seen it
always. From Delhi to Shanghai. If I watched more than
once I'd call it self-indulgence.

HAMMETT: Please don't be embarrassed on my account, old chap,
doesn't bother me, quite the opposite, gets me going.

ABEL: I'm happier to hide my eyes.

HAMMETT: Do you think I'm ashamed of what I'm doing?

ABEL: You've got to laugh, eh?

HAMMETT (*dead*): Ha ha.

ABEL: No, really. The best bit was undoubtedly on the common.
No. Seriously. You were great.

HAMMETT: Thank you.

ABEL: You should have seen their faces, Charlie.

HAMMETT: I saw their faces.

ABEL: How they love it. Gives them something to latch on to.
There's the anxious moment of shall-I, shan't-I, is-it-real,
how-long-have-I-got, then wham they're away like rabbits.
All but one. I bet you weren't half surprised. When the last
one stayed.

HAMMETT: I was touched.

ABEL: The bloke with the blond rinse was amused. What put
you on to flashing in the first place?

HAMMETT: You must go.

ABEL: It looked like some kind of opinion poll. I'd never do it
personally. We carry within us things that are better not

134

revealed. Is that not so?

HAMMETT: That is so.

ABEL: Amen.

(CATRIONA *comes in wearing a dressing-gown and glasses.*)
Catriona.

CATRIONA: Hello. I'm afraid we haven't met.

HAMMETT: Er Labour member for Paddington, dear. Say hello.

CATRIONA: Hello.

HAMMETT: Thanks for calling.

ABEL: How do you do?

HAMMETT: I'll show you out.

CATRIONA: Doesn't he have a name?

HAMMETT: Er d'Avignor Goldschmidt.

ABEL (*bowing*): Labour member for Paddington, Mam.

HAMMETT: This way.

(HAMMETT *swings open the cupboard door next to the main
entrance, and beckons* ABEL *in.*)

ABEL: I'll take the other way out, I think.

HAMMETT (*closing the cupboard door, opening the main door*): I'm
terribly sorry.

ABEL: Thank you.

HAMMETT: And good-bye.

ABEL: 'Bye, Charlie.

(ABEL *goes out.*)

CATRIONA (*waving some papers*): I've got the proofs of my next
issue. "Should young people sleep together?"

HAMMETT: Ah.

CATRIONA: A picture-probe. "We asked a hundred priests."

HAMMETT: Have I got a collar?

CATRIONA: I don't know. Main feature. "How is VD communi-
cated?"

HAMMETT: Lavishly.

CATRIONA: "The causative organism of syphilis is the treponima
pallidum, a long thread-like wavy organism with pointed
tapering ends."

HAMMETT (*searching about*): I can't go to the House without a
collar.

CATRIONA: "Syphilis affects only human beings though it has

135

been experimentally produced in anthropoid apes."

HAMMETT (*picking up the collar from the floor*): Thank God for that.

CATRIONA: How do you like my article?

HAMMETT (*fixing his collar and tie*): Very sparky.

CATRIONA: "At first there is only slight skin eruption. Then—rise of temperature and feverishness, loss of appetite, vague pains, sores in the mouth and throat, mucous patches, painful swellings of the bones, general enlargement of the lymphatic glands. Then—some months go by, maybe years. Meanwhile we see the growth here and there of granulation tissue known as gummata, appearing in the skin as hard nodules, or developing in the brain or spinal chord. Or they may lie beneath the skin or under a mucous membrane where they break down and form deep ulcers with characteristic thickened, sharply cut edges."

(HAMMETT *turns round, fully dressed but for shoes—the complete man.*)

HAMMETT: How do I look?

CATRIONA: Do you never listen?

HAMMETT: Emperor of all he surveys.

CATRIONA: You never listen.

HAMMETT: I listen. Thread-like wavy things. I've been listening. How do I look?

CATRIONA: You look the part.

HAMMETT: You just have to tuck your personality under your arm and face the world. Is that not right?

CATRIONA: That's right.

HAMMETT: Go in and fight them on your own terms. Damn your procedures and points of deference to the right honourable impostor from Lilliput. It's people that we're here to talk about. People's lives. Is that not right?

CATRIONA: Right.

HAMMETT: Good.

(*He shadow-boxes briefly in the air.*)

Stuff your constitutional palaver and down to the business of people. Do you hear me, Mother?

CATRIONA: "Are virgins redundant? We asked a hundred police-

136

men."

HAMMETT: I'm here to help the poor, the witless, the deprived. Help them towards a real life.

CATRIONA: "Do cosmetics spoil your skin?"

HAMMETT: That sounds a bit feeble for your magazine. A bit soft-core.

CATRIONA: I was bullied into it. A horrible man from a cosmetics company forced me into writing a piece about him.

HAMMETT: When was this?

CATRIONA: Yesterday.

HAMMETT (*stands over her, his fingers in her hair*): Oh.

CATRIONA: Marching into the office and saying, "Write about me." Incredible cheek.

HAMMETT: So what did you do?

CATRIONA: I fucked him.

HAMMETT: Ach so.

(*He stands over her. Then takes a couple of steps back.*)

You mean he fucked you?

CATRIONA: By no means.

HAMMETT: Why is there no phrase a liberated woman can use to describe her part in the business?

CATRIONA: There is.

HAMMETT: What?

CATRIONA: "To have a fuck." As in the phrase "we had a fuck". It's perfectly impartial.

HAMMETT: That sounds ridiculous. "Here, have a fuck." It sounds like some kind of *fondue*.

CATRIONA: We made love.

HAMMETT: To a man from a cosmetics company?

CATRIONA: Well, perhaps not love.

HAMMETT: Well.

CATRIONA: I balled him.

HAMMETT: In your case, fair enough.

CATRIONA: We balled.

(*Pause.* HAMMETT *turns back to her, iced over.*)

HAMMETT: And was he at all taken aback?

CATRIONA: It shot some of the bullshit out of him.

HAMMETT: And did he persuade you to write the article?

CATRIONA: Yes.

HAMMETT: Well, that's not what I'd call having your bullshit shot, it's what I'd call achieving your aims. Sounds as if he got a sight more out of it.

CATRIONA: You weren't there. You can't tell.

HAMMETT (*low*): Angelcake.

CATRIONA: Tweety-tweety-yummy-cheery-chops.

HAMMETT: Oh.

CATRIONA: Sorry.

HAMMETT (*going gleefully over to the drinks tray*): Cocktail time.

CATRIONA: Hardly. With my headache.

HAMMETT (*stops*): What else is in there?

CATRIONA: My feature on pop stars. All the greats.

HAMMETT: Did you meet Cliff Richard?

CATRIONA: Yes.

HAMMETT: Did you meet Lulu?

CATRIONA: Yes.

HAMMETT: What were they like?

CATRIONA: Different.

    (*Pause.*)

    And the article on VD clinics.

HAMMETT: Sometimes it was a bit more cheerful with Maud. It wasn't so bloody unfriendly.

    (HAMMETT *puts on a top hat to complete the effect and kicks his unshod leg out, but very seriously, sadly.*)

    Kerpow. How would you describe our relationship?

CATRIONA: Disaster.

HAMMETT: Yes, disaster is fair. I'd thought fiasco but disaster will do.

CATRIONA: I can't see any point really at which we connect.

HAMMETT: Bracing, isn't it?

CATRIONA: I'm only staying because I want to see Maud.

HAMMETT (*spitting on his shoes and rubbing them*): You think she'll turn up?

CATRIONA: Bound to.

HAMMETT: Ah.

CATRIONA: You're still scared of her.

HAMMETT: You've never been frightened of anyone, have you?

CATRIONA: Not really. My riding master perhaps.

HAMMETT: On Clapham Common you seemed to me gallant and realistic. I rather admired your dash. But six days on it can feel pretty grubby. Both ways. Sharing you out with cosmetics men. To you the idea of being frightened of someone, well, it's just ridiculous, it's like all neurosis—it should be vanquished. There's nothing to be nervous about. But to my generation—well—we rather pride ourselves on our neurosis. Really, it's all we've got. It's——

CATRIONA: You——

HAMMETT: I've always used it as a kind of proof of my integrity. Do you understand? In the mornings the only way that I knew I was awake was that I was worried, I was desperately worried. My life of course is barren and wasteful and all those things, but as long as I can sustain a decent level of upset, I'm somehow above it, do you see? I don't quite have to own up.

CATRIONA: My head aches.

HAMMETT: Suffering—the way I suffer—is only an excuse. It's only a way of not doing things.

CATRIONA: You look dicky in your little suit.

HAMMETT: I'm a different man.

(*The bell goes.*)

(*Quickly gathering* CATRIONA's *scattered stuff.*) Come on. Out.

CATRIONA: Don't be ridiculous.

HAMMETT: I'm sorry but it's out.

CATRIONA: Really.

(CATRIONA *at once throws everything he's just thrust at her up in a great fountain in the air, and sweeps into the bathroom. He at once starts scrabbling on the ground again.*)

(*Off.*) I'm listening.

HAMMETT: All right.

(*As* HAMMETT *crawls round the floor, the bathroom door is flung open and from it fly a number of rubber ducks and animals.*)

CATRIONA (*off*): And take your wretched rubber ducks.

(*He stoops down to collect those, as the main door flies open and* JERRY *is thrown into the room. Followed at a distance by* MAUD.)

MAUD: This is mine. Where's yours?

HAMMETT: Maud.

MAUD: Let's see what you've picked up with. (*Moving over.*) Natty line in lingerie, I'll say that for her. It's like some nineteenth-century bordello.

(ABEL *comes in behind them.*)

He won't tell me what you've gone down with.

HAMMETT: Good for him.

MAUD: This says Christian flaming Dior.

JERRY (*apologetically*): She's finally high.

MAUD: I am not. Is she there in the bath? All I've seen is a rather blurred photo of her back.

HAMMETT: I'm sleeping with the Moderator of the Church of Scotland.

MAUD: Well, where is he?

HAMMETT: Evensong.

MAUD (*tossing back the clothing*): Well, give him back his accessories.

HAMMETT: Thank you.

MAUD: Search the house.

ABEL: Not my style.

MAUD: Charlie.

HAMMETT: Shall we all settle down to a drink?

JERRY: Hic.

HAMMETT: There's tangerine gin for those who can manage it.

(*He turns. The four are suddenly at once acutely embarrassed, and the hysteria vanishes at once.*)

MAUD: Oh, dear.

(*Everyone except* HAMMETT *sits down.*)

How are you, Charlie?

HAMMETT: Fine.

MAUD: I'm sorry about this.

HAMMETT: That's O.K.

MAUD: I thought it would be better if I had an audience.

(MAUD *and* HAMMETT *laugh appreciatively. The others look dumb.* ABEL *takes a photograph.*)

ABEL (*taking another*): Smile.

HAMMETT: My love. Still got your acolyte in tow?

MAUD: We're having a mature relationship, aren't we, Jerry?

JERRY: Well, we're——

MAUD: Shut up. There you are.

HAMMETT: Still on the dole?

JERRY: Of course.

MAUD: How long can we expect this bath to last? I've got an appointment here at seven.

HAMMETT: What do you mean?

MAUD: Wait and see. I like your suit.

HAMMETT: Thank you. My parliamentary suit.

MAUD: Plunging back in?

HAMMETT: Tonight. Did you cast that play? *King Lear?*

MAUD: I left that job. Got bored. Rounded off the cast with two cripples and a queen and then packed my bags and off.

HAMMETT: What are you doing now?

MAUD: I'm a freelance person. Am an attendant lord, one that will do to swell a progress, start a scene or two——

HAMMETT: Gee, Maud, dat's poetry.

JERRY: T. S. Eliot. Spelt backwards toilets. Almost.

HAMMETT: Ah, a classical education.

JERRY: Thanks. Can I have a gin, please, Maud?

MAUD: Not until you've washed your hands.

HAMMETT: Well, this is nice.

ABEL: The smell of toads is 100 per cent distinctive.

MAUD: I finally got out of the rotten theatre. I will divide my kingdom, Lear will say, between a lisping ingénue, an ageing light comedy actress of uncertain sexual inclination, and a dwarf. And good luck to the lot of you.

HAMMETT: Have you really left?

MAUD: That is my legacy. To leave the company in the hands of of an alcoholic Lear.

HAMMETT: You were a cracking Cordelia yourself.
(*They laugh alone.*)
Tell me you love me, Daughter. Love you? Smile. You must be joking. Wobble.

MAUD: I'm good at unrealistic scenes.

HAMMETT: Yeah.
(*Pause.*)

Plunge in.

MAUD: Very little that can't be done with a deep breath.
(*Pause.*)
I'm giving her just thirty seconds.

HAMMETT: Your boy friend's looking unnaturally sober.

MAUD: He's dehydrating.

JERRY: I was standing in Marks and Spencers earlier today—I'm
standing there like a human being and suddenly I thought
there's not a grain in my body. I look round the shop. It's
the old enemy—reality. So this is how other people see it.

HAMMETT: Day after day.

MAUD: Withdrawal symptoms. He'll have to be wrung out like
an old dishcloth before he's a human being again.

JERRY: This woman's like an anti-addiction centre. (*Displays
himself.*) The new man.

HAMMETT (*pouring one out*): Have a gin, please. I can't bear you
without it.

MAUD (*getting up*): Thirty.
(*She goes over to the bathroom door.* ABEL *slips out of the main
door, unnoticed by all.*)

HAMMETT: Really not a good idea.
(MAUD *puts her hand on the handle of the door.*)

MAUD: All right, stranger, I'm coming in.
(*She throws open the door. She stands at the door amazed.
You can't see into the bathroom at all, but some steam comes
out.* HAMMETT *is over the other side of the room.*)

HAMMETT: Roy Rogers, meet the Cisco Kid.

MAUD: God.

JERRY (*the bottle tucked under his arm*): I think I'll just phase out.

HAMMETT: Hold steady.
(MAUD *has gone in. No noise.*)

JERRY: Can I take a look in there?

HAMMETT: Certainly not.
(MAUD *comes back in. Closes the door.*)

MAUD: I didn't know you'd kept in touch with Catriona.

HAMMETT: I didn't. I met her the other evening. Out walking.

JERRY: Who's Catriona?

MAUD: By accident?

HAMMETT: More or less.

MAUD: Where?

HAMMETT: Clapham Common. I was walking on Clapham Common.

MAUD: And so was she.

HAMMETT: Yes.

JERRY: Who's Catriona?

HAMMETT: She——

MAUD: We came out together.

HAMMETT: Debutantes.

MAUD: Take that stupid grin off your face. I don't believe you just bumped into her.

(CATRIONA *comes out of the bathroom wet in the robe* MAUD *wore in Act I.*)

CATRIONA: I'd traced him.

MAUD: How?

CATRIONA: Charlie calls him D'Avignor Goldschmidt.

HAMMETT: Jesus.

CATRIONA: I don't know why.

(HAMMETT *swings open the cupboard door. But it's empty.*)

HAMMETT: The bastard.

(*He closes it.*)

That's three separate sets of wages.

CATRIONA: I know.

HAMMETT: Shit.

CATRIONA: He's the first one you come to in the Yellow Pages.

HAMMETT: You were lying in wait for me lying in wait.

CATRIONA: I wanted to help.

MAUD: Good for you, Charlie. Laying into the upper classes.

HAMMETT: I——

MAUD: From the start I'd stipulate the size of the dowry.

HAMMETT: So I'm meant to be free, my darling, to do anything I want. But I pick up with an ambling aristocrat who you happen to have been at Swiss finishing school with, and you're out with your claws at a moment's notice.

MAUD: Feel free.

JERRY (*a lot gone*): Please, sir, I'd like to be excused.

MAUD: Shut up.

HAMMETT: I haven't complained about your taking up with this evacuee.

MAUD: I'm not complaining. I'm just squeezing as much satirical bad taste out of the situation as I can.

CATRIONA: I want a good clean fight. No scrapping——

MAUD: I'm pointing out that far from breaking away from me, you've chosen to lumber yourself with a great fruity slice of my past history.

HAMMETT: It was not deliberate. Jesus, I step on the 137, drive for half an hour through South London, choose the most god-forsaken, inaccessible piece of open ground in the whole city, make an entirely random selection of London's four million vaginas, and what happens? The long arm of the Abel detective agency is waiting to hoist me right back into the same old hole. And slam the lid on.

JERRY: We carry reality within us, Charlie.

HAMMETT: And no more twittering from you.

CATRIONA: It was rotten bad luck.

HAMMETT: I don't need any of you.

(*He goes out and sharply closes the door.* CATRIONA's *still standing.* MAUD *runs her hands over the tops of the bottles, but just parts them at the end.*)

MAUD: I was recently offered a part in a film with a lesbian scene in a ski-lift.

CATRIONA: You didn't do it?

MAUD: It was a bit physically ingenious for me.

JERRY: If you'll.

(*He nods and takes a couple of steps backwards. Exit.*)

M'm. Excuse me.

CATRIONA: How long have you been a casting director?

MAUD: Couple of years.

CATRIONA: Do you enjoy it?

MAUD: It's embarrassing. It puts people unfailingly in your debt.

CATRIONA: You must do well.

MAUD: And your magazine?

CATRIONA: Thrives.

MAUD: Daddy bought it?

CATRIONA: It was a birthday present.

MAUD: And how's Charlie?

CATRIONA: We don't really dovetail. We got off somewhere on the wrong foot. Since when he's been—the opposite of depressive——

MAUD: Manic.

CATRIONA: Yes. Unnatural energy. The pace is terrific. At nights he does what he calls a ton up the old M4. He drives out to the airport. Works off his energy trying to push planes out of hangars.

MAUD: Drag for you, I suppose?

CATRIONA: Oh, no.

MAUD: No.

CATRIONA: I really wanted to help. (*Pause.*) You can imagine.

MAUD: Yes.

CATRIONA: Charlie puts it charmlessly as he puts everything, but you make people feel they have a stake in you, do you understand?

MAUD: No, I don't. I think it's insolence.

CATRIONA: If that's what you think.

MAUD: It's called a mind of my own. Installed, I admit, by Professor Frankenstein out there, but now working very much on its own.

CATRIONA: Has Charlie gone?

MAUD (*opening a window*): It smells disgusting in here.

CATRIONA: I did slip into your wedding, Maud. With a rather weary symbolism I sat on Charlie's side of the aisle. The windswept side. I'm surprised you didn't see me.

MAUD: Couldn't see anything under the veil. Couldn't see Charlie. I was bent double anyway humping my virginity up the aisle like a boulder.

CATRIONA: Had you never slept with him?

MAUD: We slept. We never consummated. We were always apparently in sleeping bags. Then later we practised what Charlie quite wrongly used to call the rhythm method. Premature withdrawal. Called the rhythm method, so he said, for its Latin-American flavour. To me it was more like musical chairs. When the music stops——

(MAUD *clicks her fingers.*)

I think to this day of millions of Catholics cha-cha-cha-ing to the rhythm method. Charlie had read a book, you see, by George Orwell—you know the bloke who used to pretend he wasn't middle-class. Anyway the book said contraception was an insult to our bodies. Well, for Charlie, that finished contraception. You have to understand that CND in 1962 was of a very literary turn of mind. And it wasn't just Orwell we had to follow. We had a very damp period, for instance, of fucking in fields. Very unpleasant. No doubt how Lawrence got tuberculosis. I got a nasty cold myself. I don't really think you'd have understood. I—never wanted you to meet him. You being so—everything he'd have hated then.

CATRIONA: He hates me now.

MAUD: Good old Charlie.

CATRIONA (*listening hard*): Can you hear him?

MAUD (*the same*): No.

CATRIONA: I don't understand what happened last Friday. Why you left.

MAUD: You forget what you feel. You lose touch. Ask me what I feel about Charlie, I have to reach up to a very high shelf. I just wanted a way of forcing things through. You get to the stage when you can't believe this is the complete size of your life—tailor-made, as far as it goes. You can't believe that.

CATRIONA: You remember that night at the Connaught Hotel?

MAUD: Of course.

CATRIONA: I swallowed eighty-six pills.

MAUD: I knew you would.

CATRIONA: After you'd gone I lay with one foot poking out from under the lavatory door. They dragged me out from under. A dowager duchess put two cracked old fingers down my throat. I was sick all over the pink and white parquet. Splashed her silk stockings, I remember. She sent me the bill.

MAUD: Histrionics.

CATRIONA: You were my only friend, that's all.

(MAUD *shrugs*.)

I'd calculated you were bound to pee. I'd watched you
knock back about three pints of brown ale. I waited. It
remains—just about—the most distinctive day of my life.
To kill yourself in the Connaught powder room—it did
seem glamorous.

MAUD: I couldn't have watched. I deplore hypocrisy. Can't bear
it.

CATRIONA: At the Connaught the lavatory paper is overprinted
with roses. I remember dipping it in the bowl to see if they
would run. But they stay firm, even when soggy.

MAUD (*nervous*): Christ where has he got to?

CATRIONA: Calm down.

MAUD: He can't really have gone off to the Commons. It'll be
catastrophic.

CATRIONA: He's happy there. Let him go. He likes the skulls and
the geriatrics.

MAUD: But everyone knows he's been behaving like a child.
Clough told them.

CATRIONA: Do you really think they'll know the difference?

MAUD: I meant Charlie. I was thinking of him.

CATRIONA: I should never have let you——
(*Pause.*)

MAUD (*softly*): What was it we were going to do? Trip lightly
over the surface of the earth?

CATRIONA: Yes.

MAUD: Jumping from jet to jet. Did you go to South America?

CATRIONA: No.

MAUD: Thailand, Indonesia, Mozambique?

CATRIONA: No.

MAUD: Missed out there.

CATRIONA: I love you.
(HAMMETT *walks in with two dead pigeons with a rope tied
round their necks. Blood drips freshly from them.*)

HAMMETT: Supper, my children.

MAUD: I thought you'd gone to work.

HAMMETT: Not before dinner.

MAUD: What are those?

HAMMETT: Pigeons. I caught them in the street.

MAUD: Why?

HAMMETT: All the shops were shut.

MAUD: You can't eat pigeons off the street.

HAMMETT: Why not? It's mostly their lungs that are polluted. Otherwise they're just like ordinary pigeons. Tonight it's pigeons in chocolate sauce. Don't be alarmed. I know it sounds disgusting, but it's quite delicious.

(HAMMETT *sits down by the door, leaving it open so he can see into the hall. Then puts a newspaper on his knee and a waste-paper basket in front of him and begins to pluck.*)

MAUD: How did you catch them?

HAMMETT: Put some grain on a plate just under the ventilator, they stick their heads through the railings, clunk with your fist and slit their throats with the bread-knife. Poor little buggers don't know which way to look.

MAUD: Eeugh.

HAMMETT: What's wrong?

MAUD: My God, is it pigeons?

(MAUD *moves round to* HAMMETT's *desk sniffing. From the compartment in which the filthy letters used to be, she takes twelve dead pigeons.*)

Oh, no.

HAMMETT: Not bad for one day's work. Last Saturday. But I thought we'd eat them fresh tonight. Keep those to casserole.

(MAUD *takes them over to the wastebin.*)

Hey they're good meat.

MAUD (*going back for the rest*): They're all going out.

HAMMETT: I had plans for them.

MAUD: Too bad.

HAMMETT: Watch out. There's a sparrow in there. It was suffering from a crisis of identity.

MAUD (*taking the other basket out the door*): There, that's better.

(CATRIONA *is taking no part. She's at the front of the stage with her aching head in her hands.* MAUD *goes back to close the desk door.*)

What happened to your fan mail?

HAMMETT: Burnt it.

MAUD: And what have you done with my co-respondent?

HAMMETT: I left him in the kitchen breathing ether.

MAUD: We're meant to be going to the theatre later.

HAMMETT: Ah—La Mama Nairobi?

MAUD: No.

HAMMETT: You didn't let that slip by, did you?

MAUD: I did.

HAMMETT: What then?

MAUD (*smiles*): Not saying.

HAMMETT: Come on, out with it.

MAUD (*shy*): La Mama Birmingham.

HAMMETT: Oh, no.

MAUD: All right.

HAMMETT: Honestly they have La Mamas like Hilton hotels. How do you get away from them?

MAUD: It's an international movement, Charlie.

HAMMETT: Not like you to let one slip by, though. Fancy missing the old Nairobi. My wife is always worried that while her back is turned some sort of culture is going to happen and she's going to miss out. She can hear Yehudi Menuhin getting his violin out two miles downwind.

MAUD: Look what you're up to with that thing.

(*There's a great mess by now of blood and feathers.*)

HAMMETT: They're like vacuum cleaners. (*Demonstrates.*) You can turn them upside down and out will pour the shit of the city. Full of soot and petrol deposit. Bloke I knew shook one out.

(*He puts his hand up it and draws out its innards.*)

Disgorged a complete Tory Party Manifesto. "A better tomorrow."

MAUD: I'm going to try and find Jerry.

(*He stops her.*)

HAMMETT: What's wrong with her?

MAUD: She has migraine. An upper-class version of the headache.

(*She goes out.* HAMMETT *works at his bird.*)

HAMMETT: Has she been going at you?

(CATRIONA *nods. Tears are pouring from her eyes, but completely silently.* HAMMETT *is behind her and can't see.*)

149

I thought so. Would go at you myself but—(*he holds up the straggly, bloody bird*)—I'm compensating.

(*Pause.*)

It was a golden moment of my life, meeting you on Clapham Common. No exaggeration. It's silly to say, but you *do* make mistakes in the dark. When we left the Common, I realized the day's effort had scarcely begun. I'd flung the dart—you see—and scored nineteen. That's what I was doing in the first place. By the time I'd flashed fifteen women I was up to the necessary total. You were number nineteen. Hence the golden glow. I'd done the hardest thing I could imagine. Taken my trousers down. But that turned out to be the easy bit. Quite different when we got home.

CATRIONA: Ah.

HAMMETT: Did I fail?

CATRIONA: No.

HAMMETT: Thank you.

(*He's staring hard at her from behind, just catching the hurt in her voice. She's expressionless.*)

It's not success or failure that I care about. I believe I'm capable of anything. It's just a matter of getting round to it. I'm sure there is such a thing as impotence, I've read about it, though I privately believe it's only so much palaver. It's only laziness, you know—and, of course, glory. I once tried to convince myself that I was impotent, but your cock is not fooled. It rises like that other daily miracle. It would be nice, of course, to be impotent. It's a very glamorous affectation. It admits you to the élite of suffering and no one's keener on that club than I am. But—(*smiles*)—the damage was done elsewhere that night. Hauling my thoughts uphill. Close your eyes and think of—well—I only ever had one thing to think of.

CATRIONA: Maud.

HAMMETT: Right. She's acquired monumental status.

(*Pause. He holds the bird above his head.* CATRIONA *turns.*)

Do you like it?

CATRIONA: No.

HAMMETT: I'll do the other one. (*He puts them both aside.*) I married—would you believe it?—with a slight sneer. Thinking I could help the poor girl. (*He gets up.*) As Della Street said to Perry Mason, there's only one thing I don't understand.

CATRIONA: Yēs.

HAMMETT: Two hours after my marriage collapses, you're waiting for me on Clapham Common. That's a great detective service. I'd only employed Abel that day. How long had he been watching me?

(*Pause.*)

CATRIONA: Eight years.

HAMMETT (*faintly*): Eight.

(*Pause.*)

CATRIONA: A week at a time maybe, every six months. It wasn't continuous. I can't say I've lived every moment of your marriage. Maybe one minute every hundred thousand. But, strung together, there's a graph.

HAMMETT: Abel already knew me when I came to employ him.

CATRIONA: It's the thing of the—Yellow Pages.

HAMMETT (*moving away*): Nothing I've ever done has been private.

CATRIONA: I wouldn't say that.

HAMMETT: Nothing.

(*Pause.*)

CATRIONA: It's only edited highlights, Charlie.

(*Pause.*)

Listen, after a time I never even read what he wrote, I promise you.

HAMMETT: That's even more bloody insulting.

CATRIONA: I don't mean that.

HAMMETT: No doubt after a bit it all got so inevitable, five fucks a week and the same jokes.

CATRIONA: I don't really think you're trying to understand. I know it sounds awful——

HAMMETT: It sounds awful——

CATRIONA: But I just think it was careless. I should have stopped earlier.

HAMMETT: Round about 1963.

CATRIONA: Exactly.

HAMMETT: Before we started to repeat ourselves.

CATRIONA: Listen, I'm trying to explain——

HAMMETT: It's silly of me not to be more sympathetic——

CATRIONA: Yes——

HAMMETT: Right——

CATRIONA: I didn't attach undue importance to it. I didn't go about crabbed with jealousy, do you see? It was an incidental. I was simply concerned for your welfare. I get lots of mail. I'm a perfectly normal, normally busy sort of person. Abel's reports came in with just the same thud as the Paris fashions or the Chrysler shareholders' annual report. I just forgot to cancel my subscription. I didn't take them home to warm them under my pillow. I read them and filed them away.

HAMMETT: All on company expenses.

CATRIONA: You've never tried to understand other people.

HAMMETT: Is that what you think?

CATRIONA: You've never tried to listen to them.

HAMMETT: You seem to have done very little else.

(*Pause.*)

CATRIONA: If I told you that Clapham was not my idea. I was never going to interfere with your marriage. I hadn't for eight years. But—listen—everyone in politics knew you'd gone into your shell, it was common knowledge—once you're in politics, you can't get out, not really—so also people knew I'd been great friends with Maud, and Daddy as you may know, is Chairman of the Confederation of British Industries and it was actually him—not me—that suggested it might be a good idea if I just seek you out, because you'd been so hard to find lately, and see if you wanted—well—the idea was more or less that I'd ask you if you'd like to join the Tory Party.

HAMMETT: When I flashed you on the Common—is this what you're saying?—you took up my offer on behalf of the Conservative Party.

CATRIONA: It's called a propaganda *coup*.

HAMMETT: Jesus.

CATRIONA: I'd warned them in advance it was highly unlikely.
But if you can persuade someone it's called good publicity.
It was worth a go. Poor Daddy couldn't hope to know I'd in
fact been keeping track of you for the last eight years——
HAMMETT: You should have told him. Got Abel on to the Gestet-
ner, duplicated copies. Harold Wilson, Edward Heath,
they'd have liked to be in on it——
CATRIONA: How could I tell Daddy about Abel?
HAMMETT: You told me.
CATRIONA: I'd allowed the whole thing to get out of hand.
HAMMETT: Eight years out of hand.
CATRIONA: Listen, it's Daddy's job to know what people are
thinking. Personally I'm apolitical——
HAMMETT: When people say that, I know they're lying.
CATRIONA: Listen——
HAMMETT: All your most corrupt sentences start "Listen".
CATRIONA: Listen——
    (*Pause.*)
HAMMETT: There's a whole chain of idiots stretched across this
country. They're beckoning me, asking me to hold hands.
CATRIONA (*sitting*): My head.
HAMMETT: Was Maud unfaithful?
CATRIONA: Jerry.
HAMMETT: Apart from that?
CATRIONA: No.
    (*Pause.*)
HAMMETT: Shit.
    (*Pause.* CATRIONA *goes into the bathroom to dress.*)
Maud used to appear in plays by Ibsen in which the
characters would come on stage and tell each other what they
perfectly well knew already. "It is ten years today, Mrs.
Rummell, since the terrible snowdrifts during which Little
Eywolf fell off the kitchen table while Gregers and I were
copulating thereby damaging the nerves in his leg, which
account for the limp with which he now walks." And in
would come Eywolf, limping like mad. That's how I feel
with you, Catriona. It was called exposition. But it turned
out you already knew.

(*Pause.* CATRIONA *reappears at the bathroom door.*)

Maud played the character parts. (*Laughs with great delight.*) She was quite awful.

(*Enter* MAUD *with a Penguin Special.*)

MAUD (*in Wilson's voice*): "The Labour Party is a moral crusade or it is nothing."

HAMMETT: It is nothing.

MAUD: I'm swotting up on election promises.

HAMMETT: Where's Jerry?

MAUD: He's gone. I put some grass in his hand and rolled him downstairs.

HAMMETT: No sign of your friend yet.

MAUD: No. He's late. (*Again in Wilson's voice.*) "In the modern world it is the quality of ruggedness, not smoothness that we need."

HAMMETT: We were just talking about your acting career.

MAUD: Oh, yes.

HAMMETT: How you started at the bottom and worked your way upwards. My bottom, your upwards.

MAUD: Ho ho.

HAMMETT: Catriona couldn't hope to understand. Apparently she didn't want me for my body.

MAUD: She wanted you for mine.

HAMMETT: Not quite.

CATRIONA: Don't tell Maud.

MAUD: Those pigeons will stain the carpet, Charlie.

HAMMETT: She turned out to be in loco parentis.

CATRIONA: Untrue.

HAMMETT: She was performing on her father's behalf.

MAUD: I refuse to believe the Chairman of the Confederation of British Industries gets his sex through another party.

(HAMMETT *goes to pick up the birds. With him and* MAUD *now it's an old double-act.*)

HAMMETT: All the time I have apparently been thrilling to the blandishments of the Tory government.

CATRIONA: Let's leave it.

HAMMETT: It transpires they import lapsed socialists to tot up their back-bench quota of certifiable insane.

CATRIONA: You all hate me.

HAMMETT: She does have these rare moments of perception.

MAUD: She's going to pack.

HAMMETT: I'll get her suitcase.

CATRIONA: Don't bother: you can have it all.

MAUD: You can't leave your Dior necklaces and your Fabergé suspenders.

HAMMETT: Is it the pigskin suitcase?

CATRIONA: You can have the lot. Just get me my magazine proofs.

HAMMETT: *Venereology Weekly*. Anyone seen it?

(MAUD *has it.*)

MAUD: "Don't give yourself away too easily. A man will respect you for holding out."

HAMMETT: Holding out what?

CATRIONA: Give me those.

(MAUD *escapes* CATRIONA, *who's getting hysterical, and passes the proofs to* HAMMETT.)

HAMMETT: "My husband makes unreasonable demands."

(*As* CATRIONA *throws herself at him, he tosses them to* MAUD.)

MAUD: "You are right. Do not give way. What he is advocating is more than you can be expected to endure."

(CATRIONA *is grappling with her, but she gets them to* HAMMETT who screws them up.)

HAMMETT: Take your filth. Your lies. Your unspeakable magazine.

(*He holds them out quite gently.*)

Here. Get that printed. It'll sell.

(CATRIONA *takes the pages, then goes over and opens her pigskin suitcase and gets out a huge bundle of papers, which she puts down on the coffee table.*)

CATRIONA: The transcript of the proceedings. Eight years. You can have them.

(CATRIONA *goes out with the case. A long pause.*)

HAMMETT: She loves you.

(*Deep silence.* HAMMETT *moves first over to beside the table.*)

Put me right off my pigeons that did.

(*He sits down and puts his hand on top of the pile of papers.*)

You should phone her or something.

MAUD: I've spent my life not helping people and I'm certainly not going to start now.

HAMMETT: I didn't know she was a friend of yours.

MAUD: You just fell into conversation.

HAMMETT: I picked her up.

MAUD: Abel told me.

HAMMETT: Did he tell you how?

MAUD: No.

(*Pause. As he speaks he lifts the corner and peeks indifferently inside the pile of papers.*)

HAMMETT: I exhibited myself. Not just to her. To fourteen others.

MAUD: Was this some sort of Dutch auction?

HAMMETT: It was on the common. I was determined to display myself.

MAUD: The night you left me?

HAMMETT: Yes.

MAUD: You did well to choose Catriona. Rather like showing a pebble to a cement grinder.

HAMMETT: I didn't know she'd been trained at your school. If I'd known she'd been to a Swiss finishing place, I'd have greased the item beforehand.

MAUD: I suppose you thought everyone would scream and run away.

HAMMETT: I would.

MAUD: I know. So would I. But we're not typical. Lots of people are inquisitive.

(CLOUGH *has come in at the main door.* HAMMETT *is obviously surprised. The evening is getting dark.*)

HAMMETT: Hello.

CLOUGH: I'm late.

MAUD: That's all right.

CLOUGH: I'm sorry.

MAUD: Please. Sit down. ·

HAMMETT: Was it John you were expecting?

MAUD: Charlie. I didn't tell you——

CLOUGH: You tell him.

MAUD: I've been to Sunderland. About being their next M.P.

HAMMETT: Oh.

(*Pause.*)

MAUD: You were ill.

HAMMETT: *Am* ill. I'm allowed my bloody illness, aren't I?

MAUD: You have the illness, I'll have the seat.

HAMMETT: I'm not going to abdicate.

MAUD: What?

HAMMETT: Let the thing roll into the hands of my wife.

MAUD: You don't want it.

HAMMETT: Neither do you.

MAUD: I'm sick of watching weaklings and desperadoes bungle the business of socialism.

HAMMETT (*amazed*): Whoof, don't be absurd.

MAUD: I'm not.

HAMMETT: How can you say such ridiculous things? (*To* CLOUGH.) Begging your pardon.

MAUD: It's what I believe.

HAMMETT: Maud, I'm ashamed of you.

MAUD: Socialism has been betrayed chiefly by skyvers and bourgeois cynics like you.

HAMMETT: Now I know you're serious.

MAUD: I'm serious.

HAMMETT: You are not serious.

MAUD: I am. Deadly.

HAMMETT: You appall me.

(MAUD *bursts out laughing*.)

MAUD: It's a great game.

HAMMETT: Thank you.

MAUD (*at once serious*): But I'm serious.

HAMMETT (*to* CLOUGH): In this marriage I had cornered the market in brains. That's where I pitched my stand. On things intellectual. She pitched hers on the body. On the body I could never hope to compete. Now look.

MAUD: It's called a mind of my own, Charlie.

HAMMETT: It's a dangerous anomaly.

CLOUGH: You're going to have to come to terms.

HAMMETT: I couldn't live with her brain in action. Grinding away at nights beside me on the pillow. Chuddering and ticking over in the next door armchair. It's what I loved

about you, Maud: your superbly useless brain, like some
gorgeous ornament on the top of your neck. Like a vase or
a Chinese ginger jar. Art for art's sake. It would spoil it to
find out it worked as well.

MAUD: We are rich, we are white, we are middle-class, we are
English. We are the single most over-privileged group of
people in the world. Without exception, Charlie.

HAMMETT: Well?

MAUD: We have no right to complain.

HAMMETT: I can complain.

MAUD: What about?

HAMMETT: For a start I want my constituency back.

MAUD: Tough. You have no logical right to be unhappy. Has he?

CLOUGH: None.

HAMMETT: Your opinions are like the beats of the lash.

MAUD: Good.

HAMMETT: Quite delightful.

CLOUGH (*looking unhappily out of the window, very distant*): The
point is surely which of you is better suited to the job.

HAMMETT: Exactly.

MAUD: Right.

CLOUGH (*turning back*): Your talk about people always amuses me.
Real human beings. How you've kept your humanity. How
you're not part of the same circus. Not like actors or politicians——

HAMMETT: I don't mean——

CLOUGH: It's a bit of a doubtful privilege.

(*Pause.*)

Don't you think?

(*A long silence.*)

The bloke who was naked last time I came is now lying on
your front door step.

MAUD: I'll go and sweep him up.

CLOUGH: In a moment.

(*Pause.*)

I think you would both decorate the Labour Party. In
different ways. But Sunderland, I think, needs something
a little more—authentic.

MAUD: I was told I was going to be elected.

CLOUGH: They were being more or less polite. The secretary of the local branch of the engineering union is going to be elected.

(*Pause.*)

MAUD: Christ.

HAMMETT: Class warfare.

CLOUGH: I think——

HAMMETT: All right, sod it, I understand. After all we've done. Bloody workers.

CLOUGH: I think that's the attitude that rather upset them.

MAUD: Bloody workers always let you down.

CLOUGH: They want someone with roots in the place.

HAMMETT: What is this about roots? I've been rootless all the length of my life and felt better for it.

CLOUGH: That's what makes you so irresistibly cheerful.

HAMMETT: Oh Sunderland. Those lost week-ends.

MAUD: The black and tan.

HAMMETT: We could have been knocking back gin and tonic in Surrey casinos, all those years. We could have been enjoying ourselves.

CLOUGH: You rather chose the wrong constituency.

HAMMETT: Why do I have to be representative? It's a hopeless idea. Where are you honestly going to find a group of people *I* can represent? Should all the country's vicious, paling schizophrenics be gathered within one county's bounds so that I can be their M.P.?

CLOUGH: It's an idea.

HAMMETT: The member for the lunatic conservation area will now make his maiden jibber.

MAUD: I had plans for that place. After all we've done.

CLOUGH (*going*): I only came to tell you what they'd decided.

MAUD: All right.

(HAMMETT *ignores him, as* MAUD *leads* CLOUGH *to the door. He stands quite still at the front of the stage.* MAUD *comes back in almost at once.*)

HAMMETT: Ah shit.

(*Pause.*)

Ah fuck.

(*Pause.*)

Ah fucking shit.

MAUD: The nerve of these people. Really.

HAMMETT: Ah shit.

MAUD: That really got me. Do you know? It really——

HAMMETT: Ah.

MAUD: It really surprised me.

HAMMETT: Yeah.

MAUD: That really, really——

HAMMETT: I know.

(*Pause.*)

MAUD: Really——

HAMMETT: O.K. My love. Was that your idea? To steal my constituency?

MAUD: It just occurred to me the other day.

HAMMETT: Just because we're middle-class.

MAUD: Would you like a drink?

HAMMETT: I'd be sick. I mean, people are people, aren't they, Maud?

MAUD: So they say.

HAMMETT: I mean, it's class discrimination.

MAUD: Or perhaps they just don't like us.

(*Pause.*)

I don't like us.

(*Pause.*)

HAMMETT: No. No.

(*Pause.*)

It would be easier if there were some specific objection. I mean, like I'm off my head. Though I don't feel mad any longer. I just feel hurt. I can understand them refusing me —but you——

MAUD: Well——

HAMMETT: You. Of all people.

MAUD: Yes.

HAMMETT: Everyone likes you. Don't they?

MAUD: Well——

HAMMETT: Oh, come on, even Clough likes you.

MAUD: Yes.

HAMMETT: You're——

(*Very limp after a pause.*)

Everything I ever wanted.

(*A long silence as they just stare.*)

It seems so hurtful.

(*Pause.*)

Do you remember how in books people used to have what they called crises of identity? I could never believe in those. I've always known exactly who I am. Never had a moment's doubt. Who am I? What am I doing here? Two questions so easily answered it's frankly insulting to ask them.

(*Pause.*)

MAUD: I know two days doesn't sound very much, but my political period was very *intense*. It all seemed so clear.

(*Pause.*)

HAMMETT: It's clear.

MAUD: If we could just shift the load . . . like eight years ago we slammed down all our chips, everything we had on one bloody number. And do we have to wait the rest of our lives for one bloody number to come up?

HAMMETT: Maud——

MAUD: Charlie——

HAMMETT: Maud——

MAUD: I was brought up—you—didn't bother about what you did, it was true what you were. You—well—and it's still true. My aim is superb, my does is non-existent. People's personalities——

HAMMETT: Maud——

MAUD: Are little more than affectations. I suppose. If we could just bleach ourselves, lie out in the sun and lose our colour—— Charlie——

HAMMETT: Maud.

MAUD: Charlie. Lose our personalities.

HAMMETT: Maud.

MAUD: Charlie.

(*A long pause.*)

BLACKOUT

TEETH 'N' SMILES

for Joe

Teeth 'n' Smiles, with music by Nick Bicât and lyrics by Tony Bicât, was first performed on 2 September 1975 at the Royal Court Theatre, London. The cast was as follows:

ARTHUR	Jack Shepherd
INCH	Karl Howman
LAURA	Cherie Lunghi
NASH	Rene Augustus
WILSON	Mick Ford
SNEAD	Roger Hume
PEYOTE	Hugh Fraser
SMEGS	Andrew Dickson
ANSON	Antony Sher
MAGGIE	Helen Mirren
SARAFFIAN	Dave King
RANDOLPH	Heinz

Directed by the author
Designed by Jocelyn Herbert

The play is set during the night of 9 June 1969.

The playing area is mostly bare. Design is minimal. The band's equipment is on a stage which, for the musical numbers, trucks down to the front. In the first act the band are housed in a college room; in the second they are on a lawn behind their stage.

Of Mr Blake's company I have very little.
He is always in Paradise.

Mrs William Blake

NOTE

When *Teeth 'n' Smiles* was first played it ran just
under three hours. It was then cut during previews
to what the English think is a more palatable length.
This text accommodates most of those cuts, but not
all of them. The text was further re-written for a
West End production. I don't think plays are ever
finished, and the version you read is one of several.

SCENE ONE

As the audience come in INCH *is building the amplifiers into a bank of equipment on the band's platform. He is twenty, in leather and jewellery. Downstage there are a couple of benches, representing an undergraduate's room that has been specially emptied.* ARTHUR *is lying on one bench, staring. He is wearing a silver top hat and a silk suit but the effect is oddly discreet. He is tall, thin and twenty-six.*

INCH *disappears.*

The play begins.

INCH *comes in carrying two suitcases which he puts down in the middle of the room.*

INCH: Right. Let's smash the place up.

(*He turns and sees* ARTHUR.)

'Allo, Arfer, din know you was comin'.

ARTHUR: Motorbike. How is she?

INCH: All right. They're liftin' 'er out the van now.

(INCH *goes out.*)

ARTHUR: You're the top, you're the Coliseum
You're the top, you're the Louvre Museum
You're a melody from a symphony by Strauss . . .

(INCH *returns with a Samuelsons box from which he takes a plug. Then* LAURA *appears, a small dark girl with lovely skin.*)

LAURA: Are you set up, Inch, it's very late?

INCH: Got Maggie out?

LAURA: They're getting her down the drive.

ARTHUR: And hello, Laura.

LAURA: And hello, Arthur. Some bastard put sugar in the petrol tank, that's why we're late.

ARTHUR: It's good to see you.

LAURA: How long can you stay?

ARTHUR: How long do you want?

LAURA: Well . . .

(WILSON, *a small, bearded cockney, and* NASH, *a spaced-out black drummer, appear, look round the room and sit down.* WILSON *gets out a bottle of green lemonade.* LAURA *begins to unpack the bags she has brought in.*)

ARTHUR: Saraffian said he thought she might be on the way down.

LAURA: How Saraffian's meant to know, sitting in that office all day . . .

ARTHUR: He has a manager's nose. He's like a truffle pig, he can smell heroin at fifty paces.

LAURA: Don't be absurd, dumbo. It's not smack, it's booze. Liquid boredom. Twice a day she flips out.

WILSON: Game.

NASH: Wot's it to be?

WILSON: Pope's balls. The game is the most borin' and useless piece of information you can think of. Thus the Pope 'as balls.

NASH: Right.

WILSON: Away you go.

(LAURA *arranges a series of dresses on the back of the bench. Then starts sewing one of her choice.*)

NASH: The town of Nottingham was once called Snottingham.

WILSON: Yeah, that's borin'.

NASH: Thank you, pal, your go.

(INCH *returns with eight bottles of scotch, which he sets out on a bench.*)

WILSON: Efrem Zimbalist's first wife's name was Alma Gluck.

NASH: Well done, Wilson, that's really dull.

INCH: Diana Dors' real name was Diana Fluck.

NASH: Hello, Arthur.

ARTHUR: Nashy. How are you?

INCH: Or Diana Clunt, I can't remember which.

WILSON: The capital of Burundi is Bujumbura.

INCH: Or possibly Diana Clocksucker, but I think I would've remembered that.

(INCH *goes.*)

LAURA: She starts drinking at breakfast, she passes out after lunch, then she's up for supper, ready for the show. Then after the

show she starts drinking. At two-thirty she's out again.
Morning she gets up. And drinks. She's a great professional.
Never misses a show.

ARTHUR: Pills?

LAURA: No.

ARTHUR: Reds?

LAURA: No. Blue heavens, no. Yellow jackets, no. Bennies, no. No goofballs, no dexies, no dollies.

ARTHUR: Still no acid?

LAURA: No.

ARTHUR: And the heroin?

LAURA: No. She just drinks.

ARTHUR: What is she, some kind of pervert?

(PEYOTE *enters with an electric kettle and sits down. A moment later* INCH *appears with an extension cable from the stage, and they plug the kettle in.*)

LAURA: No aeroplane glue, no household cement, no banana peel, no fingernail polish remover, no nutmeg, no paintstripper. No one in the world but her and Johnny Walker.

ARTHUR: And the singing?

LAURA: The singing's O.K.

(LAURA *goes out.* INCH *hails* SNEAD *who is carrying* MAGGIE *into the room over his shoulder.* SNEAD *is forty-five, in top hat and black tails, this side of his first coronary. We do not see her.*)

INCH: Waiter, can you take 'er up to a bathroom?

SNEAD: Sir.

ARTHUR: You're the Nile
You're the Tower of Pisa
You're the smile
On the Mona Lisa . . .

(SNEAD *has taken* MAGGIE *away.* PEYOTE *arranges a plastic funnel and two glass tubes, which he then sets out with care on the bench.* NASH *gets up.*)

NASH: And where the 'ell are we?

(*Pause. Then he starts changing his shirt.* INCH *begins mending a plug.*)

WILSON: At this moment in time on planet earth the dead outnumber the living by thirty to one.

(LAURA *returns, distributing pork pies.*)

LAURA: She doesn't speak very warmly of you.

ARTHUR: I'm not meant to drag round the country, am I?

LAURA (*smiles*): Or of me.

ARTHUR: Still sings my songs.

LAURA: She'd prefer not to.

ARTHUR: I'm sure.

LAURA: She'd prefer to get up there and scream.

ARTHUR: You're a Moscow view
You're oh so cool
You're Lester Young . . .

(SMEGS *appears. He is dressed like a very baggy matelot. He never raises his voice.*)

SMEGS: Couple of slags here say anyone fancy a blow-job?

(ARTHUR *gets up as if to consider.*)

ARTHUR: A blow-job. Do I want a blow-job?

LAURA: How did they get in here?

SMEGS: Inch? Blow-job?

ARTHUR: Bound to turn out like a Chinese meal. Half an hour later and you need another.

INCH: Butterfly flicks, do they do butterfly flicks?

SMEGS: Ask them.

INCH: Sure.

LAURA (*to* PEYOTE): Do you have to do that in here?

PEYOTE: Fuck off.

INCH (*laughs*): But will they do butterfly flicks with a roadie?

(*He goes to find out.*)

SMEGS: Not a chance.

ARTHUR: Isn't he meant to be . . .

SMEGS: What?

ARTHUR: Setting up. You're an hour late.

LAURA (*holding a dress up*): Does this look all right?

SMEGS: It's up to him.

ARTHUR: Why don't you go and help him?

SMEGS: Because we're artists.

ARTHUR: All right.

SMEGS: See?

LAURA: Artists don't set up.

SMEGS: You don't ask Oistrakh to go out and strangle the cat.
(INCH *reappears, picks up the plug.*)

INCH: They do blow-jobs wiv singers, but nothin' below bass
guitar.

ARTHUR: That's right, love, keep your standards up.

PEYOTE: I play fuckin' bass guitar.
(*He hurries out.*)

SMEGS: Artists. I mean. Keith Moon's chauffeur got run over, he
said chauffeurs are two a penny, it's blokes like me what are
irreplaceable.

WILSON: There is no word in the English language as rhymes
with 'orange'.

NASH: Hey, these valiums, do they go with my shirt?
(*He tosses one in.* SNEAD *reappears.*)

SNEAD: Is that to be everything, sir?

INCH: No, you gotta get 'er clothes off and get 'er into the bath.

SNEAD: Sir?

INCH: You think I'm jokin'?
(*He heads out, his arm round* SNEAD.)

INCH: I'm doin' you a favour. You should be a member of the
stevedores' union.

SNEAD: Sir?

INCH: We're gonna 'ave to wash 'er. Do you wanna know wot
that's like?

SNEAD: Sir?

INCH: Well, 'ave you ever seen 'em cleanin' St Paul's?
(*They go out.*)

ARTHUR: Is that what happens every day?
(LAURA *just looks at him.*)

ARTHUR: What does everyone do?

LAURA: Pretend not to notice, what would you do?

ARTHUR: What . . .

LAURA: There's no choice. Stoke tomorrow. Then Keele. Bradford.
Southampton. Quick one in Amsterdam. Back to Glasgow.
Then they claim California, but nobody believes it.

ARTHUR: Saraffian's mad.

LAURA: Not Saraffian's idea. It's her. She wants to hit San

Francisco on her knees.

ARTHUR: What's the money?

LAURA: A hundred and twenty, no more. It won't cover overheads, whatever it is. But she . . . likes to keep busy.

SMEGS: All this jumping on the spot makes you feel famous. But it's no real substitute for people knowing your name.

(SMEGS *goes out.*)

WILSON: Arfer.

ARTHUR: Yes.

WILSON: Your contribution.

(*Pause.*)

ARTHUR: H. G. Wells was attractive to women because his breath smelt of honey.

(*Pause.*)

WILSON: Very nice.

NASH: I enjoyed that.

WILSON: Very nice.

(ANSON *appears. He is nineteen, unusually short with long frizzy black hair. He carries a clipboard and wears evening dress with a velvet bow tie.*)

ANSON: Are we nearly . . .

ARTHUR: There's a plug.

ANSON: What?

ARTHUR: We're waiting to mend a plug. Look. Over there.

(*They look at the plug.*)

ARTHUR: And then we'll be ready.

ANSON: I'm the organizer. The booking. You are . . . ninety minutes late you know. Couldn't someone . . . one of you mend it yourselves?

ARTHUR: Arms like penguins I'm afraid.

ANSON: I see.

(*He goes out.* PEYOTE *reappears with a piece of gauze.* INCH *and* SNEAD *appear.*)

NASH: Three-quarters of all children are born before breakfast.

INCH: 'Ave you got 'er dress?

LAURA: Here. Tonight Miss Frisby is in peach.

SNEAD: Will that be everything, sir?

INCH: Why not lie down there and I'll walk all over yer?

SNEAD: Sir.

INCH: Jus' can't get any decent room service round 'ere.

(*He goes out.* LAURA *cuts a pork pie neatly in four.*)

NASH: Every time we breathe we inhale several million molecules that was exhaled by Leonardo da Vinci . . .

WILSON: No, no, Nashy.

NASH: Wot?

WILSON: You don' understand, that's really quite interestin', Leonardo, I mean, it's far too interestin' . . .

ARTHUR: I'm thinking of marketing a pork pie, a new kind of pork pie, which when you put the knife through the pastry will let out an agonized honk, as of a pig being slaughtered. It would do well.

(*He looks at the hovering* SNEAD.)

ARTHUR: A tip is it Mr Snead, is that what you're after?

SNEAD: Sir?

ARTHUR: Don't look at us, pal, we're too famous, we're like the Queen, we don't carry actual money.

SNEAD: Sir?

WILSON: An' you're playin' it far too fast.

(INCH *calls from offstage.*)

INCH: She says will Arfer 'elp 'er out the bath?

PEYOTE: Waiter.

SNEAD: Sir?

PEYOTE: Fuck off.

(ARTHUR *pulls at an imaginary dog on a lead.*)

ARTHUR: Come on, Arthur, come on boy, come and meet Maggie. Come on, come on boy.

(ARTHUR *and* SNEAD *go out different ways.* PEYOTE *sterilizes the tubes with boiling water which he then throws on the floor.*)

PEYOTE: Wot's that creep doin' 'ere?

LAURA: If . . .

PEYOTE: Never said it.

(*Pause.*)

LAURA: Where the others?

PEYOTE: I 'ate Canterbury. Every time we come to Canterbury I swear never to come again.

LAURA: So do I. Except this is Cambridge.

PEYOTE: Yeah. Look.

> (PEYOTE *holds up a fresh hypodermic in a sterilized packet.*)

PEYOTE: The cleanest needle in showbiz.

LAURA: T'rific.

WILSON: It should be *dull*.

PEYOTE: The bag.

LAURA: What?

PEYOTE: The bag. Pass me the bag.

LAURA: This is Maggie's.

PEYOTE: Pass me the fuckin' bag.

> (LAURA *hands the carpetbag to* PEYOTE. *He lightly tears the lining. Takes out an envelope.*)

PEYOTE: Jus' borrowed 'er bag.

LAURA: That . . .

PEYOTE: Uh. Jus' borrowed 'er bag.

> (ANSON *returns.*)

ANSON: Has there been any . . .

LAURA: Progress? No.

PEYOTE: She en't bin busted as often as me.

LAURA: That would be quite hard, Peyote. I mean, you would have to stand on street corners stuffing tabs up traffic wardens' nostrils to get yourself busted quite as often as you.

PEYOTE: Fuck off.

ANSON: Is Miss Frisby with you?

LAURA: She's just being sandblasted next door. Why don't you sit down?

ANSON: Thank you.

> (ARTHUR *wanders back.*)

LAURA: Did you see her?

ARTHUR: What is she on?

LAURA: Huh, did she recognize you?

ARTHUR: She said, who let this pieca shit in here?

LAURA: She recognized you.

ARTHUR: Yes.

LAURA: I must call Saraffian. Do you know where there's a phone?

ANSON: In the porter's . . .

LAURA: Lodge? Thank you.

ARTHUR: He doesn't care. As long as they stagger on to the stage.

Get their hands somewhere near the guitar. Yes, Peyote?

PEYOTE: Fuck off.

ARTHUR: I don't care either. Butcher my tunes. Forget my lyrics. Steal my royalties. I expect it.

(*Pause.*)

Thought she . . . thought she wanted to see me.

LAURA: Sure.

ARTHUR: Just tell me what she's on.

LAURA: Arthur, you lived with her . . .

ARTHUR: Have you let her get hooked? Well? Have you let her get hooked again?

LAURA: Have I?

ARTHUR: Well?

(LAURA *storms out, furious.* ARTHUR *turns away.* PEYOTE *has melted twenty pills in boiling water and is now pouring them through the funnel and gauze into the other tube.* WILSON *and* NASH *are flat out, probably asleep, possibly concentrating.*)

ANSON: Have you had a look where you're . . .

(*Pause.*)

ARTHUR: Peyote, do you know what she's on?

PEYOTE: She's mainlinin' string. Pullin' it through 'er veins.

ANSON: Do you want to have a look at . . .

ARTHUR: Little fella, why don't you ever get through a . . .

ANSON: Sentence. I know. It's . . . I just hear what I'm saying and it always sounds so dreary and second-hand I just am . . . too fastidious to . . .

ARTHUR: Finish.

ANSON: Right.

(*Pause.*)

I'm hoping to interview Miss Frisby.

ARTHUR: She's in the bathroom, walk right up.

ANSON: Does she have any clothes on?

ARTHUR: It's never stopped her before.

ANSON: Ah.

ARTHUR: What you going to ask her?

ANSON: Oh . . . general things. About the role of popular music in society.

(*Pause.*)

ARTHUR: Yes, well, that's a very good subject. Very good subject. You could even ask Peyote here about that. He has a lot of words to say on that. Well, not a lot. Acually he has two. Off and fuck. Only usually he contrives to put them the other way round.

(ARTHUR *goes out.* PEYOTE *and* ANSON *are now as if alone.* PEYOTE *ties a rubber tube round his upper arm, teases the liquid in the hypodermic.* ANSON *is embarrassed.*)

ANSON: Hmph.

PEYOTE: Ah.

(ANSON *gets up and moves away.* PEYOTE *shoots up.*)

ANSON: Squeamish. Grotesquely squeamish for a medical student. It's a problem. Really. You call that shooting up?

PEYOTE: Uh-huh.

ANSON: Is that heroin?

PEYOTE: Preludin.

ANSON: Ah. Preludin is a fuck-pump, I think I'm right. I know that much. It enlarges your sexual capacity. You're meant to stay hard for twenty-four hours, is that not . . . I believe that's right.

(*Pause.*)

It's none of my business but I think you may be taking rather a chance. I mean in Cambridge. Knowing the overall standard of skirt in this town I'd say twenty minutes would be pushing your luck.

(*Pause.*)

I had a guitar once. When I was young. Had a guitar. And a drum.

(*Pause.*)

You make conversation seem a little unreal. I suppose the silence is what . . . turns you on.

(*Pause.*)

Yes. I know. Fuck off. Certainly. By all means.

(*He moves towards the plug.*)

PEYOTE: Don't touch it.

(INCH *returns.*)

INCH: Right.

ANSON: Are you nearly . . .

INCH: Jus' gotta change this plug.

ANSON: Will it take very long?

INCH: Don't know, it's a technical thing.

ANSON: Is it going to be good tonight?

(*Pause.*)

INCH: It's gettin' really nasty out there.

ANSON: What?

INCH: The audience. They're stamping all over the lawn.
Fuck.

ANSON: What?

INCH: Forgotten the flowers.

(INCH *goes out again, putting the plug down.* SNEAD *appears at the same time.*)

ANSON: Are you . . .

SNEAD: Everyone's now ready for the orchestra, sir.

INCH: Tell 'em they're jus' gettin' inta their dickies.

(INCH *gone.*)

SNEAD: I think you'll have to make some announcement, sir.
They're getting very restless having to wait.

ANSON: Tell them . . . er . . . tell them they're coming just as fast
as they can.

(ARTHUR *comes on, goosing* LAURA *who is wearing his top hat
and laughing.*)

ANSON: Ah . . . do you think they're almost . . .

ARTHUR: Listen, they got the place right, didn't they? That's
three-quarters of the battle. The time, the time is a
sophisticated detail.

ANSON: I don't know, Mr Snead.

PEYOTE: Wot is this place, anyway?

ARTHUR: You are in what scientists now know to be a black hole,
Peyote. Floating free, an airless, lightless, dayless, nightless
time-lock, a cosmic accident called Jesus College Ball.

PEYOTE: Jesus.

ARTHUR: College Ball.

PEYOTE: What does it mean?

ARTHUR: It means the college at which I was educated. Yes, Mr
Snead?

LAURA: It means undergraduates.

ARTHUR: Narcissists.

LAURA: Yahoos.

ARTHUR: Intellectuals.

(ARTHUR *embraces* LAURA *from behind, his hands on her breasts.*)
Rich complacent self-loving self-regarding self-righteous
phoney half-baked politically immature neurotic evil-
minded little shits.
(*He stares at* SNEAD.)
Expect nothing and you will not be disappointed.
(*Silence.* SNEAD *turns and goes out.* ANSON *looks at his hands.*
ARTHUR *turns his back to us.*)

WILSON: Internal memorandum. Rhyl Town Hall. The life
expectancy of a civic deck chair is now a season and a half.

LAURA: He used to clip tickets.

ARTHUR: I was at this college. I know Mr Snead of old. Give me
that.
(LAURA *gives him her current cigarette.*)
Where I first met Maggie. She was singing in the Red Lion.
She was sixteen, seventeen, a folk singer. Let us go a pickin'
nuts, fol de ray, to Glastonbury fair, a tiddle dum ay. I had to
carry her over the wall, can you imagine, to get her to my
rooms. They build walls here to stop undergraduates making
love. Well, we got caught, of course, by this very Mr Snead
coming in satirical German manner, even shining a torch, an
English suburban stormfuhrer. He hauled me up to my
tutor, who said, do you intend to marry the girl? I said, not
entirely. He said, as this is a first offence you will not be sent
down, instead I fine you ten pounds for having a girl on the
premises. I said what you mean like a brothel charge? I was
furious, I was out of my mind. Do you have another?
(LAURA *lights him another.*)
Thanks. And everyone told me: don't waste your energy.
Because that's what they want. They invent a few rules that
don't mean anything so that you can ruin your health trying
to change them. Then overnight they re-draft them because
they didn't really matter in the first place. One day it's a
revolution to say fuck on the bus. Next day it's the only way
to get a ticket. That's how the system works. An obstacle

178

course. Unimportant. Well, perhaps.

(*Pause. He stands a moment.*)

NASH: The word Cicero literally means chick-pea.

ANSON: Oh God. I think I'd better . . . go and . . .

LAURA: Don't. Don't go away.

ARTHUR: Sit down, tell us something about yourself.

ANSON: I'm sorry. It's just so late. I . . .

ARTHUR: People appreciate things more when they've had to wait.

ANSON: That's not how we advertised . . .

ARTHUR: Let them suffer.

ANSON: We didn't sell the tickets on the quality of the suffering we could offer.

ARTHUR: Well done. Whole sentence. This band has converted more people to classical music than any other human form of torture.

ANSON: I don't understand why . . .

ARTHUR: They come out saying, please, please, give me a drip in a bucket.

(INCH *returns.*)

INCH: She says she's not going on tonight.

ANSON: Oh no.

ARTHUR: Uh, it's fine. Don't panic.

INCH: It's quite all right, it's fine.

ARTHUR: The nights she's not going on are fine. It's the nights she can't wait to get on, they're the ones to watch for.

WILSON: Right.

(INCH *goes.* SMEGS *wanders back on.*)

SMEGS: How we doing?

LAURA: Fine.

ARTHUR: Fine.

WILSON: Fine.

SMEGS (*sits*): Must be almost time.

ANSON: Yes.

WILSON: Only one man 'as actually died on television. In a television studio. 'E was on a stool, talkin' about 'ealth food, about honey, an' 'e jus' fell over an' died.

NASH: Fantastic.

WILSON: Yeah.

(PEYOTE *stretches out.*)

PEYOTE: It's so good, it's so very good . . .

SMEGS: I wouldn't have minded a sound check.

ARTHUR: When did you last have one of those?

SMEGS: Barnsley. Halifax. I don't know. They carry me about in a
sealed container. And sometimes the seasons change. Or we
run over a dog. Or they change the design on my cigarette
pack.

ARTHUR: Well . . .

SMEGS: I don't know.

ARTHUR: It seems to be what she wants.

SMEGS: It's needless you know. It just makes her feel good.

ARTHUR: How is she to you?

LAURA: Unspeakable.

ARTHUR: Ah.

LAURA: She treats me barely human.

ARTHUR: Still?

LAURA: More than ever. She is jealous.

ARTHUR: I don't see . . .

(PEYOTE *sits up suddenly. Panic.*)

PEYOTE: There's a wheel comin' off the van.

ARTHUR: It's all right, Peyote, it's just a brain cell dying.

PEYOTE: It's comin' off.

SMEGS: It'll be horses in a minute, on sweeties he always has
horses.

ANSON: I'm sorry but I really do have to insist . . .

WILSON: What is wrong with you?

ANSON: I . . .

WILSON: I don't think I've ever met a man wiv so little karma.

ANSON: How can I . . .

WILSON: You should leave your brain to a Buddhist 'ospital, they'd
be very interested in you.

ANSON: We are waiting for one plug to be connected.

WILSON: Correct.

ANSON: It's ridiculous.

WILSON: Don't touch it.

ANSON: It's absurd.

(*Pause.*)

ANSON: I'm sorry, I just can't . . .

    (ANSON *moves towards the plug.*)

WILSON: Don't fuckin' touch it, you miserable little turd.

    (*Pause.*)

ARTHUR: Just leave it to Inch.

LAURA: Inch changes a mean plug.

WILSON: Right.

ARTHUR: Inch is a great roadie. Inch is the Panama Red of roadies.

ANSON: I'm . . .

ARTHUR: Just . . .

    (*He holds up his hands. Pause.*)

    It's just best. O.K.?

    (INCH *returns.*)

INCH: She says she's goin' on.

ARTHUR: Ah.

INCH: She says she can't wait to get out there.

ARTHUR: Fine.

INCH: Now. What? I'm almost ready. There was somethin'.

ANSON: Plug.

INCH: I jus' gotta change this plug.

ARTHUR: Fine. No hurry. Enjoy it.

    (INCH *sets to. Then stops.*)

INCH: I can't work if I'm watched.

    (ANSON *turns away.*)

WILSON: A pullet is a pullet till the first time it moults. Then it's a
hen.

SMEGS: Sussex have never won the County championship.

NASH: Marilyn Monroe was colour blind.

ARTHUR: Oscar Wilde died Sebastian Melmoth.

WILSON: Two gallons to one peck. Four pecks to one bushel.
Eight bushels to one quarter. Four and a half quarters to a
chaldron. One hectolitre per hectare equals one point one
bushels per acre.

INCH: Right. Ready when you are.

ANSON: I think we're ready.

INCH: O.K., band?

WILSON: You might plug it in first, then we'll join yer.

INCH: Fine.

(INCH *goes*.)

WILSON: Not gonna walk across there if the plug's not gonna work.

NASH: Get yer sneakers dirty.

WILSON: Quite.

ANSON: Well, everyone . . . let me say . . . go out there and break a leg.

(ANSON *goes*.)

WILSON: Wot an 'orrible little man.

NASH: 'E's very *short*, in' 'e?

WILSON: Yeah, an' that 'orrible black 'air. Makes 'im look like a lavatory brush.

SMEGS: Are we playing outside?

LAURA: Yes. On the lawn.

WILSON: Wot if it rains?

ARTHUR: Somebody had better . . .

SMEGS: Yes.

ARTHUR: Peyote.

(ARTHUR *wakes him*.)

PEYOTE: Horses.

SMEGS: Told you.

WILSON: Come on, Peyote, once through the Christmas oratorio.

NASH: You take one arm.

WILSON: Yeah, come in loud, eh Nashy? Drum all over 'im if you find 'e's on the floor.

NASH: Will do.

PEYOTE: Horses poundin' down the Mall.

WILSON: Right, right, Peyote.

SMEGS: Off we go.

(PEYOTE *is guided towards the stage. The rest drift with him. They disappear behind the equipment*.)

WILSON (*as he goes*): I wish we'd found somethin' more, well, more kinda staggeringly borin'.

(ARTHUR *and* LAURA *left on their own*.)

LAURA: Are you going to watch?

ARTHUR: What?

LAURA: Arthur.

ARTHUR: Yes, of course.

LAURA: I'll see you later.

182

ARTHUR: Good.

LAURA: Arthur. Don't drift away from me.

> (*She goes.* ARTHUR *alone at the front. Then at the back you see* INCH *raise his arm. He is holding the mended plug.*)

ARTHUR: Paganini played the violin so well . . . people said he was in league with the devil.

> (*The plug goes in. The music crashes on.*)

The First Set

The band's truck rolls downstage, the music already on the way. The band is PEYOTE (*bass*), WILSON (*keyboard*), SMEGS (*lead*), NASH (*drums*).
> *Standing about watching and talking are* INCH, LAURA *and* ARTHUR. *The band sing by themselves.*

Close To Me

In a cafe called Disaster
Photos of the movie stars
Looked down upon the customers
As if they came from Mars
In a cafe called Disaster
Shelter from the rain
You said you couldn't love me
That we should never meet again

Will you always be this close to me
When you're far
When you're far
When you're far away from me
And will you always
Will you always be this close to me
When you're far
When you're far
When you're far away from me
And will it always be the same

In an age of miracles
In the heat of the afternoon
Falling on your funny face

183

The shadow of the moon
In an age of miracles
As sharp as any knife
I felt a touch of winter
In the summer of my life

And will you always etc.

(Then without a break the band go straight into the next number.
Dazzling light. MAGGIE *joins them, singing, burning off the fat as*
she goes.)

Passing Through

Mamma said I had the morals
Of an alley cat
Just because I wanted more
Sister fuckin' Rita
Was a mean child beater
But she said I was a high street whore

Burning down the freeway
Like a shootin' star
Bitching how my life is run
Learning how to shake it
In the back of a Bedford
Taking it from every mother-fucker's son

Shut your mouth honey
I don't wanna know your name
Shut your mouth honey
I don't care why you came
Pass me the bottle
Roll over let's do it again

Say you gotta save it
For someone special
And you know that that's a lie
If you don't holler
When the lights go out
Life is gonna pass you by
Gotta reputation as a
One night stand
Kinda precious too
If you let a greaser
Stay another night
They're gonna get a lease on you

Shut your mouth etc.

I'm a sunflower lady
With a sweet electric band
I'm a sunflower lady
With a bottle and a man
Don't want quiet
I don't want care
When the sun comes up
And the lights blaze out
If you don't scream honey
How do they know you're there

(*The truck goes back almost before the song ends.* ARTHUR
wanders down and sits quietly at the front.)

PASSING THROUGH

SCENE TWO

ARTHUR *sits staring out front. Then* WILSON *and* NASH *come in, both fuming to a standstill.*

ARTHUR: Sorry about that.

WILSON: Necrophilia. Like fuckin' the dead.

NASH: Amateur night at 'Arrods staff canteen.

WILSON: Like floggin' a corpse.

NASH: The bastards.

WILSON: Fuck 'em.

NASH: Bastards.

    (SMEGS *comes in.*)

SMEGS: What bastards.

WILSON: Do you know, some woofter comes up to me after the set, says I expectin' somethin' altogether more Dionysiac, I says Thursdays we're Dionysiac, Fridays we're jus' fuckin' awful.

ARTHUR: Right.

WILSON: Not that I care.

NASH: Right.

WILSON: Fuckin' penguins.

ARTHUR: Right.

WILSON: I'm sittin' there, I'm thinkin' the Marshall Stack's up the spout an' the Vox AC30 'as gone on the blink, an' not even the cloth-ears of Cambridge are fooled.

ARTHUR: And that's just the first set.

NASH: Right.

WILSON: 'Ow long till the next one?

ARTHUR: One o'clock. And the last at three-thirty. Then you can go to bed.

    (NASH *hands out joints.* INCH *comes in carrying a guitar which he sets about mending.*)

NASH: And you . . .

INCH: Sorry, lads, bit o' wobble on the Vox.

NASH: Wobble?

INCH: I've smeared it with pork fat, usually does the trick.
    (ANSON *appears*.)
ANSON: I've come to interview Maggie. She told me . . .
WILSON: Last month in Miami, Florida . . .
NASH: Again.
ANSON: . . . to wait here.
WILSON: Jim Morrison of the Doors got it out. Not the only
    occasion this 'as 'appened. By no means. There is the
    example of our own P. J. Proby in the Croydon Odeon,
    splittin' 'is velvets from knee to crotch.
SMEGS: A great moment.
WILSON: The. Great. Moment.
ARTHUR: Yes.
WILSON: Slightly spoilt, it must be said, by the fact 'e then
    spontaneously split 'em every night till 'e was thrown off the
    tour.
ARTHUR: A mistake.
WILSON: Certainly. That bit. A mistake.
NASH: That's right.
    (*Pause.* WILSON *inhales deeply*.)
WILSON: Fuck 'em. An' I know 'ow 'e feels.
ANSON: How do you think it went?
    (*Silence. They all smoke.* MAGGIE *appears talking from a long
    way off.* LAURA *dancing attendance*.)
MAGGIE: Mother born in Hitchin, father born in Hatfield, so they
    met half way and lived all their life in Stevenage. That's how
    my interview begins.
ARTHUR: Oh, Jesus.
    (NASH, WILSON, SMEGS *and* INCH *rise as a man, and leave as
    quickly as they can*.)
MAGGIE: Guess I must have been unhappy as a child . . .
ARTHUR: Oh, my God.
MAGGIE: Laura, I would love something to eat.
LAURA: Sure.
    (LAURA *goes off*.)
MAGGIE: Well, hello, Candy Peel, I thought it was you.
ARTHUR: Hallo, Maggie.
MAGGIE: Do you know why I call him Candy Peel? Because he has

a small scrap of that substance hanging where real men . . .

ARTHUR: Thank you, Maggie, do the same for you.

MAGGIE: Do you know how you survive in Stevenage? You say this isn't happening to me. That's what you say. You say I may appear to be stifling to death in this crabby over-heated mausoleum with these cringing waxworks who claim to be my parents. But it's not true. I'm not here. I'm really some way away. And fifty foot up.

ARTHUR: Right.

MAGGIE: In fact I'm a Viking.

ARTHUR: Have you got this?

ANSON: I . . .

ARTHUR: I would write it down if I were you.

MAGGIE: In another age. I was a Viking. Reincarnation. I had a dream last night, I was called Thor, and I was wrapped in furs and I had strips of dried meat tied round my waist.

ARTHUR: Well, I think we can guess what the dried meat means, honey.

MAGGIE: No nourishment in Stevenage. You draw no strength. It's like living on the moon.

ANSON: I have heard you saying that before.

MAGGIE: Listen, kid, you ask for an interview, I give you an interview. If you wanna *new* interview you gotta pay more, understand?

ANSON: Yes. Sorry.

MAGGIE: Like to rub my back, Arthur?

ARTHUR: Give me the bottle.

MAGGIE: I won't drink before the show, Arthur. I just like to hold it, O.K.?

(*Pause.*)

MAGGIE: Ask us another question.

ANSON: Would you say . . .

MAGGIE: Yes?

ANSON: Would you say the ideas expressed in popular music . . . have had the desired effect of changing . . . society in any way?

(*Pause.*)

MAGGIE: Hamburger. Dill pickle. That's what I want.

(LAURA *returns with* SNEAD.)

LAURA: I got the gay boy back.

ARTHUR: Ah, come in, waiter.

MAGGIE: Hallo, ringer, must have been you in the tub just now.

SNEAD: Sir?

ARTHUR: Did you say sir?

MAGGIE: That's all right, I'm just one of the boys.

ARTHUR: Hamburger, please, Mr Snead. With dill pickle.

MAGGIE: And relish and french fries. Coca-cola. And a banana
pretty. And a vanilla ice with hot chocolate sauce. Chopped
nuts. And some tinned peaches. And tomato sauce for the
hamburger. With onion rings. And mayonnaise. And
frankfurters. Frankfurters for everyone, O.K.? With French
mustard. And some toasted cheese and tomato sandwiches.
With chutney. On brown bread, by the way, I'm a health
freak.

ARTHUR: Got that, Mr Snead?

SNEAD: I'm afraid I'll have to send out for this. Do you think you
could give me some money?

LAURA: Money?

MAGGIE: Don't make with the jokes, ringer, they don't go with the
grovelling.

SNEAD: I can get you something from the college kitchen.

ARTHUR: O.K., just get us whatever's nice and greasy and
answers to the name of Rover, O.K.?

SNEAD: Sir?

MAGGIE: Then the first time I heard Bessie Smith, that was
somethin'.

ARTHUR: Off you go.

SNEAD: Sir.

(SNEAD *goes out.*)

MAGGIE: That was really somethin'. In a record shop, I was
fourteen. Did you know that as well?

ANSON: Actually I . . . read your press release.

MAGGIE: Did you?

(*Pause.*)

LAURA: I reckoned he should . . .

MAGGIE: Yes, well I do have some sort of life outside my press release. I can't remember where I put it, but I do know I have it.

(MAGGIE *gets up and slips the scotch bottle back in the rank of eight.*)

LAURA: Do you want to change for the next set?

MAGGIE: What you gawpin' at?

ANSON: Looking at you.

(MAGGIE *points to where she had been sitting.*)

MAGGIE: Still looking at the tragedy? That was over there. The girl with no life of her own. I left her over there.

ANSON: That easy?

MAGGIE: Tragedy's easy. I pick it up, I sling it off. Like an overcoat.

(*Pause.*)

ARTHUR: What is she on?

LAURA: Arthur.

ARTHUR: Will somebody please tell me what this girl is on?

(*Pause.*)

MAGGIE: So I tell you the story of my life. Everyone in Stevenage hated me, they hated me when I was a child. Cos I was big and fat and rich and took no shit from anyone. What's this for?

ANSON: A university paper.

MAGGIE: So they sent me to a convent. Anything you heard about randy nuns, forget it. They have tits like walnuts and leathery little minds. But me, I'm like a great slurpy bag of wet cement waiting to be knocked into shape. Everybody at the convent, they hate me too.

ANSON: You . . .

MAGGIE: How did I lose it, is that what you want to know?

ANSON: I didn't . . . get . . .

MAGGIE: I lost it to an American airman on top of a tombstone in Worthing cemetery. He was very scared. I was only thirteen and he didn't want to lose his pilot's licence. Write this down for Chrissake, it's good.

(ANSON'*s pencil obeys.*)

MAGGIE: So then even the American gets to hate me, yes, Laura?

LAURA: Oh, yes.

193

MAGGIE: She was at school with me, you see. We both had it, this English education. Takes a long time to wipe that particular dogshit off your shoe.

ANSON: And Arthur?

MAGGIE: Arthur I meet when I'm seventeen. A case of Trilby. Which is Trilby? I never know.

ARTHUR: The woman is Trilby.

MAGGIE: And the monster is Frankenstein.

ARTHUR: No.

MAGGIE: The doctor is Frankenstein.

ANSON: The monster doesn't have a name.

LAURA: The man is Svengali.

MAGGIE: Anyway. He invents me.

(ARTHUR *smiles and shrugs*.)

LAURA: Do you want to change?

MAGGIE: Yeah, I'll change.

(LAURA *organizes a new dress from the bags*.)

ANSON: Are there . . . any other singers you greatly admire?

MAGGIE: Well, it's a funny thing you'll find . . . singers mostly admire Billie Holliday, same as jazzmen admire Charlie Parker. Conductors say they admire Toscanini. It's something to do with how they're all dead.

ARTHUR: No competition.

MAGGIE (*smiles*): Yes.

ANSON: Among the living?

(MAGGIE *stands behind* ANSON *and puts her hands on his shoulders*.)

MAGGIE: This is all real you know, kid. None of the others can say that. Never had a nose-job. Or a face-lift. Or my chin pushed in. Or my jaw straightened. No paraffin wax, no mud-packs. All my own teeth. This is it. The real thing. I am the only girl singer in England not to have been spun out of soya bean.

ANSON: You never seem very happy to have been English. What would you rather have been?

MAGGIE: American.

ANSON: Why?

(MAGGIE *smiles at* ARTHUR.)

MAGGIE: America is a crippled giant, England is a sick gnome.

(ARTHUR *makes an o with his fingers.*)

MAGGIE: I sing of the pain. Do you understand?

ANSON: No.

MAGGIE: The words and music are Arthur's but the pain is mine. The pain is real. The quality of the singing depends on the quality of the pain.
(*Pause. She smiles.*)

MAGGIE: Yeah. What you study?

ANSON: Oh . . . medicine.

MAGGIE: Great.

ANSON: Well, yes, in a way except I don't seem very suited. It's not my . . . anyway . . . I don't want to bore you with my problems.

MAGGIE: What would you like to be?

ANSON: Well . . . I don't know. If I was free . . .
(MAGGIE *stares at him.*)

MAGGIE: Round the back of the Odeon? Yes? After the show? Would you like that?

ANSON: Odeon?

MAGGIE: It's a figure of speech. Kid.

ARTHUR: You could stand on a beerbox, reach up to her.

LAURA: Shake hands with Saigon Charlie.
(MAGGIE *smiles at them. Then cuffs lightly the top of* ANSON's *hair.*)

MAGGIE: First man I knew played rock music, he was nobody, a real nothing. I say rock music, but really it was all that hoopla and fag dancing the groups used to do. This boy got his big break, bottom of the bill with the Who, national tour. At the end of the tour he came back to Stevenage, he threw it in. I said, you got depressed because they're so good? He said, I got depressed because they're so very good, and yet even they ask the same questions I do every night: where is the money and where are the girls?
(*Pause.*)
And that is it. Where indeed is the money? And where are the girls?
(*Silence.* PEYOTE *walks into the room and lies down, says nothing.*)

MAGGIE: You know Jimi Hendrix gets depressed, he gets livid, because he says people don't come to hear his music, not really to listen, but simply because they've all heard he's got a big cock and plays the guitar with his teeth.

ARTHUR: Yar.

MAGGIE: And I say, sure Jimi, you're right to complain, people are cunts, but wouldn't it be a better idea to stop wearing tight trousers and give up clapping your mouth round the strings?

LAURA: I think I'd better keep an eye on Peyote tonight.

MAGGIE: He'll be O.K.

LAURA: He may need looking after.

MAGGIE: If it makes you feel good.

(*Pause.*)

MAGGIE: The hat.

LAURA: What?

MAGGIE: I'd like that hat, Laura. Gonna wear that hat tonight.

(LAURA *hands it to her.*)

MAGGIE: Does Peyote have any chicks lined up?

ARTHUR: He didn't say so.

MAGGIE: Well, where's he gonna put it then?

ARTHUR: Can't guess.

MAGGIE: Can't go around with blue balls all night. Laura.

LAURA: I get sentimental about my body. Maggie. Everything else I give to the band, but the body . . . you know . . . I still like to choose.

(MAGGIE *laughs, turns to* ANSON.)

MAGGIE: You couldn't make her with a monkey wrench. Arthur will tell you all about . . .

LAURA: End of interview.

MAGGIE: Laura here is my press secretary.

LAURA: End of interview. Anything else you need to know . . .

(MAGGIE *rides in over her, definitive.*)

MAGGIE: I only sleep with very stupid men. Write this down. The reason I sleep with stupid men is: they never understand a word I say. That makes me trust them.

(ARTHUR *gets up, moves away, turns his back.*)

So each one gets told a different secret, some terrible piece of my life that only they will know. Some separate . . . awfulness.

But they don't know the rest, so they can't understand. Then the day I die, every man I've known will make for Wembley stadium. And each in turn will recount his special bit. And when they are joined, they will lighten up the sky.

(*She picks up the dress* LAURA *has laid out.*)

MAGGIE: Come on, kid, I'll change after. No point in getting another dress dirty.

ANSON: No.

(*She leads* ANSON *out. On the way they pass* SNEAD *wheeling in a huge trolley of steaming food. Salvers, tureens, etc.*)

LAURA: Hey, Maggie, the food.

MAGGIE: Not hungry.

(*She and* ANSON *go out.*)

LAURA: Just . . . leave it there will you, Mr Snead?

SNEAD: Madam.

LAURA: And thank you.

(SNEAD *goes.*)

ARTHUR: She knows exactly what she's doing. Always. That's what I learnt.

LAURA: Yes.

ARTHUR: She knows the effect she's having. Even when she's smashed, when she's flat out on the floor, there is still one circuit in her brain thinking, 'I am lying here, upsetting people.'

LAURA: Yes.

ARTHUR (*smiles*): There you are.

LAURA: Arthur.

(INCH *reappears with* NASH, *then* WILSON. *They check the place.*)

INCH: 'As she gone?

ARTHUR: Yes.

INCH: All right everyone, you can come out now.

LAURA: The little fellow with her.

ARTHUR: She swallowed him up like a vacuum cleaner.

(LAURA *dips a plastic cup in the tureen, drips green lumps of soup on the floor.*)

INCH: Did she tell the Jimi Hendrix gag?

LAURA: Of course.

INCH: Did she say . . .

LAURA: Yes, she said it.

INCH: You 'aven't 'eard it yet.

LAURA: I haven't heard it but she said it. Just terrible.

NASH: 'I sing of the pain.'

LAURA: She said that.

INCH: 'The pain is real.'

NASH: The pain is bloody real.

INCH: Mostly in the arse.

ARTHUR: All right.

> (PEYOTE *gets up from the bench and leaps into the air. At the last moment he catches hold of an iron bar across the roof. He hangs there swinging slightly, eight feet above the ground, joint between his teeth.* WILSON *appears and opens a large book.*)

WILSON: Readings from the London telephone directory.

INCH: Oh no.

WILSON: The game is:

INCH: No.

WILSON: The game is: I read from the London telephone directory. You lot remain completely silent. The first person to make a sound is disqualified. The winner is the person who can stand it longest.

ARTHUR: Oh, my God.

WILSON: Arfer, you'll get yerself disqualified before we begin.

ARTHUR: Is that a . . .

WILSON: Now, where shall I begin? I think I was jus' gettin' inta the Smiths . . .

> (SARAFFIAN *enters. He is in his early fifties with a paper hat, camel hair coat and streamers round his neck.*)

SARAFFIAN: Saraffian comes.

> (*He releases a balloon full of water which squirts away into the air.*)

SARAFFIAN: And at once we have a party.

ARTHUR: Saraffian. My God.

> (RANDOLPH *follows on. He is heavily made up, you cannot tell his age. He is carrying a crate of champagne.* SARAFFIAN *takes a chicken from inside his coat.*)

WILSON: 'Ello, Boss.

SARAFFIAN: Poulet farci aux champignons. Loot from the ball, my

dears. And twelve bottles of a bleak little non-vintage Dom
Perignon. Za za.

INCH: Fantastic.

NASH: Za za.

SARAFFIAN: Just in case we don't get paid. Wilson, you old dog,
I've come to show you this . . . thing.
(*He gestures at* RANDOLPH.)
Put the crate down. Come here. Look. Look at my glittering
pigeon-chested youth. How do you like it? My future star.
(*They all look at* RANDOLPH.)

NASH: Great.

SARAFFIAN: Beautiful, isn't it? I'm really proud. He's going to
wipe up the queer market, no question.

RANDOLPH: I . . .

SARAFFIAN: Uh, don't risk it, just don't spoil it, lad. Don't mess
with the words, O.K.? Don't risk them, they only get you
into trouble.

RANDOLPH: Pl . . .

SARAFFIAN: He wants to protest his heterosexuality. Just don't
mention it, underplay it and we might believe in it. Might.
(*Pause.*)
Much better. So. Hallo, Peyote, don't bother to come down,
just stay up there if you want. So. I'm a fine surprise.

LAURA: Saraffian.

SARAFFIAN: My dear.

LAURA: What are you up to?

SARAFFIAN: Come to hear the band.

LAURA: I've been trying to ring you these last few days.

SARAFFIAN: Ah.

LAURA: Have you seen her?

PEYOTE: The sun goin' da'an. A tha'asand golden chariots.
Leather. Metal. Horseflesh. Careerin' da'an through the sky.
(*He drops from the beam simply to the floor.*)

PEYOTE: Ten tha'asand angels in a single file.

LAURA: Have you seen her?

SARAFFIAN: Well . . .

WILSON: Did you 'ear the first set?

SARAFFIAN: Certainly I heard it. I heard it all. From beginning to end. And I'm hoping it will have earned me some small remission in hell.

(*to* RANDOLPH.)

Look lively, open the bottles, son.

LAURA: When are you going to talk to her?

SARAFFIAN: Well, this is nice. Peyote, I saw your old woman last night. Would you believe it, she has another husband, she's still only nineteen.

WILSON: Wot's 'e like?

SARAFFIAN: Very charming. Easygoing bloke. Nose-flute player in a monastery band.

LAURA: She's not very well, Saraffian.

NASH: Let's 'avva game.

SARAFFIAN: Snap.

WILSON: Poker.

NASH: Monopoly.

WILSON: Lost the board.

LAURA: Saraffian.

WILSON: And Peyote swallowed the boot.

SARAFFIAN: Poker.

LAURA: And she's drinking again.

SARAFFIAN: Yes.

LAURA: Arthur will you tell him?

ARTHUR: I . . .

LAURA: Why do you think she drinks?

SARAFFIAN: I never ask, in my profession you expect to spend a portion of your time sitting by a hospital bed . . .

LAURA: Listen . . .

SARAFFIAN: I've got very good at it. I think the ultimate accolade of my profession should not be a disc, it should be a golden hypodermic.

LAURA: Saraffian.

SARAFFIAN: What is this? I pay a courtesy call on one of my bands . . .

LAURA: Don't be stupid. Courtesy call. When did you last see a band on the road?

SARAFFIAN: Glen Miller, I think.

LAURA: Saraffian, why does she drink?

SARAFFIAN: Why do we discuss her all the time? That's why she drinks. So we'll discuss her. You know, so we won't have time to do things like cut our fingernails or make love to our wives. That's why she drinks. So as to stop any nasty little outbreaks of happiness among her acquaintances. Are there any glasses for this stuff?

(INCH *goes to get some.*)

LAURA: So tell me why you thought Arthur should come.

SARAFFIAN: Kid.

ARTHUR: Please.

LAURA: Why does he have to come and see her again, it only screws her up.

SARAFFIAN: Please leave it, Laura, there are no answers and there is absolutely no point in the questions.

LAURA: I see. Can I say anything at all?

SARAFFIAN: No.

LAURA: Can anyone say anything?

SARAFFIAN: No.

(*A long pause.*)

I'm very grateful, Laura, for all the work you've done.

LAURA: Don't crawl up my arse, Saraffian, what is Arthur doing here?

SARAFFIAN: He . . .

ARTHUR: I wanted to come.

LAURA: What?

SARAFFIAN: He wanted to see her.

LAURA: Arthur?

SARAFFIAN: His own idea.

ARTHUR: Yes. Just to see her for Chrissake. I wanted to see her. Is that . . . just to see her.

(ARTHUR *goes out. A pause.*)

SARAFFIAN: Everyone should love everyone. Take the global view, Laura, please. Champagne.

(INCH *back with beer mugs.* SARAFFIAN *pours out.* LAURA *as if about to cry.*)

Ease up will you, Laura, you're doing Joan Crawford out of a job.

LAURA: Listen . .

SARAFFIAN: Shit, Laura, a man can love two women at once. I've
seen it done. The human heart. Shall we ever understand it,
Tone?

RANDOLPH: I . . .

SARAFFIAN: The answer is no. The boy adored her. Now he feels
responsible. So.
(LAURA *gets up. Moves. Stops dead. The rest are sitting, staring
into their mugs. Almost all comprehensively stoned now.*)

WILSON: And . . .

LAURA: Well . . .

INCH: There.
(*Pause.*)

SARAFFIAN: Look at it this way, Laura. I knew a Viennese teacher
who said that desperate people who try to kill themselves but
only succeed in shooting their eyes out, never, ever attempt
suicide again. It's the sense of challenge you see. Once you've
lost your eyes, it gives you something to live for.
(*He laughs.*)

PEYOTE: Dubbin. Brass. Bells.

NASH: Wot's up wi' 'im?

PEYOTE: Streakin' through the sky. The 'ouse'old cavalry itself.

WILSON: 'E's on 'orses again.

PEYOTE: Pomades. The royal 'orses.

WILSON: Said in the paper seventy per cent of adult males dream
regularly of fuckin' Princess Anne.

INCH: Quite right. I mean, what's a royal family for if not to . . .

WILSON: . . . dream.
(*They smile. Pause.*)

PEYOTE: An' a cry of 'allelujah.
(SARAFFIAN *sits back. They all drowse.*)

LAURA: It's just possible anywhere, any time to decide to be a
tragic figure. It's just an absolute determination to go down.
The reasons are arbitrary, it may almost be pride, just not
wanting to be like everyone else. I think you can die to avoid
cliché. And you can let people die to avoid cliché.

SARAFFIAN: Quite.
(*Pause.*)

WILSON: Shall we play the telephone game?

SARAFFIAN: I can't tell you the beauty of this profession. Years ago when I was young. It was full of people called Nat and Harry and Dick in brown suits and two-tone shoes. With thick chunky jewellery as if someone had splattered hot melting gold over their bodies with a watering can, and it had set in great thick blobs. And golden discs on the walls. And heavy presentation ballpoint sets, on their desks. Would sell you their grandmother's wooden leg; Nat did sell his grandmother's wooden leg, after she died, admittedly. And they muttered the totem phrases of the trade like, 'Tell him I'll get back to him.' There was no higher compliment an initiate could be paid than to be taken out for pickled brisket and beetroot borscht and be told in perfect confidence, 'The real dough's in sheet music. My son.' And they snapped great white fingers round the piano and used words like 'catchy' and 'wild'. And the artists . . . the artists bore no connection to the world I knew. When Nat travelled he carried them in the back of the van with a sliding glass compartment between him and them so he wouldn't have to listen to their conversation. He talked about installing sprinklers, as in Buchenwald. It was organized crime. Really. Those days. That's what interested me. The blatancy of it. The damnfool screaming stupidity of popular music. I loved it.

(*Pause. His eyes are closed.*)

You want me to sack her, you all want her to go.

(*Pause. He opens his eyes.*)

You are making the Mafia sign.

(*Pause. Nobody moves a muscle.* LAURA *looks furious.*)

O.K.

(*The band's equipment comes down silently and* SCENE TWO *scatters.*)

SCENE THREE

The abandoned stage. Just LAURA. *She walks behind the bank of speakers. She gets out a packet of fags. Lights two. Hands one down behind the amplifiers where it disappears. She moves away.*

LAURA: Where the people?

MAGGIE'S VOICE: In the dinner tent.

LAURA: Ah.

MAGGIE'S VOICE: They're having dinner. In the dinner tent.

> (LAURA *goes behind the organ, picks up the clean dress and throws it behind the speakers.*)

LAURA: You ought to . . . put this on. The other's got dirty.

MAGGIE'S VOICE: Laura.

LAURA: Yeah.

MAGGIE'S VOICE: The boy, the student . . .

LAURA: Yes, I can imagine.

> (*Pause.*)

MAGGIE'S VOICE: The journalist.

LAURA: Yes, yes, I know who you mean.

MAGGIE'S VOICE: He was in a bit of a state, I couldn't believe it. I think he must have juiced himself up.

LAURA: Yes.

> (MAGGIE *sits up behind the amplifiers.*)

MAGGIE: He said your thighs are so beautiful, your thighs are so beautiful, well, Laura, you seen my thighs . . .

LAURA: Yes.

MAGGIE: I said please let's not . . . I'd rather you just . . .

> (*Pause.*)

LAURA: You better go on.

MAGGIE: He said your body is like a book in which men may read strange things, a foreign country in which they may travel with delight. Your cheeks like damask, the soft white loveliness of your breasts, leading to the firm dark mountain peaks of your, Laura, now I am dreading which part of my body he will choose next on which to turn the great white beam of his fucking sincerity. Between your legs the silver comets spiral through the night, I lose myself, he says . . . he says . . . how beautiful you are Maggie and how beautiful life ought to be with you.

> (*Pause. She cries.*)

LAURA: Don't.

MAGGIE: So. I don't want to know.

LAURA: No.

(*Pause. She begins to recover.*)

MAGGIE: Then eventually . . . I say please, faking. He says yes of course, he stops talking. We wait. For thirty minutes. For thirty minutes it is like trying to push a marshmallow into a coinbox.

(*Pause.*)

Then he manages. In his way. Afterwards he says it's his fault. I say no mine, perhaps the choice of location . . . he says it can't be your fault, you have made love to the most brilliant and beautiful men of your generation, you have slept with the great. I say, there are no great, there is no beautiful, there is only the thin filth of getting old, the thin layer of filth that gets to cover everything. So. Off he goes. Za za.

(*Pause. Then a complete change.*)

MAGGIE: Where's Arthur? God, how I used to love that man.

LAURA: Yeah.

MAGGIE: He used to make me feel good, you know, he made me want to curl up foetal.

LAURA: Across the way they . . . talking about you.

MAGGIE: I'm a zeppelin. I'm fifty foot up.

LAURA: Saraffian's here.

MAGGIE: No kid.

LAURA: That's right.

MAGGIE: Why'd he come tonight?

LAURA: I don't know.

(LAURA *reaches down for a near-empty Johnny Walker from behind the speakers.*)

MAGGIE: Bum set. Bum gig. Think he noticed?

(*They look at each other.*)

Gimme the bottle will you, Laura?

LAURA: Arthur has travelled quite a long way.

MAGGIE: Yeah.

LAURA: Say seventy miles. I think he's entitled to a little of your time. If you can fit him in between . . .

MAGGIE: Do you know Arthur was a good man? When we first met? Really good man. He used to leave half-finished joints in telephone booths just so passers-by could have a good time.

LAURA: Listen . . .

MAGGIE: But he's become a little over-earnest for me, don't you think? I mean, if there was going to be a revolution it would have happened by now. I don't think 1970'll be the big year. I mean the real revolution will have to be . . .

LAURA: Inside?

MAGGIE: Gimme the bottle.

LAURA: Why do you talk like that, Maggie?

MAGGIE: Gimme the bottle.

LAURA: Where does that stupid half-baked bullshit come from?
(LAURA *holds on to the bottle.*)

MAGGIE: Well . . .

LAURA: If you really wanted rid of him you wouldn't sing his songs. And you wouldn't be afraid to tell him to his face.
(*Pause.*)

MAGGIE: All my life I've noticed people in telephone booths, in restaurants, heads down, saying things like, 'I don't want to see you again.' Once you start looking, they're everywhere. People rushing out of rooms, asking each other to lower their voices, while they say, 'You've got to choose between her and me.' Or, 'Don't write me, don't phone me, I just don't want to see you again.' People bent over crawling into corners at parties, sweating away to have weasely tearful little chats about human relationships. God how I hate all that. It seems so clear. I've finished with Arthur. And I'm fed up with his songs. I'm resentful and jealous and I want to be left alone. And I don't want to look in his lame doggy eyes.
(*Pause.*)
God, the singing is easy. It's the bits in between I can't do.
(*They look out from the stage into the void. At the back* INCH *comes on and starts preparing the equipment.*)

LAURA: They're coming back.

MAGGIE: Look at carrot-top over there.

LAURA: Must be almost time.

MAGGIE: Look, he's laughing.

LAURA: And his hand's coming up. Look . . .

MAGGIE: Yes.

LAURA: No, she's wriggled out of it.

MAGGIE: She's saying something.

LAURA: I think his name's Rodney.

MAGGIE: What did she say?

LAURA: Dunno. Something like don't touch me, Rodney.

MAGGIE: Christ, look at him.

LAURA: He's taking it badly.

MAGGIE: They're funny the rich . . .

LAURA: He's standing there gasping.

MAGGIE: They do it all so slowly.

LAURA: Like someone hit him with a cricket bat. He's . . .

> (*Pause. Appalled.*)

Jesus.

> (*Pause. Relief.*)

Ah no, he's seen a friend. Look, he's all right. He's trotting away into the paddock. Hallo, Roger, hallo, Rodney. He's quite frisky now. Lifting his fetlocks. Ha, ha, ha. All well.

INCH: You can't 'elp wonderin' . . . wot a bomb would do.

SARAFFIAN: Hallo, my dear.

> (SARAFFIAN *has crept in silently and is staring at* MAGGIE. *Towards the back of the stage a conga of* WILSON, NASH, PEYOTE, ARTHUR *and* RANDOLPH *snakes down; then the band begin to set up.*)

CONGA: 'Ow do yer do what yer do to me
         'Ow I wish I knew . . .

MAGGIE: Saraffian. Come to check on your investment?

SARAFFIAN: That's right.

MAGGIE: Just merchandise to you.

SARAFFIAN: Sure are.

MAGGIE: We could be anything. Soapflakes we could be. Well, that's fine. Yes. That's fine by all of us. Yes, Arthur?

> (*She looks at him for the first time.*)

ARTHUR: I don't know. It's not so easy of course. I believe the acid dream is over, it said in the *Daily Express*. But you and I, Maggie . . . we still want to say something. Yes?

> (MAGGIE *smiles and leans over him.*)

MAGGIE: Love you. Where my shoes?

> (*She moves away.* LAURA *goes to get her shoes.*)

SARAFFIAN: At the present rate if you lot go on working for another three years, you'll just about cover the advance I gave you.

(ARTHUR *plays a few chords of 'My Funny Valentine'.* MAGGIE *turns and stares.*)

ARTHUR: Leonardo da Vinci drew submarines. Five hundred years ago. They looked pretty silly. Today we are drawing a new man. He may look pretty silly.

MAGGIE (*to* ARTHUR): You still want it to mean something, don't you? You can't get over that, can you? It's all gotta mean something . . . that's childish, Arthur. It don't mean anything.

LAURA: Do you want the flowers?

MAGGIE: Fuck the flowers.

(MAGGIE *disappears.*)

ARTHUR: Haven't I seen Randolph before?

SARAFFIAN: Used to be a drummer. Year or two ago. Use to lay down a beat for Eve Boswell.

ARTHUR: Eve Boswell?

SARAFFIAN (*beaming*): Well, he is nearly thirty-five you know. They all come round. It all comes round again.

(MAGGIE *goes to collect her scotch. The band quiet and almost ready.*)

SARAFFIAN: I first knew Randolph in the fifties. My generation. The golden days of British rock. Crêpe soles, a tonic solfa and a change of name. That was all you needed. He was . . .

RANDOLPH: Tony Torrent.

SARAFFIAN: Right. It never got better you know. It'll never get better than 1956. Tat. Utter tat. But inspired. The obvious repeated many times. Simple things said well. Then along came those boys who could really play. They spoilt it of course. Ruined it. They were far too good. Before that . . . very fine my dears.

MAGGIE: Saraffian.

SARAFFIAN: Yes.

MAGGIE: Shut up.

(MAGGIE *walks to the back of the stage. Silence.* SMEGS *comes in and picks up his guitar. She lifts her bottle, drinks. Turns. The band look one to another.*)

SARAFFIAN: Rock me baby till my back ain't got no bone.
  (*He gets up.*)
  After that the rest was downhill.
  (*He walks away. She comes down.*)

The Second Set

ARTHUR, RANDOLPH, LAURA and SARAFFIAN *all wander out of
sight during the first song. The band start an aggressive rock
number; at the point* MAGGIE *should come in, they stop. Nothing.
Then* MAGGIE *speaks.*

MAGGIE: Just try and forget, eh? Forget who you are. Don't think
  about it. Pack your personality under your arm an' have a
  good time. I really mean it.
  Mama, take yer teeth out cos Daddy wanna suck yer gums.
  (*Pause. Then the band begin again. At the moment of entry,*
  MAGGIE *wanders away from the microphone and picks up her
  bottle. Pause.*)
  It's enough to make a haggis grow legs, man.
  (*An abrupt drum solo from* NASH *and a couple of chords from*
  WILSON. *Then silence.*)
  Now listen, kids, call you kids, so far you're schlebs and
  secret assholes. What you say, sir?
  (*She listens.*)
  Yeah, well, what you do with it is your business. Just don't
  ask me to hang it in my larder. Now this is meant to be a
  freak-out not a Jewish funeral. Let me make this plain. I
  don't play to dead yids. What you say, what are you saying,
  madam?
  (*She leans forward, her hand in front of her eyes.*)
  Sure. If that's what you want. Meet you in the library in
  half an hour. Bring your knickers in your handbag.
  (*She leans forward again.*)
  I am what? What is that word? I have not heard it before.
  What is stoned? (*She holds up the whisky bottle.*)
  This is a depressant, I take it to get depressed.

Now I have some very interesting stuff to say. First we're gonna talk about me. Then we're gonna talk about me. Then we'll change the subject. Give you a chance to talk . . . about what you think about me.

Right. So. It's mother born in Hitchin, father born in Hatfield. So they met half way and lived all their life in . . .

WILSON: Get on with it.

(*Long pause. The band look bored and regretful at her behaviour. She turns to* WILSON.)

MAGGIE: Wilson here . . . this is Wilson . . . on keyboard. Wilson has always entertained the notion of taking his trousers down. On account of the pain. So let's have them, Wilson.

(MAGGIE *lurches at the organ.* WILSON's *seat crashes over. She climbs on top of him and tries to rip his jeans off.* INCH *pulls her off, the others stand on one leg, play the odd note.*)

Right, let's have it, that's it, that's it, that's it, that's it, let's have it, that's it, that's it, that's it, that's it.

INCH: Come on, come on now.

(WILSON *stands well away.* INCH *has his arms round* MAGGIE. *Then* WILSON *slips nervously back to the organ.* INCH *slowly lets go of* MAGGIE *then stands behind her like a puppet master. Pause. Then superb coherence.*)

MAGGIE: Ladies an' genel'men . . .

(*Brief drum from* NASH.)

The acid dream is over lezzava good time.

(*The next number begins shatteringly loud. Where the words should be* MAGGIE *sings tuneful but emphatic.*)

Yeah yeah yeah yeah yeah yeah yeah yeah yeah . . .

(*The truck pulls back upstage. The music fades and falters as it goes.*)

YEAH YEAH YEAH

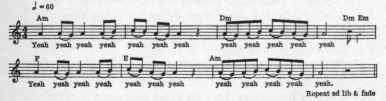

Repeat ad lib & fade

SCENE FOUR

SARAFFIAN *and* ARTHUR *straight in at pace. The music stops.*

ARTHUR: Great stuff.

SARAFFIAN: Really terrific.

ARTHUR: Where is she?

(LAURA *comes in.*)

SARAFFIAN: Getting her head kicked in.

LAURA: Didn't get us very far.

(WILSON *comes in.*)

WILSON: My jeans.

LAURA: Where did she get to?

WILSON: My beautiful jeans.

SARAFFIAN: Winner of the 1969 Judy Garland award for boring boring boring . . .

(INCH *comes in.*)

INCH: Wot the fuck was that about?

WILSON: Somethin' to do with the pain.

INCH: Wot pain?

LAURA: Go and get a shower ready.

INCH: Wot fuckin' pain?

SARAFFIAN: The pain, you know, the pain that makes her such a great artist.

(NASH *comes in carrying* MAGGIE *over his shoulder.*)

INCH: I'm not washin' 'er again.

LAURA: Put her down.

NASH (*swivelling* MAGGIE *round*): Anyone want 'er?

INCH (*stands on the table*): Will somebody tell me wot fuckin' pain?

WILSON: The pain.

(NASH *puts her down.* INCH *stands belligerently above them.*)

INCH: It's meant to be somethin' ta do with the pain. But wot pain? She can't even remember wot it was 'erself. Somethin' ta do with 'er upbringin'. Well, my upbringin' was three in a

bed and jam if yer lucky on Sundays, but I rub along.
Somethin' ta do with bein' unloved, but she don' wanta be
loved, she wants to be flattened by a Sherman tank.

ARTHUR: Leave it alone.

INCH: Of course, bloody Arthur thinks it's wonderful.

LAURA: Tell her now.

SARAFFIAN: What?

LAURA: Tell her, for God's sake, get it over with. It can't get
worse. She'll understand, she'll pretend not to, but get it
over with.

INCH: Wot a cow.

SARAFFIAN: Shut up.
(SARAFFIAN *goes over to* MAGGIE *who is propped up, lolling. You
don't know if she's faking.*)
Maggie?
(*Pause.*)
Maggie . . .
(*He slaps her face.*)

LAURA: She's listening.

SARAFFIAN: Some pressure building up, my dear, amongst us all.
The boy . . .

ARTHUR: I . . .

SARAFFIAN: Shut up. In his stumbling way. I, in mine. The band,
all in theirs. Arthur would like to be free of you. He would
like to set up a home with Laura. Yes. And you're sacked.
(*He puts his hand under her chin.*)
All right?
(SNEAD *appears with an Alsatian and a* POLICEMAN.)

SNEAD: This is a raid. You're all busted.

(*Blackout*)

INTERVAL

212

The equipment stands deserted on its rostrum at the back of the stage. The speakers now have their backs to us.

  ARTHUR *speaks from the absolute dark.*

ARTHUR: What matter? Out of cavern comes a voice
            And all it knows is that one word: rejoice.

SCENE FIVE

The light comes up on ARTHUR *who is sitting at the front of the stage on a pile of champagne crates, staring at a small white box of potato salad in his hands.*

  The stage merges into darkness at the sides so that the characters come and go in the night. First ANSON *approaches, jacket over arm.*

ANSON: I saw the second set. She rather . . . pushed the boat out,
            I thought.
ARTHUR: Yes.
ANSON: I saw the police about.
ARTHUR: We were busted.
ANSON: Gosh, I'm sorry.
ARTHUR: Mmm.
ANSON: That's terrible. Vicious.
ARTHUR: Vicious.
ANSON: Terrible.
            (*Pause.*)
ARTHUR: What's everyone doing?

ANSON: Who?

ARTHUR: Everyone.

ANSON: Oh, you mean the revellers.

ARTHUR: Yes.

ANSON: They've scattered. It rather loses its focus, you know. Till the champagne breakfast. It's . . . all over the place. The dinner tent's a disco and . . . they've got a Deanna Durbin in the buttery.

ARTHUR: Of course.

(*Pause.*)

ANSON: I did have a partner, you know.

ARTHUR: Yes.

ANSON: I rather lost track of her, I'm sure she's . . .

ARTHUR: Yes.

ANSON: You were at this college?

ARTHUR: I read music.

ANSON: What happened?

ARTHUR: I met Maggie. It seemed academic just to go on reading it.

ANSON: Yes.

ARTHUR: At the time troubador was the fashionable profession. It was also very good fun.

(*Pause.* ARTHUR *sets the salad aside.*)

Still the same shit-hole, eh?

ANSON: I don't like it very much.

ARTHUR: The people don't seem to have changed.

ANSON: Oh, I don't know. There are a few more totallys, you know. I should think. I share digs with a totally. I mean, I call him a totally, what happens is he has his friends to tea, I never stay, I just occasionally have to let them in the door and I overhear them, they're always sitting there saying, 'The whole system's totally corrupt an's gotta be totally replaced by a totally new system', so I just stand at the door and say, 'Couple more totallys for you, Tom.'

(*A Dietrich figure goes by in a long silver evening dress. It is* PEYOTE. *He is radiant.*)

ARTHUR: Hallo, Peyote.

PEYOTE: If ya 'appen to see a chick wiv jus' a pair o' jeans an' a leather waistcoat, say 'ello from Peyote, will ya?

ARTHUR: Sure thing.

(PEYOTE *passes*.)

ANSON: I'm hoping to drop out, you know. When I get my
degree. I just want to groove.

ARTHUR: Course you do. But it's not so easy is it? I mean, the
rules are so complicated, it's like three-dimensional chess.

ANSON: Yes.

ARTHUR: Just . . . work at it, eh?

(INCH *passes through heading for the tent.* ARTHUR *tries to get
away.*)

INCH: 'Allo, Arfer.

ARTHUR: How they doing?

INCH: Still doin' the interviews.

ARTHUR: What have they found?

INCH: I don't know. I think Peyote swallowed a certain amount of
the evidence. 'E's very quick.

ANSON: I wonder . . .

ARTHUR: Where you off to?

INCH: Look for some crumpet.

ARTHUR: Can I come with you?

INCH: You'd cramp me, Arfer. Somewhere in that tent is my ideal.

ARTHUR: What's that?

INCH: A short dirty-minded blonde.

(*He goes out.*)

ANSON: I've got a finger in my pocket.

ARTHUR: Ah.

ANSON: You know I'm a medical student?

ARTHUR: Yes.

ANSON: Can I show it to you? I think it's rather a good joke.
Handshake, you know, and one drops off.

(*He shows* ARTHUR *the severed finger.* ARTHUR *takes it and looks
at it seriously.*)

I cut it off a corpse in the lab. Here. It's quite a good joke.

ARTHUR: Yes. Yes.

(SARAFFIAN *comes in with a silver candlestick which he tucks
away in the crates.* RANDOLPH *follows.*)

SARAFFIAN: Here we are, lads. Za za. Small advance. In lieu of. It's ten grand to a spent rubber we don't get paid.

ARTHUR: You must be mad, the police are everywhere.

(ARTHUR *hands over some silver spoons.* SMEGS *on from the other direction.*)

SARAFFIAN: Well?

ARTHUR: Here, you can guard your own loot now.

SARAFFIAN: What did they say to you?

SMEGS: Same as everyone. Name and address and not to leave the area.

SARAFFIAN: Do you know what they found?

SMEGS: Apparently that Alsatian went berserk. It found so much stuff its eyes kept crossing and its knees caved in.

SARAFFIAN: Where's Nash?

SMEGS: Gone for a smoke in the bog. Said he needed a joint to calm himself down.

(SMEGS *takes loot from his pocket.*)

SMEGS: Pepperpot.

SARAFFIAN: Ta.

ARTHUR: And Maggie?

(SARAFFIAN *looks at* SMEGS.)

SARAFFIAN: They can't find her. Disappeared. Don't say 'oh God', that's what she wants you to say. That's what you're programmed to say, Arthur.

(SARAFFIAN *holds up a hand to interrupt.*)

ARTHUR: Where is she?

SARAFFIAN: After the bust she just slipped off . . .

ARTHUR: Saraffian.

SARAFFIAN: Listen. She is sacked. Keep your nerve. Arthur.

(*Pause.* ARTHUR *glares at him.*)

RANDOLPH: Guv, can I . . .

SARAFFIAN: Here's something. Look. You have to get the little ball in the hole.

(SARAFFIAN *has taken a toy from his pocket.* RANDOLPH *sits down and tries to get the ball in the hole.* ARTHUR *watches, then turns to* ANSON.)

RANDOLPH: Right.

ARTHUR: Do you know how Saraffian made his money?

SMEGS: Not us.

ARTHUR: No, real money.

SARAFFIAN: Go on.

ARTHUR: He used to wait for some black group to do well in the States, you know like the Temptations, then he says he's bringing them over. Sell out, of course. Except when they arrive they aren't quite the same people they are in the States. They're just five guys he's met in a bar.

SARAFFIAN (*smiles*): This is true.

ARTHUR: Who he calls the Fabulous Temptations, then teaches them the songs the real group plays.

SARAFFIAN: I've brought over some great sounds this way.

ARTHUR: And in England nobody knows the difference.

SARAFFIAN: Seeing how they're black.

(*He laughs.*)

ARTHUR: Yeah, you wouldn't try it with the Beach Boys would you?

SARAFFIAN: Well, one or two cheap tricks it's true. People expect it. The odd artist hung upside down from a third-floor window. It's part of the show.

ARTHUR: No doubt.

SARAFFIAN: And Arthur feels strongly that . . .

ARTHUR: All right.

SARAFFIAN: No, come on, you feel strongly that . . .

ARTHUR: It's not worth saying. Nothing's worth saying. It's all so obvious.

SMEGS: Anyone got a fag?

(*Pause.*)

ANSON: Gertrude Stein never put her car in reverse.

(*Pause.*)

ARTHUR: Yes, there is the inkling of an objection, just a smudge, perhaps the feeling Al Capone might greet you in the street.

SARAFFIAN: I told you.

ARTHUR: Of course, it's a big organization, fair number of clients, so if some junior oddball wants to drive her band until they're catatonic with fatigue, with pills, with petrol fumes, well, at least that is her taken care of, until you choose to flick her off your balance sheet.

(WILSON *comes in.*)

ARTHUR: And if the damage is in the head and irreversible, well at least you were many miles away.

WILSON: Wot's 'appenin'?

SMEGS: Cambridge Union Debate.

WILSON: Oh. Wot's the subject?

ARTHUR: Ethics.

WILSON: County Championship?

SMEGS: No, no, not Ethex like Thuthex, ethics like—what you're meant to do.

ARTHUR: I'm going to go and find her. Take this.

(ARTHUR *hands* SARAFFIAN *the finger. Goes out.*)

ANSON: It's my finger.

SARAFFIAN: Course it is, lad.

ANSON: I get screwed up you know. If you can imagine my life.

SARAFFIAN: Mmm.

(*He smiles at him and wanders away.*)

ANSON: I just long to get away. Join a band. On the road. Eh? I wouldn't mind how menial . . . anything. It's just every day here I know what the next day will be like. Isn't that dreadful? Going to lectures. Work in the lab. And all the time I want my mind to float free, I want it above me like a kite, and instead it's . . . why have I no friends? And why does nobody talk to me?

(*Pause. He looks round.*)

And, of course, I'm being boring.

(*He turns and goes out.*)

WILSON: Bloody 'ellfire.

SARAFFIAN: Well.

WILSON: Never go to the piss'ouse wiv that one, 'e'd chop it off soon as look at yer.

SARAFFIAN: He's just lonely.

WILSON: Wot else 'as 'e got in 'is pocket, bits of old toe 'n' little chunks of earlobe?

SARAFFIAN: He's trying to be interesting, you know. Have some character. The man who goes round with a finger in his pocket. Very casual, very interesting. Rather dark. He just wants to be liked.

WILSON: You know the real killers?

SARAFFIAN: Yes.

WILSON: The ones who jus' wanna be liked.

(ARTHUR *reappears upstage*.)

ARTHUR: Where is she? She's not in the tent.

SARAFFIAN: Nobody knows.

WILSON: 'Where is she, wot is she on?'

ARTHUR: Where is she?

SARAFFIAN: Look in the common room. Or the cricket pavilion.
She might be there. But don't let her know you're looking.

(ARTHUR *goes out*.)

Nice boy.

SMEGS: Yeah.

WILSON: Let's 'avva look at that.

SMEGS: How long till we play?

(WILSON *wanders upstage with the finger*.)

SARAFFIAN: The first day they met he drove her to the north of
Scotland. The northern sky was wide and open so that strange
Hebridean light came through white blinds on to their bed in
a perfect square. A perfect white square in a dark hotel room.
And they felt that first night they were almost not in the
world at all.

(*He smiles.*)

I can give you more. Much more. Many more moments of . . .
one thing or another. Arthur is obsessed. What happened in
rooms. On trains. The telegram she sent. Some pair of shoes.
Everything.

SMEGS: How do you know?

SARAFFIAN: Oh, she used to tell you.

SMEGS: Why?

SARAFFIAN: To make you think it didn't matter to her. That's why
she told you. As a hedge against disaster. Like her whole life.

SMEGS: What gets me is, it's her we talk about all the time, but it's
Peyote'll actually kill himself.

(LAURA *appears*.)

LAURA: Has anyone seen Arthur?

SARAFFIAN: Oh jeepers.

WILSON: Where is 'e? Wot is 'e on?

LAURA: I just wondered if anyone had seen him.

SMEGS: The footsteps go from left to right. Stop there briefly. Then we say . . .

SARAFFIAN: Try the common room.

SMEGS: Or the cricket pavilion.

SARAFFIAN: But don't let him know you're looking.

SMEGS: You look puzzled and depart.

LAURA: What?

SMEGS: Next.

WILSON: Laura. Jus' let me show you somethin'.

(WILSON *turns round. The finger is now sticking through his fly.*) You see doctor . . .

LAURA: Wilson . . .

(*It drops from his fly to the ground.*)

WILSON: Whoops, there it goes again.

LAURA: Very funny.

(*She goes out.* WILSON *calls after her.*)

WILSON: Laura, I promise to concentrate next time.

SARAFFIAN: Where did you stash it?

SMEGS: What?

SARAFFIAN: The stuff.

WILSON: Oh, we only 'ad some giggle-weed, it 'ad nearly all gone.

SMEGS: Shouldn't we talk about the future of the band?

WILSON: Yeah.

SMEGS: Do something different, what do you think?

WILSON: I'd like to do some songs about Jesus Christ.

SMEGS: Wilson, he's been done to death.

WILSON: Ah—'is own complaint exactly.

SARAFFIAN: And who carried the rest, the hard stuff, who carried that?

(*Pause.*)

SARAFFIAN: Don't tell me.

WILSON: Well . . .

SARAFFIAN: Did she know?

WILSON: She 'ad a carpetbag. It's only Peyote. 'E used to . . .

SARAFFIAN: Did she know?

(*Pause.*)

She was the bagman and she didn't know.

WILSON: Yes.

SARAFFIAN: You think the police are going to believe that?

WILSON: It's true.

SARAFFIAN: Of course it's true, that's not the point. The point is, who gets to go to jail.

(PEYOTE *comes in.*)

PEYOTE: I jus' bin propositioned by the rowing eight.

WILSON: Wot did you tell them?

PEYOTE: I told 'em I wasn't that sort of girl.

SARAFFIAN: Listen, Peyote, you're going to have to come with me to the police, you're going to have to tell them about this bag . . .

PEYOTE: I said I'd smash a bottle in their face.

(PEYOTE *smashes the bottle he is holding against the crates. It shatters, leaving him with nothing but the smallest neck.*)

WILSON: Never works that. I never believe it when they do it in the films . . .

PEYOTE: Jus' who the hell do they think I am?

(*Pause. He is out of his mind and commands a sudden healthy respect.*)

SARAFFIAN: Yes, Peyote.

PEYOTE: I'm not anybody's.

(*Pause.*)

SARAFFIAN: No, Peyote.

PEYOTE: I'd rather busk, I'd rather play free gigs, I'd rather busk in the foyers of V.D. clinics than play to these cunts.

SARAFFIAN: Yes.

WILSON: It's pointless.

(PEYOTE *throws his wig violently to the ground.*)

PEYOTE: An' they've ruffled my fuckin' wig.

(*Pause.*)

WILSON: It's pointless. You'll never get through to him now.

SARAFFIAN: All right everyone. Find the girl.

(*Blackout. At once* SMEGS *plays acoustic guitar and sings amazingly fast in the complete dark.*)

Don't Let the Bastards Come Near You

I come from the rulers you come from the ruled
We were making the film of our lives
And the media dwarves were howling for masterpieces
People were dropping like flies
The crew were on librium I was on brandy
Struggling hard to get through
And the days and the nights were alive
With the hatred directed at you

(*Eight single spots come up on* SMEGS, WILSON, NASH, PEYOTE, RANDOLPH, ARTHUR, LAURA, INCH *as they join in the chorus.*)

> *Don't let the bastards come near you*
> *They just want to prove you're sane*
> *To eat up your magic and change you*
> *So I'll help keep the bastards away*

(*The spots fade and we are back in complete black.*)

It was in your dark night of disaster
We watched as you smashed up your room
And Spanish and I we decided
We just couldn't stay in your tomb
In the morning I drove for the border
And Spanish he stayed till the end
But he has resources of humour
To which I cannot pretend

(*The spots come up again on the eight suspended faces.*)

> *Don't let the bastards come near you*
> *They just want to prove you're sane*
> *To eat up your magic and change you*
> *So I'll help keep the bastards away*

(*The spots fade.*)

Now I don't like singing with sailors
And I don't like drinking with fools
But I'll do anything that I have to
Because I know those are the rules
I know that the pain is like concrete
And the road is lonely it's true

And the load that we carry is studded with nails
So this is my message to you
(*The spots return.*)
　　Don't let the bastards come near you
　　They just want to prove you're sane
　　To eat up your magic and change you
　　So I'll help keep the bastards away

BASTARDS

♩ = 116
Very fast

I come from the ru-lers You come from the ruled We were mak-ing the film of our lives And the me-di-a dwarves were howl-ing for master-pie-ces Peo-ple were drop-ping like flies The crew were on Li-bri-um I was on bran-dy Strug-gling hard to get through And the days and the nights were a-live with the ha-tred Di-rec-ted at you Don't let the bas-tards come near you They just want to prove you're sane To eat up your ma-gic and change you So I'll help keep the bas-tards a-way A-way. way. A-way. way. A-way.

SCENE SIX

The deserted equipment. At the front of the stage MAGGIE *is sitting reading a book. Her lips are moving. A bottle stands by the chair.*
Then SARAFFIAN *finds her.*

SARAFFIAN: Looking for you. Everyone. Everywhere.

MAGGIE: In the library.

SARAFFIAN: Didn't think of that. There are some things you should be told.
(MAGGIE *holds up the tiny book.*)

MAGGIE: Thoughts of St Ignatius. Look. Pretty thin, eh?

SARAFFIAN: Yeah.

MAGGIE: Poor value. Just whatever came off the top of his head.
(*She throws it to him.*)

SARAFFIAN: Maggie . . . there's a problem with the bust . . .

MAGGIE: And I got you a trinket.
(*She tosses him a napkin ring.*)

SARAFFIAN: Thank you.

MAGGIE: You can melt it down.

SARAFFIAN: I will.

MAGGIE: And pour it down your throat.

SARAFFIAN: Maggie . . .

MAGGIE: You really got me Saraffian.

SARAFFIAN: I know.

MAGGIE: You did well.

SARAFFIAN: The timing . . .

MAGGIE: I was going to quit.

SARAFFIAN: I'm sure. But I sacked you first.
(*Pause.*)
Are you hurt?

MAGGIE: Not in my overself.

SARAFFIAN: What does your overself say?

MAGGIE: My overself says: everything's O.K.
(*Pause.*)

224

SARAFFIAN: Maggie about the bust . . .

MAGGIE: Why are girls who fuck around said to be tragic whereas guys who sleep about are the leaders of the pack?

SARAFFIAN: Why do people drink?

MAGGIE: Can't stand it?

SARAFFIAN: Wrong. Need an excuse.

MAGGIE: Ah.

SARAFFIAN: They want to be addicted so's to have something to blame. It's not me speaking. It's the drink. The drugs. It's not me can't manage. They want to be invaded, so there's an excuse. So there's a bit intact.

MAGGIE: I've never been addicted.

SARAFFIAN: No?

MAGGIE: This goes through me like a gutter. Even on heroin I knew I could beat it. I did beat it. There's something in me that won't lie down.
(*Pause.*)
You know I've always pitied schizophrenics.

SARAFFIAN: Oh yes.

MAGGIE: Struggling along on two personalities. I have seventeen, I have twenty-one.

SARAFFIAN: Like everyone else.
(*She doesn't hear.*)

MAGGIE: Do you know the purpose of reincarnation?

SARAFFIAN: Not exactly.

MAGGIE: You get sent back because you failed last time.

SARAFFIAN: I see.

MAGGIE: I believe all we're doing here is trying to avoid coming back. I think you get sent back because you didn't get it right last time. Basically. You get sent back for having blown it the time before. Well, this time . . . I'm not coming back.
(*Pause.*)
I was a Viking, I was a Jew . . .

SARAFFIAN: Ah.

MAGGIE: I could get you through the Sinai desert, no map, no compass. I'd know. Just like that.

SARAFFIAN: Really?

MAGGIE: Why don't people take more care of their overselves?

They just rub them in the mud.

SARAFFIAN: Yes.

MAGGIE: Why is that?

SARAFFIAN: It's a failing people have.

MAGGIE: You don't believe a single word I say.

SARAFFIAN: No. Nor do you.

MAGGIE: Con safos.

(*Pause.*)

Go to San Francisco, sing in a bar.

SARAFFIAN: You never would.

MAGGIE: Well, what am I going to do tomorrow? Tonight?

SARAFFIAN: I thought you had the little fellow . . .

MAGGIE: Don't patronise me, Saraffian.

SARAFFIAN: . . . the finger freak. What happened to him?

MAGGIE: I don't know. I gave him some acid, told him to get high.

SARAFFIAN: How did you get it?

MAGGIE: What?

SARAFFIAN: The acid.

MAGGIE: Oh, some creep. Liked the way I sang.

SARAFFIAN: Have the police talked to you?

MAGGIE: I'm O.K. Don't worry. I'm cool. This is legal and it's all
    I've got.

(*She shows him the bottle and smiles.*)

SARAFFIAN: Maggie.

MAGGIE: You're not my manager now.

SARAFFIAN: No.

(*They both smile.*)

MAGGIE: Do you know why I liked you as my manager?

SARAFFIAN: I have a fairly shrewd idea.

MAGGIE: Because you were such an unspeakable shit.

SARAFFIAN: That's right. I was aware of that. You'd say to people,
    I'd love to do your charity gig, play free in the streets of
    Glasow, great but—er—that bastard Saraffian would just
    never let me. And everyone says, poor girl.

MAGGIE: You're right.

SARAFFIAN: I know. That's why everyone likes to be handled by
    me. I'm an excuse. Any artist stands next to me looks like a
    saint. Canonization. Cheap at twenty per cent.

MAGGIE: Then why did you like me?

SARAFFIAN: I don't know. Two-bit band, one of five hundred, fifteen hundred. Your tunes were better and the singer had balls. But where did I get you? One week in the *Melody Maker* at number eighty-four. And what's called a minor cult. I'd rather have leprosy than a minor cult. You know, some booking manager rings you, says what've you got? I say Maggie Frisby's lot, he says, no no, I never take minor cults. You have it round your neck in letters of stone.

MAGGIE: So what happened?

SARAFFIAN: Well. What happens to everyone? Bands just break up. Travel too much. Drop too much acid. Fifty-seven varieties of clap. Become too successful—never your problem, my dear—they break up because they don't feel any need. I don't mean fame, that's boring, or money, that's a cliché, of course it goes without saying that money will separate you from the things you want to sing about, we all know that. I mean—need. Maggie. Where's the need?

MAGGIE: I don't know. What do you think?

SARAFFIAN: I don't know. I don't sing.

(*Pause.*)

MAGGIE: It's nothing to do with singing.

SARAFFIAN: No?

MAGGIE: Oh, come on, it's nothing to do with being an artist, artists are just like everyone else . . .

SARAFFIAN: Then what . . .

MAGGIE: I have this sense of arbitrariness you know. Like it was Arthur but it could have been one of ten thousand others.

SARAFFIAN: Just . . .

MAGGIE: Where did we get this idea that one human being's more interesting than another?

(*Pause.*)

Saraffian. In Russia the peasants could not speak of the past without crying. What have we ever known?

(*Pause.*)

My aunt's garden led down to a river. It was the Thames, but so small and green and thick with reeds you wouldn't recognize it. It was little more than a spring. I was staying there,

227

I was six, I think, I had a village there by the riverbank, doll village with village shop, selling jelly beans, little huts, little roads. I took the local priest down there, I wanted him to consecrate the little doll church. The sun was shining and he took my head in his hands. He said, inside this skull the most beautiful piece of machinery that god ever made. He said, a fair-haired English child, you will think and feel the finest things in the world. The sun blazed and his hands enclosed my whole skull.

(*She smiles, pours whisky over her head, down her front, and inside her trousers. Then goes over to* SARAFFIAN, *takes hold of him. Puts her hands round his head. Then she lets go.*)

Saraffian. Thank you. Great relationship. Great creative control.

SARAFFIAN: Maggie.

MAGGIE: Great help in career at time most needed. Never forgotten. Farewell.

SARAFFIAN: Maggie. The band didn't get around to telling you. They stashed all their stuff in your bag. That means the bust sort of settles on you.

(*Long pause.* MAGGIE *turns back and looks at him.*)

MAGGIE: O.K. Try prison for a while, why not?

(*She sits down where she is. Pause. Then she lies down.*)

SARAFFIAN: Ah. Is that all right?

(*Pause. You can see him thinking. Then he takes some fags out and goes over to her.*)

SARAFFIAN: Cigarette?

MAGGIE: No.

SARAFFIAN: You know . . .

(*Pause.*)

You know how people crap on about Hollywood in the thirties.

MAGGIE: Yes.

SARAFFIAN: Long books about Thalberg and Louis B. Mayer. Who laid the ice-cubes on Jean Harlow's nipples? But nobody notices they're living through something just as rich, just as lovely. And in thirty years' time they'll write books about the record business of the fifties or sixties. What it was like to have known Jerry Wexler. Or glimpse Chuck Berry at the other end of the room.

MAGGIE: You think?

SARAFFIAN: I'm banking on it. If I'm to have had any life at all. It's going to look so special. Once it's over, of course.
(*Pause. Then* INCH *comes on holding up one hand.*)

INCH: Upper-class cunt, it's in a world of its own. Smell my fingers.

SARAFFIAN: Thank you, no.

INCH: Dab some be'ind yer ears.

SARAFFIAN: Inch . . .
(INCH *sits down with a vacuum flask and a Mars bar.*)

INCH: Now I'm 'ungry.

SARAFFIAN: They should invent a machine.

INCH: Wot?

SARAFFIAN: Gratify all your senses at once.

INCH: Well, I did know someone used to eat Complan sittin' on the can. 'E was into 'is 'ead, you see, despised the body, so 'e reckoned it best to sit shovellin' it in at one end and pushin' it out at the other, an' that way get the 'ole job over with. Now I reckon if 'e coulda jus' spared 'is left 'and as well . . .

SARAFFIAN: Quite.

INCH: Do the lot in one go.

SARAFFIAN: Yes. The rest of us, well, we spread our pleasures so thin.
(LAURA *comes in.*)

LAURA: What's happening?

SARAFFIAN: Did you find him?

LAURA: No. Is she all right?
(MAGGIE *is lying still on the ground.*)

SARAFFIAN: Yes. Get ready for the third set.

LAURA: It's cancelled. There are notices all over saying it's cancelled by popular demand.

INCH: Great.

SARAFFIAN: I knew it. It's in the contract. Three sets or we don't get paid.

LAURA: So what do we do?

SARAFFIAN: Play it. Just play it, it's our only chance of the cash. I don't care if nobody's listening. Why don't you round up the band?

LAURA: It's not my job.

INCH: I'm 'avin' me tea.

SARAFFIAN: Laura. Please.

(*She goes out to start looking.*)

Getting your hands on it. I mean, actually getting your hands on the cash. That is the only skill. Really. The only skill in music.

(*From offstage the sound of* PEYOTE *playing the piano with his feet. He is wheeled on by* WILSON, NASH *and* SMEGS *as* SARAFFIAN *goes out.*)

PEYOTE: 'Ere we are.

INCH: That's not ours.

PEYOTE: Saraffian said nick somethin', I nicked somethin'.

INCH: We can't nick that, we can't get it in the van.

PEYOTE: Let's 'ave a ball of our own.

WILSON: Did yer talk to the pigs?

PEYOTE: Let's 'ave a party.

(LAURA *returns.*)

LAURA: Right. Is everyone ready?

WILSON: 'Ow yer feelin', Peyote?

PEYOTE: Fantastic. Let's 'avva party.

LAURA: It's three-thirty, let's just play the . . .

WILSON: 'E's right back up there, 'ow does 'e do it?

PEYOTE: Listen, mate, if you'd dropped as much stuff as me . . .

SMEGS: It always comes back to this.

PEYOTE: You lot'll never understand . . .

SMEGS: If there's one thing I really despise it's psychedelic chauvinism . . .

PEYOTE: I want some fun.

SMEGS: 'I've had more trips than you.'

PEYOTE: Fun.

INCH: If you like I can . . .

WILSON: Wot?

INCH: Set light to my fart.

NASH: Oh no.

WILSON: Not again.

NASH: We've seen it.

WILSON: Dozens of times.

SMEGS: One streak of blue flame and it's over.

WILSON: Can't you do anything else?

INCH: Yeah. I do bird impressions.

SMEGS: Really?

INCH: Yeah. I eat worms.

  (SARAFFIAN *returns with a conductor's baton which he taps on the piano.*)

SARAFFIAN: Right. Look lively, everyone. Third set. Any ideas? Requests?

WILSON: I would like to 'ear Richard Tauber sing 'Yew Are My 'eart's Desire.'

NASH: Wot is this?

SMEGS: Get in a line.

PEYOTE: Let's get on with it . . .

SARAFFIAN: This is the third set.

PEYOTE: I'm gonna need a fuck in about forty-five seconds.

NASH: Did you take sweeties again?

  (RANDOLPH *has appeared.*)

RANDOLPH: Guv, this little ball it just won't go in . . .

SARAFFIAN: Keep trying.

NASH: Who's the vocals?

SARAFFIAN: Just stay in a line.

PEYOTE: I'm not gonna last.

WILSON: Listen, we gotta 'ave real vocals.

SARAFFIAN: Tony. Sing with the band.

RANDOLPH: But I gotta try and . . .

SARAFFIAN: You may stop. You may sing with the band.

RANDOLPH: Wot key are we in?

  (*A photographic moment. Held for a second, the new team with* RANDOLPH *at the centre. Then the music begins with* SMEGS *on jew's harp, the rest come in one by one. An improvised jam, very inspired.*)

Let's Have a Party

PEYOTE: Ball gown baby
Bubble gum queen
Left her body
In my new blue jeans
Said hello
That was that
Didn't have time to check my hat
So

BAND: *Let's have a party, let's paint the town*
Let's have a party, chase away that frown
Let's have a party, let your hair down.
(*Instrumental verse, then.*)
Let's have a party, etc.
Ball gown baby
Bubble gum queen
Saw her picture in a magazine
Said she'd go down
The butterfly flicks
All of them changes all of them licks
So
Let's have a party, etc.
(*They leap back, challenging* RANDOLPH *to enter the song. He does, falteringly, inventing the words as he goes.*)

RANDOLPH: Ball gown baby
Bubble gum queen
Spread some sauce on my baked beans
Said hey I got you
Special treat
Be bop a lula
You eat meat
So
(*He is accepted. They all bash hell out of the piano.*)

ALL: *Let's have a party, etc.*
(SARAFFIAN *stops them.*)

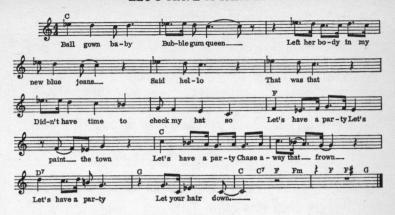

Ball gown ba-by Bub-ble gum queen___ Left her bo-dy in my new blue jeans___ Said hel-lo That was that Did-n't have time to check my hat so Let's have a par-ty Let's paint___ the town Let's have a par-ty Chase a-way that___ frown___ Let's have a par-ty Let your hair down.

SARAFFIAN: All right. Hold it. There's no one to witness the third set took place. We need that little bloke. The one that booked us.

WILSON: The one wiv the finger.

SARAFFIAN: Yes.

WILSON: You won't find 'im. Some cretin gave 'im some acid. They took 'im to 'ospital. Stupid little shit.

(*A pause.* MAGGIE *sits up. She looks at the band. A silence. Only* SARAFFIAN *doesn't see her.* MAGGIE *stands up and looks at them, then goes out. Sudden deflation.*)

SARAFFIAN: Oh dear.

LAURA: What happens next?

SARAFFIAN: Just let me think . . .

LAURA: What about . . .

SARAFFIAN: Tony, ring Mrs Saraffian, say I'm not going to get back tonight so she's to change the budgie's sandpaper, O.K.?

RANDOLPH: Will do.

(*He goes.*)

PEYOTE: Are we gonna do this or are we not?

NASH: I'm beginnin' to feel jus' a bit of a fool.

WILSON: You think there'd be somebody. Wouldn't you? Don't

you think? Jus' somebody to hear us? Wouldn't you think?
(*They stop and look out into the night. Then* ARTHUR *comes in.*)

ARTHUR: What the hell is going on?

SARAFFIAN: Arthur . . .

ARTHUR: I just talked to the police.

SARAFFIAN: Don't worry, everything's in hand . . .

ARTHUR: They seem to think Maggie was pushing the stuff.

SARAFFIAN: That's right.

ARTHUR: Well, who the hell put the stuff in her bag?

PEYOTE: I think I'll jus' phase out, you know . . .

ARTHUR: He knows bloody well what's going on.

PEYOTE: Jus' go and get laid.

ARTHUR: He's a bit fucking selective about what he blocks out.
   (PEYOTE *shrugs and giggles.*)

PEYOTE: Well.

SARAFFIAN: Arthur . . .

ARTHUR: Did you tell Maggie?

SARAFFIAN: Yes.

ARTHUR: Does she know she's going to get done?

SARAFFIAN: Oh yes.

ARTHUR: Well, what does she say?
   (*Pause.*)

SARAFFIAN: Well . . . to be honest . . . she doesn't seem to mind.
   (RANDOLPH *returns quickly.*)

RANDOLPH: You better come quick. She's burning down the tent.
   (*Blackout. Pitch black. Silence.*)

SCENE SEVEN

Pitch dark. You can see nothing at all. You just hear their voices:
MAGGIE *is very cheerful.*

ARTHUR: Maggie. Maggie. Are you there?
   (*Pause.*)
   Are you there?

MAGGIE: Arthur.

ARTHUR: Ah.

MAGGIE: I'm here. I'm naked and I'm covered in coconut oil.

ARTHUR: Oh fuck, what was that?

MAGGIE: It's a rugby post.

(*She laughs.*)

ARTHUR: You've done pretty well.

MAGGIE: Thank you very much.

ARTHUR: Yip. Police. Ambulance. Fire brigade. You just got to score the air-sea rescue service and you got a full house.

MAGGIE: Thank you. What's the damage?

ARTHUR: Not bad.

MAGGIE (*complaining*): I can't see any *flames*.

ARTHUR: No, no, they're all coping rather well. They all love it you know. Dashing about in the smoke. They're hoping to make it an annual event.

MAGGIE: Really?

ARTHUR: Bit of fun.

(*Pause.*)

ARTHUR: How've you bin?

MAGGIE: All right.

ARTHUR: Haven't seen you for a long time. Must be six months. What have you been up to?

MAGGIE: Nothing really. I had the flu.

ARTHUR: What else?

MAGGIE: Do you have some cigarettes?

ARTHUR: Sure.

MAGGIE: Can you give me the pack? It's just if I'm gonna be arrested I'm gonna need some.

ARTHUR: Of course. Here.

MAGGIE: Thank you.

(*A match flares. We see their faces as they light their fags.*)

ARTHUR: What were you doing?

MAGGIE: What?

ARTHUR: The tent. Just making sure?

MAGGIE: Oh yes. Just making sure.

(*The match out. Darkness again.*)

ARTHUR: I can get you a lawyer.

MAGGIE: Don't be stupid. What else?

ARTHUR: Oh, you know. Larry says, come and see him soon. Martha says will you cover the new Dusty Springfield for the supermarket? Derek says . . . Derek says . . .

MAGGIE: Yeah, what does Derek say?

ARTHUR: Derek says . . . I don't know what Derek says. Far out. Out of sight. Wow man. Jeez. That's what Derek says.
(*Pause.* ARTHUR *begins to cry.*)
I can't live without you. I can't get through the day.

MAGGIE: What else?

ARTHUR: You said you loved me.

MAGGIE: I did. I did love you. I loved you the way you used to be.

ARTHUR: But it's you that's made me the way I am now.

MAGGIE: I know. That's what's called irony.
(*Pause.*)
We better go back.

ARTHUR: Maggie.
(*She shouts into the night.*)

MAGGIE: Nothing's going to stop me. No one. Ever. Let me do what I want.
(*Pause.* ARTHUR *lying on the ground.*)

MAGGIE: So much for small-talk. Will you walk me back?

ARTHUR: Right.

MAGGIE: Poor Arthur. You'd like to be hip. But your intelligence will keep shining through.
(*She laughs, and they begin to go.*)
Watch where you drop that fag.

ARTHUR: Ha ha.

MAGGIE: Don't want to start a . . .
(*She peals with laughter. At once the lights come up. The stage is empty. But thick with smoke. They've gone.*)

SCENE EIGHT

At once LAURA *wheels a flat porter's barrow on through the smoke.* INCH *appears from the other side.*

236

INCH: I jus' drove the van across the cricket pitch.

LAURA: Well done.

INCH: I reckon it'll be takin' spin this year.

(*He and* LAURA *begin to dismantle the equipment.* MAGGIE *and* ARTHUR *appear.*)

INCH: There some people lookin' for you.

MAGGIE: Really? Where?

INCH: About seven 'undred and fifty of 'em. An' all round, I'd say.

(SARAFFIAN *appears squirting a soda syphon.*)

SARAFFIAN: My dear.

MAGGIE: Saraffian.

SARAFFIAN: Well done. Very educational. We have all learnt something tonight.

MAGGIE: What's that?

SARAFFIAN: Always put an arson clause in the contract. I'm going to have to pay for this.

(*He hands* INCH *the syphon.*)

Might as well nick it.

INCH: Right.

SARAFFIAN: My God, but that was fun.

(*He bursts out laughing and embraces* MAGGIE.)

Bless you my dear. At a stroke the custard is crème brulée. You've totally restored my faith in the young.

ARTHUR: Is anyone hurt?

SARAFFIAN: Can I tell you a story? I really must tell you a story now.

(WILSON *passes. He has scored a fireman's helmet.*)

WILSON: Congratulations.

MAGGIE: Thank you.

WILSON: It's really beautiful.

(*He kisses her.*)

MAGGIE: Better than taking your trousers down?

WILSON: Oh yeah. It's jus' a different thing.

MAGGIE: Right.

WILSON: If yer don't mind, I've 'eard there's a psychology tutor on fire, I'd really like to see it you know.

MAGGIE: Sure.

(WILSON *heads out.*)

237

WILSON: It's so stupid it's just wonderful.

INCH: Hey, 'old on, Wilson, I think I'll come and drag some naked women from the flames.

(INCH *leaps off the stage and follows* WILSON.)

SARAFFIAN: I'll tell you of my evening at the Café de Paris. March 9th, 1941.

(NASH *crosses with a bucket of water.*)

ARTHUR: You won't put it out with that.

NASH: This ain't for the fire. It's for Peyote.

(*He laughs and goes into the dark.*)

SARAFFIAN: I was with this girl. She's related to a Marquis on her mother's side and me a boy from Tottenham whose dad ran a spieler in his own back room. So I'm something of a toy, a bauble on her arm. And she said, please can we go to the Café de Paris, I think because she wants to shock her pals by being seen with me, but also because she does genuinely want to dance to the music of Snakehips Johnson and his Caribbean band.

(LAURA *picks up as much equipment as she can manage and goes out.* SARAFFIAN, MAGGIE *and* ARTHUR *left alone with the piano.*)

So I say fine, off to Piccadilly Circus, Coventry Street, under the Rialto cinema, the poshest . . . the jewelled heart of London where young officers danced before scattering across four continents to fight in Hitler's war. You won't believe this but you went downstairs into a perfect reproduction of the ballroom on the *Titanic*. I should have been warned. And there they are. A thousand young blades and a thousand young girls with Marcel waves in their hair. So out of chronic social unease, I became obstreperous, asking loudly for brown ale, and which way to the pisshouse, showing off, which gave me a lot of pleasure, I remember they enjoyed me, thinking me amusing. And I was pretty pleased with myself. The glittering heart of the empire, the waiter leaning over me to pick up the champagne. And then nothing. As if acid has been thrown in my face. The waiter is dead at my feet. And the champagne rises of its own accord in the bottle and overflows. Two fifty-kilo bombs have fallen through the cinema above and Snakehips

Johnson is dead and thirty-two others. I look at the waiter.
He has just one sliver of glass in his back from a shattered
mirror. That's all.

(MAGGIE *gets up and moves away to sit on the stage.*)

So we're all lying there. A man lights a match and I can see
that my girl friend's clothes have been completely blown off
by the blast. She is twenty-one and her champagne is now
covered in a grey dust. A man is staring at his mother whose
head is almost totally severed. Another man is trying to wash
the wounded, he is pouring champagne over the raw stump
of a girl's thigh to soothe her. Then somebody yells put the
match out, we'll die if there's gas about, and indeed there
was a smell, a yellow smell.

I looked up. I could see the sky. It's as if we are in a huge
pit and above at the edges of the pit from milk bars all over
Leicester Square people are gathering to look down the hole
at the mess below. And we can't get out. There are no stairs.
Just people gaping. And us bleeding.

Then suddenly I realized that somebody, somehow, God
knows how, had got down and come among us. I just saw two
men flitting through the shadows. I close my eyes. One
comes near. I can smell his breath. He touches my hand. He
then removes the ring from my finger. He goes.

He is looting the dead.

And my first thought is: I'm with you, pal.

I cannot help it, that was my first thought. Even here, even
now, even in fire, even in blood, I am with you in your scarf
and cap, slipping the jewels from the hands of the corpses.
I'm with you.

So then a ladder came down and the work began. And we
climbed out. There we are, an obscene parade, the rich in
tatters, slipping back to our homes, the evening rather . . .
spoilt . . . and how low, how low can men get stealing from
the dead and dying?

And I just brush myself down and feel lightheaded, for the
first time in my life totally sure of what I feel. I climb the
ladder to the street, push my way through the crowd. My
arm is grazed and bleeding. I hail a taxi. The man is a

cockney. He stares hard at the exploded wealth. He stares at me in my dinner jacket. He says, 'I don't want blood all over my fucking taxi.' And he drives away.

There is a war going on. All the time. A war of attrition.

(*He smiles.*)

Good luck.

MAGGIE: Bollocks. I just wanted to go to jail.

(*Silence. Then* LAURA *appears.*)

LAURA: They really do seem to want you, Maggie. Can they have you now?

MAGGIE: What a load of shit. You're full of shit, Saraffian. What a crucial insight, what a great moment in the Café de Paris. And what did you do the next *thirty years*?

(*Pause.*)

Well, I'm sure it gives you comfort, your nice little class war. It ties things up very nicely, of course, from the outside you look like any other clapped-out businessman, but inside, oh, inside you got it all worked out.

(*Pause.*)

This man has believed the same thing for thirty years. And it does not show. Is that going to happen to us? Fucking hell, somebody's got to keep on the move.

(*Then she smiles, very buoyant.*)

Laura, come here, you look after Arthur.

LAURA: Yes.

MAGGIE: You can have your hat back, all the hats he wants to give you, you can have. Anything I said about you, I withdraw. The tightness of your arse I apologize. You're Mahatma Gandhi, you're the Pope. Arthur, you're Cole Porter. Or at least you will be. Or at least nobody else ever will be.

(*She smiles again.*)

LAURA: Shall I let you know how it goes in Stoke?

MAGGIE: If you make it.

LAURA: What?

MAGGIE: I'm only guessing. But I'd take a bet this band never plays again. When did you cancel Stoke?

SARAFFIAN: About a week ago.

MAGGIE: There.

SARAFFIAN: You know me too well.

(*He goes out.*)

MAGGIE: So I go to jail. Nobody is to think about me, nobody is to say, 'How is she these days?' Nobody to mention me. Nobody to say, 'How much does she drink?' Nobody is to remember. Nobody is to feel guilty. Nobody is to feel they might have done better. Remember. I'm nobody's excuse.

If you love me, keep on the move.

(*She heads out. She makes as if to take the bottle of scotch from on top of the piano but stops dead, her back to us, and raises her hands instead. A pause. Then she goes out. Silence.* ARTHUR *and* LAURA *alone.*)

LAURA: What are you on?

ARTHUR: On?

LAURA: Transport.

ARTHUR: Oh. Motor-sickle.

LAURA: Is there room on the back?

ARTHUR: Sure.

LAURA: Will you give us a tune? One of those awful old ones you like . . .

(*He stares at her. Then* INCH, WILSON, NASH *and* SMEGS *return laughing.*)

WILSON: That was the best night I 'ad in years.

NASH: Really brightened up the evenin'.

WILSON: Yeah.

NASH: I thought we was gonna 'ave a real flop on 'our 'ands.

INCH: Funny 'ow plastic burns in' it?

WILSON: Yeah, all sorta blue wiv little fringes.

INCH: And formica doesn't.

NASH: That's right. I noticed that.

INCH: I kept 'oldin' it in the flames but nothin'.

(*He starts loading the equipment on to the barrow.*)

SMEGS: So what do we do?

LAURA: The police said we can all bugger off.

INCH: Then we go 'ome, that's what we do.

WILSON: Great.

INCH: The van's over there.

WILSON: Anyone fancy a game?

241

SMEGS: Sure.

WILSON: Seven-card stud? I got some cards in the back. Perhaps
we could try some new rules I got . . .

(NASH, WILSON, SMEGS, INCH *go off, pulling off the trolley
loaded with equipment.*)

LAURA: Where did you put your helmet?

ARTHUR: I used to think it was so easy, you know. If I leave her,
she'll kill herself. I thought she's only got one problem. She
doesn't know how to be happy. But that's not her problem at
all. Her problem is: she's frightened of being happy. And if
ever it looked as if she might make it, if the clouds cleared
and I, or some other man, fell perfectly into place, if everyone
loved her and the music came good, that's when she'd kill
herself. Not so easy, huh?

(*Pause.*)

LAURA: Play us a dreadful old tune.

ARTHUR: Laura. It just wouldn't work between us. Not now.

(INCH *returns.*)

INCH: There's 'ardly any petrol left in the van. I can't find the
spare can.

ARTHUR: Maggie took it. To burn down the tent.

INCH: That's a bit fuckin' inconsiderate, she mighta noticed we
was short o' gas. Lend us a couple a quid somebody. Arfer?

ARTHUR: Don't have it.

INCH: Well, sorry to say this, Laura, but we're gonna 'ave to sell
your body. And pretty bloody fast. Somewhere between 'ere
an' Baldock you're gonna 'ave to do it in the road.

(INCH *goes off.*)

LAURA: I've only waited six years. You might have mentioned it
before.

ARTHUR: Yes. Yes. It was silly.

(*Pause.* SARAFFIAN *returns, picks up the situation at once.*)

SARAFFIAN: I had a look at the cellars.

ARTHUR: Ah.

SARAFFIAN: The stock is remarkable. The 1949 Romanée St
Vivant is like gold-dust you know.

ARTHUR: Did you, er . . .

SARAFFIAN: Unfortunately, not. They'd padlocked the racks.

ARTHUR: Ah.

INCH (*off*): Laura, get your fat butt in 'ere.

(SARAFFIAN *looks at* LAURA *who now has tears running down her face.*)

SARAFFIAN: Of course, this college was once famous for its port.

ARTHUR: I didn't know that.

SARAFFIAN: The finest cellar of vintage port in England. Then in 1940 when the dons heard Hitler was coming . . . Hitler was coming . . .

(*They both look at her. She is now having hysterics, hitting the ground.*)

ARTHUR: Laura, can you stop crying . . .

SARAFFIAN: Hitler was coming . . .

ARTHUR: I can't hear what Saraffian is saying.

SARAFFIAN: They drank it. So he wouldn't get his fat German hands on it. Their contribution to the war effort. Four thousand bottles in just eleven months.

(SARAFFIAN *as if to move.*)

ARTHUR: Leave her.

(PEYOTE *enters.*)

PEYOTE: Fantastic.

ARTHUR: Yeah.

PEYOTE: Fuckin' on a fire engine, you wouldn't believe it.

(*He goes.*)

ARTHUR: What's the time?

SARAFFIAN: Just gone four.

LAURA: When are you going to tell them?

SARAFFIAN: Who?

LAURA: The band.

SARAFFIAN: Oh, tomorrow. Enough for one day.

(WILSON *has appeared upstage.*)

WILSON: Laura. You comin' wiv us?

LAURA: Yes. Yes. I'm coming with you.

(*She stands a moment crying.* WILSON *looks at them all as if anew.*)

WILSON: I don't know why you lot make it so 'ard for yerselves.

(LAURA *picks up* MAGGIE's *bag and goes out.*)

WILSON: Right. Well. Back into the little tin hell. Always makes

me feel like bloody Alec Guinness. You know, into the 'ot
metal 'ut. And at the other end, well we may be a little
sweaty about the lip an' doin' that funny walk, but fuck me if
we ain't whistlin' Colonel Bogey. Goodnight all.
(*He goes.*)

SARAFFIAN: Goodnight lads.

ARTHUR: Goodnight.

(SARAFFIAN *and* ARTHUR *alone.*)

ARTHUR: I knew a guy, played in a band. They were loud, they
were very loud. What I mean by loud is: they made Pink
Floyd sound like a Mozart quintet. I said to him, why the
hell don't you wear muffs? In eighteen months you're going
to be stone deaf. He said: that's why we play so loud. The
louder we play, the sooner we won't be able to hear.
I can see us all. Rolling down the highway into middle age.
Complacency. Prurience. Sadism. Despair.

(SARAFFIAN *gets out a hipflask.*)

SARAFFIAN: Don't worry. Have some brandy.

ARTHUR: What?

SARAFFIAN: Napoleon. Was waiting till those buggers had gone.

(*He offers it.* ARTHUR *refuses.* ARTHUR *sits down at the upright
piano on the deserted stage.* RANDOLPH *comes in.*)

RANDOLPH: I rung the wife.

SARAFFIAN: Thank you.

RANDOLPH: Bloke answered.

SARAFFIAN: So.

(*Pause.*)

We must go.

ARTHUR: Who's the bloke?

SARAFFIAN: Where did I put the car?

ARTHUR: Who's the bloke?

SARAFFIAN: Oh, Mrs Saraffian's friend. Called Wetherby.
Secretary of the local golf club, I'm afraid. Mean with a nine
iron. She likes his manners. I rev the Jag in the drive, rattle
the milk bottles, you know, wait ten minutes, then . . . enter
my home.

(*Pause.*)

God bless you and . . . Saraffian goes. Come on, Tony, long

way to go. Too late to count number plates, you'll just have to sit and think.

(SARAFFIAN *and* RANDOLPH *go out.* ARTHUR *alone on stage with the piano.*)

ARTHUR: Where is the money? And where are the girls?
(*Pause. Then he begins to play.*)

Arthur's Song

My relatives and friends all think I'm barmy
Because I went away and joined the Foreign Legion
My funny little ways
Have got the others in a mess
I think it's time that I came clean
Decided to explain
It isn't just the season
That has given me the opportunity to do
What I have always wanted to do
And though we're stranded in the rain
Leaving on a midnight boat
At ease upon our chairs before the mast
The world round is spinning round decidedly too much
We must hang on or lose our sense of drama

Never seen faces so empty
Never spent money so fast
You can't touch the important things
They keep them under glass
Your good friends always tel! you lies
Doing what your bad friends would never do
And nothing rhymes with orange
But
I love you

ARTHUR'S SONG

My re-la-tives and friends all think I'm bar-my Be-
-cause I went a-way and joined the for-eign le-gion My fun-ny lit-tle ways Have got the
oth-ers in a mess I think it's time that I came clean De-ci-ded to ex-plain It
is-n't just the sea-son That has giv-en me the op-por-tu-ni-ty To do what I have al-ways
wan-ted—— to do And though we're stran-ded in the rain
Leav-ing on a mid-night boat—— At ease up-on our chairs before the
mast The world is spin-ning round De-ci-ded-ly too much We must hang
on or lose our sense of dra-ma—— Nev-er seen fa-ces so emp-
-ty Nev-er spent mon-ey so fast——
You can't touch the im-por-tant things They keep them un-der glass——
Your good friends al-ways tell you lies
Do-ing what your bad friends would nev-er do And noth-ing rhymes with
o-range But I love you.

Never seen faces so empty etc.

(*Towards the end of the song* SNEAD *enters carrying two
suitcases. He comes down towards* ARTHUR *at the very end.*)
SNEAD: Sir.
> (*Pause.*)
> Left these.
> (*Pause.*)
> Left these behind.
> (*Pause.*)
> Sir.
ARTHUR: Thank you, Mr Snead. Why are you frightened? Why's
> everyone frightened?
> (*Pause. Then a blackout. Then projections large in the blackout,
> one by one.*)
> ANDREW SMITH NICKNAME PEYOTE
> INHALED HIS OWN VOMIT
> DIED IN A HOTEL ROOM IN SAN ANTONIO TEXAS
> APRIL 17TH 1973
> MAGGIE
> ARTHUR
> SARAFFIAN
> THE BAND
> ALIVE
> WELL
> LIVING IN ENGLAND
> (*Then*)

Maggie's Song

> Last orders on the Titanic
> Set up the fol de rol
> Tell the band to play that number
> Better get it in your soul
> Put the life boats out to sea
> We've only got a few
> Let the women and children drown
> Man we've gotta save the crew

Because the ship is sinking
And time is running out
We got water coming in
Places we don't know about
The tide is rising
It's covering her name
The ship is sinking
But the music remains the same

Last orders on the Titanic
Put your life belts on
We can't hear the captain shouting
Cos the band goes on and on
I only want to tell you
That you have my sympathy
But there has to be a sacrifice
And it isn't going to be me

Because etc.

Last orders on the Titanic
Get up and paint your face
Deck hands in dungarees
And millionaires in lace
I only woke you baby
To say I love you so
But the water is up around
My knees goodbye I have to go

Because the ship is sinking etc.

The music remains the same

LAST ORDERS

♩ = 58

Last or - ders on the Ti - tan - ic Set up the fol de rol

Tell the band to play that num - ber

Bet - ter get it in your soul Put the life - boats

out to sea We've on - ly got a few

Let the wo - men and chil - dren drown Man we've got to save the crew,

Be - cause the ship is sink - ing And time is run - ning out We got

wa - ter com - ing in Pla - ces we don't know a - bout The tide is ri - sing It's

cov - er - ing her name The ship is sink - ing But the mu - sic re - mains the same

between verses

The mu - sic re - mains the same.